HAMLYN
ALL COLOUR
BEST PLANTS

ANNUALS PERENNIALS TREES SHRUBS

HAMLYN
ALL COLOUR
BEST PLANTS

1000 easy-to-grow garden plants

hamlyn

First published in Great Britain in 2006 by
Hamlyn, a division of Octopus Publishing Group Ltd
2–4 Heron Quays, London E14 4JP

ISBN-13: 978-0-600-61331-2
ISBN-10: 0-600-61331-3

A CIP catalogue record for this book is available from the
British Library

Printed and bound in China

10 9 8 7 6 5 4 3 2 1

Contents

Introduction

Everyone has their own view of what a garden is for and what it means to them and their family. How you intend to use your garden will ultimately dictate your choice of plants and with so many wonderful subjects to choose from, the decision can be a difficult one.

If you have children you will want a space in which they can play safely and in which the plants are robust enough to withstand stray balls and small feet. If you are interested in wildlife you will want to grow some of the older cultivars rather than new, untested cultivars. You will be relaxed about allowing plants to go to seed and about leaving seedheads to remain uncut until spring. If you suffer from hay fever, you will want flowers that do not produce pollen. If you simply want a pleasant place to sit, you will want plants that will perform reliably and need little attention beyond the occasional trim or tidy up.

The sheer number of plants that is available today makes deciding on new plants for your garden an increasingly difficult task. Plant encyclopedias and reference books often don't help, listing every possible species and form. Garden centres and, increasingly, supermarkets and DIY stores stock masses of uniform-looking plants that are often poorly labelled with information about size and preferred conditions, so buying plants that will fit into your garden becomes something of a lottery.

The plants described in this book – mostly perennials and shrubs, but also some annuals, bulbs and trees – are not necessarily the most widely available but they are, mostly, easy to grow and easy to maintain.

▲ *Actinidia kolomikta*

▼ *Leucojum aestivum*

Buying plants can be frustrating, and it is often better to identify the plant you want to grow and then to find a reliable supplier, whether it is a local nursery or a mail-order outlet, which will despatch the plants at the most appropriate planting time.

Bulbs, especially, are best bought by mail order from a reputable supplier. Ordered in spring or summer, they will be delivered in good time for autumn planting. Specialist bulb suppliers will also have a good selection of some less usual species and cultivars, and will be accompanied by useful planting information. Although it may be tempting simply to fill a bag with a mixture of bulbs, remember that most plants look best in groups of the same cultivar. It is far better to plant 12 bulbs of a single type of daffodil than 50 bulbs, each of a different cultivar.

If you have a new garden or have recently moved house, it is always worth checking the type of soil you have. Most plants will grow in most soils, but some plants have specific requirements, and you will struggle to grow them, perhaps wasting money by replacing them over and over again if the soil in your garden is unsuitable. Although the plants growing in your neighbours' gardens will be a useful guide to whether the soil is acid or alkaline, your own garden soil may have been imported by a previous owner or your neighbours might have a passion for heathers and spent a fortune replacing their soil. Buy a simple soil-testing kit from a garden centre or DIY store and test the soil in different areas of the garden.

▲ *Prunus* x *subhirtella* 'Autumnalis'   *Taxus baccata* 'Standishii' ▶

If you have strongly alkaline soil it is simply not worth trying to grow camellias, rhododendrons, some types of heather or a few other plants. These are acid-loving plants and in an alkaline soil will soon look sick, fail to thrive and ultimately die. You can waste a lot of money that would be better spent on plants that will flourish in the conditions you can provide, but if you really cannot live without a pieris or an azalea, plant one in a large container or build a raised bed filled with ericaceous (acidic) compost.

Unless otherwise noted, the sizes given in the plant descriptions throughout the book are for mature plants grown in optimum conditions. Shrubs and trees grown in containers, for example, will rarely reach the height or spread of the same plant grown in the open garden, and plants grown in shade may not do as well as a similar plant grown in full sun, and vice versa. Sizes are given in the form height x spread.

Everybody, even experienced gardeners, will plant something unsuitable from time to time – a tree or shrub that is too large or too small, a perennial that turns out to be a hideous colour or a plant that just does not suit the conditions you can provide. Don't persevere: once you have recognized your mistake, dig it up and then find something you really like and that will like your garden.

Abelia

Abies
SILVER FIR

▲ *Abelia chinensis*

▲ *Abies balsamea* Hudsonia Group

These shrubs are grown for their abundant flowers, which appear in late summer. The deciduous *Abelia chinensis*, 1.5 x 2.4 m (5 x 8 ft), bears scented, pink-tinged, white flowers from midsummer until autumn.

The more vigorous hybrid *A.* x *grandiflora* is evergreen or semi-evergreen. The slightly scented, pinkish-white flowers open from reddish-pink buds and are borne from late summer until the first frosts. Planted against the shelter of a fence or wall, it will grow to 3 x 4 m (10 x 12 ft). 'Francis Mason', 1.5 x 1.8 m (5 x 6 ft), has dark green leaves edged with yellow-gold, which becomes more noticeable on plants grown in full sun. 'Gold Spot' (syn. 'Goldsport', 'Gold Strike') has golden-yellow leaves.

The more compact *A. floribunda* bears masses of bright pink flowers but is less hardy that others in the genus and needs a sheltered, sunny corner, when it will get to 1.8 m (6 ft) high and across. The reliable cultivar *A.* 'Edward Goucher', 1.5 x 1.8 m (5 x 6 ft), is semi-evergreen and produces deep pink flowers from summer until autumn.

KEY FEATURES
• Deciduous or evergreen shrub
• Tubular flowers
• Year-round interest

PLANT
In full sun in well-drained soil

PROPAGATE
Greenwood cuttings in early summer; semi-ripe cuttings in late autumn

HARDINESS
Frost hardy to half-hardy; zones 6–9

PESTS AND DISEASES
Trouble free

The fragrant *Abies balsamea* (balsam fir) is the parent of several dwarf forms, useful in small gardens for providing year-round colour and structure. They won't grow in shallow, chalky soil, and don't do well in heavily polluted air, so are generally better away from busy roads. The Hudsonia Group (which covers a range of plants with the name Hudson) is a variety of slow-growing, compact conifers, gradually reaching a height of 80 cm (32 in) with a spread of about 1 m (3 ft). 'Nana' is a rounded form, eventually reaching about 1 m (3 ft).

A. koreana (Korean fir) forms an attractive cone, and the dark green leaves have glaucous blue undersides, giving a shimmering appearance. The species will grow to 10 x 6 m (30 x 20 ft), but there are numerous cultivars, offering a wide range of colour, shape and height. One of the best known is the widely available 'Silberlocke', with slightly twisted leaves that reveal silvery undersides. It will very slowly reach about half the size of the species.

KEY FEATURES
• Evergreen conifer
• Year-round interest
• Suitable for small gardens
• Good in a container

PLANT
In sun in well-drained, neutral to acid soil

PROPAGATE
Ripe seed in late winter; graft in winter

HARDINESS
Hardy; zones 4–7

PESTS AND DISEASES
Adelgids, honey fungus

Acacia
WATTLE

Acanthus
BEAR'S BREECHES

▲ *Acacia verticillata*

▲ *Acanthus spinosus*

Acacias have brilliant yellow flowers and the trees have an upright elegant form, but unfortunately they are not hardy in any but the most favoured of situations. They can be grown in large containers in conservatories, when they will need regular pruning to keep them to a reasonable size, but they do tolerate drought.

The tender *Acacia verticillata* (prickly Moses), potentially to 8 m (25 ft) high and across but usually 3 m (10 ft) high and across, is an evergreen shrub, which bears lemon-yellow flowers in spring.

A. dealbata (mimosa, silver wattle), 15 x 10 m (50 x 30 ft), is slightly hardier. The tree has silver-grey, rather fern-like, evergreen leaves and pretty, fragrant, yellow flowers from winter to spring. It will grow outside in mild areas, when it will develop into a graceful feature tree.

A. baileyana (cootamundra wattle), 8 x 6 m (25 x 20 ft), has evergreen leaves and from late winter to early spring a mass of bright yellow flowers, which are borne in dense racemes. Again, this is not hardy.

KEY FEATURES
- Deciduous or evergreen climber, shrub or tree
- Fragrant flowers
- Good in containers

PLANT
In full sun in neutral to acid soil

PROPAGATE
Seed in spring; semi-ripe cuttings in summer

HARDINESS
Half-hardy to frost tender; zones 9–10

PESTS AND DISEASES
Trouble free

These handsome, clump-forming perennials should be grown in a large border or even as feature plants in an island bed, where the glossy leaves will have space to spread. Once established, they will colonize the border and you may find it difficult to clear the ground if you decide you want to grow something else. The dried flower spikes can be used in winter arrangements.

The deeply cut, dark green leaves of *Acanthus spinosus* can be as much as 1 m (3 ft) across and the spikes of distinctive, hooded white and mauve flowers are 1 m (3 ft) or more tall. Cultivars in the Spinosissimus Group, 1.2 m x 60 cm (4 x 2 ft), have grey-green, deeply cut, spiny leaves and need a position in full sun to flower well.

A. mollis, 1.5 x 1 m (5 x 3 ft), has tall spikes of mauve and white flowers above glossy green foliage, which is evergreen in mild areas. There are several cultivars.

KEY FEATURES
- Perennial
- Attractive foliage
- Unusual flowers
- Good feature plant

PLANT
In sun or partial shade in fertile, well-drained soil

PROPAGATE
Seed in spring; division in spring or autumn; root cuttings in winter

HARDINESS
Hardy to frost tender; zones 6–10

PESTS AND DISEASES
Powdery mildew but usually trouble free

Acer

MAPLE

▲ *Acer griseum*

Achillea

YARROW

▲ *Achillea* 'Moonshine'

The Japanese maples (forms of *A. japonicum* and *A. palmatum*) are all attractive and versatile small trees, mostly spreading in habit. The soft green leaves of *A. japonicum* 'Aconitifolium', eventually 5 x 6 m (15 x 20 ft), turn orange in autumn. 'Orange Dream', which turns from orange to golden-yellow in autumn, reaches only 3 m (10 ft) after 10 years, and tiny 'Mapi-no-machihime' ('Little Princess') grows to just 75 cm (30 in); its yellow-green leaves, edged with red in spring, turn golden-yellow in autumn. *A. palmatum* var. *dissectum* (cut-leaf maple) is perfect in a container or oriental garden as it grows to only 90 cm (3 ft). The finely cut leaves have purple stripes in autumn.

Although celebrated for their autumn colour, some acers are also grown for their interesting bark. That of *Acer griseum* (paperbark maple) is orange-brown and peels; it is slow-growing, eventually to 10 m (30 ft) high and wide.

Protect Japanese maples from cold winter winds. In an exposed, open garden it might be necessary to wrap them in horticultural fleece when penetrating frosts are forecast.

KEY FEATURES
• Deciduous shrub or tree
• Excellent autumn leaf colour
• Some ideal for containers

PLANT
In sun or partial shade in fertile, well-drained soil

PROPAGATE
Ripe seed; bud in late summer; graft in winter

HARDINESS
Hardy; zones 6–8

PESTS AND DISEASES
Aphids, caterpillars, honey fungus, verticillium wilt

These useful and reliable herbaceous perennials deserve to be in every mixed border and in every wildlife garden.

Although it is a common weed, there are several good cultivars of *Achillea millefolium*, providing a range of heights and colours. They all have the typically deeply divided, mid- to grey-green leaves and flattish flowerheads, borne in summer to early autumn on plants to about 60 cm (2 ft) high and across. 'Burgundy' and 'Sammertriese' have dark red flowers, and 'Cerise Queen' has pinkish-red and white flowers. The flowers of 'Paprika' are orange-red, and those of 'Lilac Beauty' are lilac-mauve.

One of the best cultivars is *A*. 'Moonshine', 60 cm (24 in) high and across; it bears flat heads, to 15 cm (6 in) across, of tiny yellow flowers. 'Terracotta', which grows to 60–90 cm (24–36 in) high and 30–45 cm (12–18 in) across, has golden-yellow to deep orange flowers

A. ptarmica 'Nana Compacta' is ideal for the front of a border. Growing to 30–45 cm (12–18 in) high and across, it bears little, pure white daisy-like flowers in mid- to late summer. 'The Pearl', 60 cm (24 in) high and across, has double white flowers in summer.

KEY FEATURES
• Perennial
• Reliable flowers
• Wide range of colours
• Aromatic foliage

PLANT
In full sun in well-drained soil

PROPAGATE
Seed; division in spring

HARDINESS
Hardy; zones 3–9

PESTS AND DISEASES
Aphids, mildew

Actinidia

Adiantum
MAIDENHAIR FERN

▲ *Actinidia kolomikta*

▲ *Adiantum pedatum*

The best-known species is probably *Actinidia deliciosa* (syn. *A. chinensis*; Chinese gooseberry or kiwi fruit), which has mid-green leaves covered in reddish hairs. In mid- to late summer it bears cream-white flowers followed, on female plants, by the familiar green-brown fruits. If you want fruit you will need to prune plants as you would a grapevine and grow both a male and a female form or a self-fertile cultivar, such as 'Blake' or 'Jenny'. 'Hayward' and 'Bruno' are both female; 'Tomuri' and 'Matua' are male.

A. kolomikta is an ornamental hardy climber. Its dark green leaves, at first tinged purple, develop unusual pink and white variegation (the leaves will remain green if in shade). Clusters of scented white flowers appear in early summer, and female plants bear small, yellow fruits.

Also hardy is *A. polygama* (silver vine), which has attractive dark green leaves with silver-white variegation. In early summer there are fragrant white flowers, followed, on female plants, by small yellow-green fruits.

KEY FEATURES
- Deciduous climber
- Colourful foliage
- Summer flowers
- Autumn fruits

PLANT
In sun, sheltered from blustery wind, in well-drained soil

PROPAGATE
Seed in autumn or spring; semi-ripe cuttings in summer; graft in summer

HARDINESS
Hardy to frost hardy; zones 4–9

PESTS AND DISEASES
Trouble free

The 200 to 250 species of fern in this genus range from reliably hardy plants to those best grown as houseplants.

The deciduous *Adiantum pedatum* (five-fingered maidenhair fern), 30 x 30 cm (12 x 12 in), has upright, pinnate fronds with black or dark brown stalks. It needs partial or full shade and, although hardy, should be given a good winter mulch. *A. aleuticum* (syn. *A. pedatum* var. *aleuticum*; northern maidenhair fern), 70 cm (28 in) high and across, can be semi-evergreen, and has slender, mid-green fronds with purplish-black stems and midribs. The dwarf 'Subpumilum' grows to only 15 x 30 cm (6 x 12 in).

A. venustum (Himalayan maidenhair fern), 30 cm (12 in) high and across, is evergreen, with triangular fronds. They are bronze-pink when they first appear in early spring and take on a bluish tinge as they age.

A. capillus-veneris (true maidenhair fern), 30 x 40 cm (12 x 16 in), will survive outdoors where temperatures hardly fall below freezing; in other areas it can be treated as an evergreen houseplant, its triangular, mid-green fronds and glossy black stems making an attractive clump.

KEY FEATURES
- Deciduous, evergreen or semi-evergreen fern
- Attractive foliage
- Will grow in shade

PLANT
In partial shade in moderately fertile, well-drained soil

PROPAGATE
Ripe spores; division in spring

HARDINESS
Hardy to frost hardy; zones 3–8

PESTS AND DISEASES
Trouble free

Agapanthus
AFRICAN LILY

Ajuga
BUGLE

▲ *Agapanthus* 'Bressingham White'

▲ *Ajuga reptans* 'Jungle Beauty'

These clump-forming perennials, some evergreen, originated in southern Africa, and not all are hardy. *Agapanthus praecox* subsp. *orientalis*, for example, needs to be moved into a frost-free greenhouse or conservatory in winter. In summer it produces clusters of bright blue, trumpet-shaped flowers on sturdy 90 cm (36 in) stems.

Several hardy cultivars have been developed, and these can be left in the ground after flowering so that they can form large clumps. Even these, however, will benefit from a winter mulch. *A.* 'Bressingham White', 90 x 60 cm (3 x 2 ft), has pure white flowers on upright stalks in late summer. Among the hardy blue-flowered forms are 'Ben Hope' and 'Blue Giant', both to 1.2 m (4 ft) tall, which produce rounded umbels of trumpet-shaped flowers, rich blue and pale blue, respectively, from mid- to late summer. The shorter 'Blue Moon', to 60 cm (24 in), has pale blue flowers from late summer into early autumn, while at the back of the border 'Loch Hope', 1.5 m (5 ft) tall, bears dark blue flowers above grey-green leaves.

Lift and divide clumps only when flowering begins to diminish; these plants seem to do best when congested.

KEY FEATURES
- Perennial
- Showy flowers
- Good in containers

PLANT
In full sun in moisture-retentive but well-drained soil

PROPAGATE
Seed in spring; division in spring

HARDINESS
Hardy to half-hardy; zones 7–10

PESTS AND DISEASES
Slugs and snails, viruses

The wild *Ajuga reptans* (bugle) is found in woodlands in spring, its small blue, occasionally pink or white, flowers borne in leafy spikes. In the garden less invasive cultivars are usually grown, their names often indicating the character of the foliage. Most have flower spikes to about 15 cm (6 in) high. They spread by runners and will colonize an area 1 m (3 ft) square in suitable conditions.

A. reptans 'Burgundy Glow' has silver-green leaves with bronze or pink margins. The large leaves of 'Catlin's Giant' are brown-purple and the flower spike about 20 cm (8 in) tall. 'Jungle Beauty' (syn. 'Jumbo') has large green leaves that turn brown in autumn and winter. 'Multicolor' (syn. 'Rainbow') has bronze-green leaves variegated cream-yellow and red. 'Variegata' (syn. 'Argentea') has green leaves splashed grey and cream.

A. pyramidalis is a clump-forming perennial about 20 cm (8 in) tall, with long, dark green leaves and blue flower spikes in early summer. The cultivar 'Metallica Crispa' is half the size, with bronze leaves and dark blue flowers.

KEY FEATURES
- Evergreen or semi-evergreen perennial
- Good groundcover
- Easy to grow
- Tolerates a wide range of conditions and poor soil

PLANT
In partial shade in moist soil

PROPAGATE
Softwood cuttings in summer

HARDINESS
Hardy; zones 3–9

PESTS AND DISEASES
Powdery mildew

Alcea
HOLLYHOCK

Alchemilla
LADY'S MANTLE

▲ *Alcea rosea 'Nigra'*

▲ *Alchemilla mollis*

Alcea (formerly *Althaea*) *rosea*, the hollyhock, is a familiar cottage-garden plant, useful for adding height and colour to a border. Because plants are susceptible to rust, they are often treated as annuals, even though the perennial forms are perfectly hardy.

The species has light green, rather rough, slightly lobed leaves, above which the slender flower spikes rise to 2.4 m (8 ft) in midsummer. The single flowers, up to 10 cm (4 in) across, are purple, pink, white or yellow. 'Nigra', 1.8 m (6 ft) tall, has dark chocolate, almost-black flowers; 'Indian Spring' has single, white, pink or yellow flowers. Several strains have double flowers. Plants in the biennial Chater's Double Group have doubles in pink, red, salmon pink, violet, white and yellow. The annual Summer Carnival Group also has double flowers in shades of yellow and red. New introductions include the soft yellow 'Park Allee', 1.8 m (6 ft) tall, and the shorter 'Park Rondell', with pink flowers veined with deeper pink and a dark centre.

A. rugosa, with large yellow flowers, is a biennial and more resistant to rust than *A. rosea*.

KEY FEATURES
- Biennial or perennial
- Colourful flowers on tall spikes
- Attracts bees and butterflies

PLANT
In full sun in well-drained soil

PROPAGATE
Seed in late winter or
early spring

HARDINESS
Hardy; zones 6–9

PESTS AND DISEASES
Aphids, capsid bugs, cutworms,
mallow flea beetles, slugs, rust

Alchemilla mollis, 50 cm (20 in) high and across, is a useful plant in the garden. It can be used to fill gaps in a herbaceous border, as groundcover, as a source of cut flowers and as a good companion underplanting for plants like roses.

The round, fan-like, softly felted pale green leaves make dense mounds in spring, and these are topped by sprays of yellow-green flowers in midsummer. The leaves are especially attractive when they hold droplets of dew or summer rain. The only possible drawback is that plants will self-seed prolifically if the flowers are not rigorously deadheaded, and you will find the little rosettes of perfect leaves appearing in the most unlikely places, especially in gravel paths.

A. alpina is more compact and neater, growing to 15 x 45 cm (6 x 18 in). It has dark green, kidney-shaped, lobed leaves and sprays of flowers that are similar to, but smaller than, those of *A. mollis*.

KEY FEATURES
- Perennial
- Good groundcover
- Attractive foliage
- Easy to grow
- Reliable

PLANT
In sun or shade in any soil

PROPAGATE
Seed in spring; divide in spring
or autumn

HARDINESS
Hardy to frost hardy; zones 3–7

PESTS AND DISEASES
Trouble free

Allium
ORNAMENTAL ONION

Alstroemeria
PERUVIAN LILY, LILY OF THE INCAS

▲ *Allium giganteum*

▲ *Alstroemeria aurea*

There are so many flowering onions that it is possible to find one for every part of the garden, from the alpine house to the mixed border. When planting, add some fine grit to the bottom of the hole to improve drainage. In a container, add a good layer of crocks in the bottom and ensure excess water can drain away.

As the name suggests, *Allium giganteum* is one of the tallest, at almost 1.5 m (5 ft). In summer it bears dense round heads of tiny, star-shaped, lilac flowers. At the other extreme is *A. karataviense*, only 25 cm (10 in) tall. Unlike most alliums it has attractive foliage, grey-green with red margins; the globular flowerheads are pale pink. 'Ivory Queen' is similar, with ivory-white flowers.

One of the most eye-catching is *A. christophii*, 60 cm (24 in) tall, which in early summer bears flowerheads almost 20 cm (8 in) across composed of lilac-purple flowers with a glistening metallic sheen. These are popular with flower arrangers and in dried-flower arrangements, but they are just as attractive left in the garden as they dry.

KEY FEATURES
- Bulb or rhizomatous perennial
- Wide range of flower colour, shape and size
- Good cut flowers

PLANT
In full sun in well-drained soil

PROPAGATE
Seed in spring; divide in spring; offsets in autumn

HARDINESS
Hardy to frost hardy; zones 4–10

PESTS AND DISEASES
Onion fly, downy mildew, white rot

The striking flowers of alstroemerias grow from tubers, which will, in the right conditions, spread to form clumps 1 m (3 ft) across. The funnel-shaped flowers appear in summer and are borne in clusters at the ends of the stems. These flowers look so exotic that it is hard to believe that they can be grown outside, but in a sheltered, sunny spot they will thrive in all but the very coldest of gardens. Apply a good mulch in winter, especially to young plants.

Alstroemeria aurea (syn. *A. aurantiaca*), 90 x 45 cm (36 x 18 in), has bright yellow and orange flowers, splashed with dark red. 'Dover Orange' has deep orange flowers and 'Lutea' bright yellow. *A.* 'Apollo', 60 cm (24 in) high and across, is one of the best hybrids. From midsummer into autumn it bears large white flowers streaked with yellow and brown inside. 'Charm' bears pale pink flowers, the insides cream-yellow flecked with brown, and 'Marina' has dark pink flowers, yellow inside and splashed with brown.

The popular Ligtu Hybrids, developed from *A. ligtu*, include plants that grow 60 cm (24 in) high and across and have variable flowers in pinks, oranges and yellows.

KEY FEATURES
- Perennial
- Colourful flowers
- Good cut flowers

PLANT
In sun or partial shade in well-drained soil

PROPAGATE
Ripe seed; divide in autumn or early spring

HARDINESS
Hardy to almost hardy; zone 8

PESTS AND DISEASES
Slugs and snails, viruses

Amelanchier

JUNE BERRY, SHADBUSH, SNOWY MESPILUS

Anemone

WINDFLOWER

▲ *Amelanchier alnifolia*

▲ *Anemone blanda*

Amelanchiers are large enough to be grown as a feature but small enough to be grown in a large mixed border.

Amelanchier lamarckii, 10 x 12 m (30 x 40 ft), is a lovely multi-stemmed small tree. The young leaves emerge bronze in spring, turn dark green and become fiery in autumn. In spring white flowers are borne in racemes to 12 cm (5 in) long, and these are followed by purple-black fruit. *A. alnifolia* (alder-leaved serviceberry), 4 m (12 ft) high and across, has fragrant, cream-white flowers in erect racemes in spring, and these are followed by purple-black fruits. 'Alta Glow' is a useful columnar form, to 6 m (20 ft) tall. *A. grandiflora*, 8 x 10 m (25 x 30 ft), is a spreading bush that makes a good feature plant. The starry white flowers appear with the bronzy new foliage in spring, and the leaves turn red and purple in autumn. *A. canadensis* (shadbush), 6 x 3 m (20 x 10 ft), is a rather suckering shrub, which bears erect racemes of white flowers in spring, followed by berries and good autumn colour.

KEY FEATURES
- Deciduous shrub or tree
- Pretty spring flowers
- Good autumn colour
- Fruits attract birds

PLANT
In sun or partial shade in moisture-retentive but well-drained soil

PROPAGATE
Ripe seed; greenwood or semi-ripe cuttings in summer

HARDINESS
Hardy; zones 4–8

PESTS AND DISEASES
Fireblight

The brilliantly coloured forms of *Anemone coronaria*, the De Caen and St Bridgid Groups, have red, blue and white single or double flowers borne on erect stems above ferny leaves. 'Lord Lieutenant' has deep blue flowers, and 'The Bride' white blooms. All grow to 45 x 15 cm (18 x 6 in); plant tubers in light, well-drained soil and mulch in winter.

For early-spring flowers plant tubers of the low-growing *A. blanda* under deciduous trees and shrubs in sun or partial shade in fertile, well-drained soil. There are several cultivars with flowers in white, red, blue or purple. 'Radar' has deep red flowers with a white centre, and 'White Splendour' has white flowers. Flowering from spring to early summer, *A. nemorosa* (wood anemone) is good for naturalizing under trees and shrubs. The species has pink-white flowers; 'Robinsonia' has large pale blue flowers.

The herbaceous perennials *A. hupehensis* and *A. x hybrida* produce flowers from summer to early autumn. *A. x hybrida* 'Honorine Jobert' has lovely white flowers, and 'Max Vogel' bears pale pink flowers; both are 1.2 m (4 ft) high. Grow in sun or partial shade in fertile, well-drained soil.

KEY FEATURES
- Perennial
- Long flowering period
- Good for naturalizing

PLANT
Avoid waterlogged soil

PROPAGATE
Ripe seed; divide in spring or autumn; divide tubers in summer

HARDINESS
Hardy to half-hardy; zones 4–9

PESTS AND DISEASES
Caterpillars, leaf eelworms, slugs, powdery mildew

Anthemis

Armeria
SEA PINK, THRIFT

▲ *Anthemis tinctoria* 'E.C. Buxton'

▲ *Armeria maritima* 'Vindictive'

The long-lasting, freely borne flowers of anthemis make them indispensable in the flower garden. The daisy-like flowers attract beneficial insects. The perennial forms are not long lived, so take cuttings every couple of years.

Anthemis tinctoria is instantly recognizable as the golden marguerite, a clump-forming perennial with golden-yellow, daisy-like flowers, each to 3 cm (1¼ in across), above fern-like leaves. The cultivar 'E.C. Buxton', which can get to 60 cm (24 in) tall, produces pale lemon-yellow flowers with darker yellow centres. 'Sauce Hollandaise', 90 x 60 cm (36 x 24 in), bears cream-yellow flowers for weeks. 'Wargrave Variety', 60 cm (24 in) high and across, has creamy-yellow flowers with deep golden centres.

Other cultivars include *A.* 'Beauty of Grallach', which has deep golden-yellow flowers, and 'Grallagh Gold', which has large golden-yellow flowers and dark green foliage. Both grow to about 60 cm (24 in) high and across.

A. punctata subsp. *cupaniana* rarely gets to more than 30 cm (1 ft) high; it has silver-grey foliage and white, daisy-like flowers. It needs well-drained soil and full sun.

KEY FEATURES
• Annual or perennial
• Free flowering
• Long-lasting flowers for cutting

PLANT
In sun in well-drained soil

PROPAGATE
Seed in spring; divide in spring; root cuttings in spring

HARDINESS
Hardy to frost hardy; zones 4–8

PESTS AND DISEASES
Aphids, slugs, powdery mildew

The easy-going *Armeria maritima*, 20 x 30 cm (8 x 12 in), forms dense hummocks of narrow, dark green leaves. From late spring to summer round flowerheads, which may be white, pink or red-purple, are borne on erect stems. The species is found in the wild on cliffs and mountains throughout much of the northern hemisphere.

Several cultivars have been developed to provide strongly coloured flowers. *A. maritima* 'Alba' has large white flowers. 'Bloodstone', to 20 cm (8 in) tall, has dark red flowers. 'Corsica' has salmon flowers, 'Düsseldorfer Stolz' has crimson flowers. 'Vindictive' bears large, pink-red flowerheads on 15 cm (6 in) long stems.

A. juniperifolia is a plant for a rock garden. It grows to about 8 x 15 cm (3 x 6 in), forming hummocks of dark grey-green leaves, which are covered in late spring by purple-pink to white flowerheads, borne on short stalks. 'Bevan's Variety' is even smaller, at 5 cm (2 in) high, and bears bright rose-pink flowers.

KEY FEATURES
• Evergreen perennial or subshrub
• Dense white or pink flowers
• Compact, neat mounds of foliage

PLANT
In sun in well-drained soil

PROPAGATE
Seed in spring or autumn; divide in spring; basal cuttings in summer

HARDINESS
Hardy; zones 4–7

PESTS AND DISEASES
Trouble free

Artemisia

MUGWORT, WORMWOOD

Arum

CUCKOO PINT, LORDS AND LADIES

▲ *Artemisia ludoviciana* 'Silver Queen'

▲ *Arum creticum*

This large genus contains plants that are suitable for rock gardens as well as those for a herb garden, a mixed border or for groundcover. *Artemisia ludoviciana* (western mugwort), 1.2 m x 60 cm (4 x 2 ft), is a clump-forming perennial, with pretty, aromatic, silvery leaves and, in late summer to early autumn, clusters of yellowish flowers. The compact 'Silver Queen', which grows to about 75 cm (30 in) tall, has larger leaves and fewer flowers. 'Valerie Finnis', to 60 cm (2 ft) tall, has sharply cut, silver-grey leaves.

One of the most widely planted artemisias is *A.* 'Powis Castle', 1 x 1.2 m (3 x 4 ft), a woody based, semi-evergreen perennial. It has feathery, silver-grey foliage, and in late summer it bears plumes of silver-yellow flowers.

The evergreen perennial *A. stelleriana* 'Boughton Silver', 15 x 45 cm (6 x 18 in), is useful for groundcover or for edging a border. It has silver-grey, deeply cut leaves. In late summer and early autumn insignificant yellow flowers are borne on erect stems. *A. schmidtiana*, 30 x 45 cm (12 x 18 in), is an evergreen with finely cut, silvery leaves. The compact 'Nana', 8 x 30 cm (3 x 12 in), is ideal for edging.

KEY FEATURES
- Deciduous or evergreen perennial or shrub
- Aromatic foliage

PLANT
In sun in well-drained soil

PROPAGATE
Seed in autumn or spring; divide in autumn or spring; greenwood cuttings in summer

HARDINESS
Hardy to frost hardy; zones 5–8

PESTS AND DISEASES
Aphids, powdery mildew

The most familiar of these tuberous perennials is the wildflower *Arum maculatum*, which grows in hedgerows, producing glossy, arrow-shaped leaves and unusual flowers within a large spathe. The flowers are followed by spikes of poisonous red berries.

The half-hardy *A. creticum*, 50 x 15 cm (20 x 6 in), has large dark green leaves and yellow or cream-white spathes. It will do best in full sun.

The hardy *A. italicum*, 30 x 15 cm (12 x 6 in), has large, white-veined leaves and greenish-white spathes. The berries that follow the flower spike are orange-red. *A. italicum* subsp. *albispathum* has pure white spathes and all-green leaves. The most decorative form, however, is *A. italicum* subsp. *italicum* 'Marmoratum' (syn. *A. italicum* 'Pictum'), which has large leaves, veined with cream or pale green, and white spathes, enclosing a flower spike that is followed by red berries. The leaves of this cultivar are larger when it is grown in shade.

The berries are a good source of autumn and winter food for birds.

KEY FEATURES
- Perennial
- Colourful spathes
- Attractive foliage

PLANT
In sun or shade in fertile, well-drained soil

PROPAGATE
Seed in autumn; divide after flowering

HARDINESS
Hardy to half-hardy; zones 7–9

PESTS AND DISEASES
Trouble free

Aruncus

Arundo

▲ *Aruncus dioicus*

▲ *Arundo donax*

The light green, toothed and fern-like leaves of *Aruncus dioicus* (goat's beard) grow to 1 m (3 ft) long, and the cream-white flowers of this herbaceous perennial are borne in large panicles, to 50 cm (20 in) long, in early to midsummer. Plants get to 1.8 m (6 ft) tall and to 1.2 m (4 ft) across, so make sure they have plenty of space. The smaller cultivar 'Kneiffii', to 1.2 m (4 ft) high and 45 cm (18 in) across, has dark green, ferny leaves and tiny, cream flowers. 'Glasnevin' is similar.

This is a good plant for near a natural pond in reliably moist soil, although when it is planted in full sun it will tolerate drier soil. In shady, woodland settings it needs moisture-retentive soil. It will self-seed around, so deadhead where necessary.

A. aethusifolius is a compact perennial, 40 cm (16 in) high and across, with leaves that are tinged with pink or red in autumn. In summer it bears panicles to 15 cm (6 in) long of cream-white flowers.

KEY FEATURES
- Perennial
- Large flowerheads
- Will grow in shade
- Good for naturalizing around a pond

PLANT
In sun or partial shade in moist soil

PROPAGATE
Seed in autumn or spring; divide in autumn or spring

HARDINESS
Hardy; zones 4–8

PESTS AND DISEASES
Aphids but usually trouble free

Of the two or three species in the genus, only *Arundo donax* (giant reed) is widely grown. Its sturdy stems can grow to about 5 m (15 ft) high, and the clump will eventually spread to 1.5–1.8 m (5–6 ft) across. This is not a plant for a small garden – grow it at the back of a large border, where the attractive seedheads can be a feature in winter when other plants have died back. The stout stems bear broad, blue-green leaves, each to 60 cm (24 in) long. The panicles of pale green to purple spikelets are up to 60 cm (24 in) long and are borne in autumn, turning white as they age. Flower spikes are borne on two-year-old stems and rarely appear in cool climates.

A. donax var. *versicolor* (syn. 'Variegata'; striped giant reed), 1.8 m x 60 cm (6 x 2 ft), has leaves boldly striped with cream-white. 'Variegata Superba', 1 m (3 ft) tall, has wide leaves that are edged and striped in white.

A. formosana (Taiwan grass) is smaller than *A. donax*, growing to about 2.4 m (8 ft) tall and having pink-tinged panicles that turn golden-brown as they age. 'Golden Fountain' has green-striped, yellow leaves; 'Green Fountain' makes a neat, rounded clump.

KEY FEATURES
- Evergreen grass
- Attractive seedheads
- Bamboo-like foliage

PLANT
In sun in moist soil

PROPAGATE
Seed in spring; divide in spring

HARDINESS
Hardy to half-hardy; zones 7–10

PESTS AND DISEASES
Trouble free

Aster

Astilbe

▲ *Aster alpinus*

▲ *Astilbe* 'Hyazinth'

Aster alpinus is a clump-forming perennial, about 25 cm (10 in) high, bearing purple, daisy-like flowers with bright yellow centres in early to midsummer. It needs full sun. Cultivars have deep purple, pale pink or white flowers.

Better known are *Aster novae-angliae* (New England aster) and *A. novi-belgii* (Michaelmas daisy) that flower in summer to autumn. New England asters include 'Andenken an Alma Pötschke', 1.2 m (4 ft) tall with pink flowers, 'Barr's Pink', 1.3 m (4 ft 6 in) tall with double pink flowers, and 'Herbstschnee', 1.2 m (4 ft) tall with white flowers.

There are dozens of cultivars of *A. novi-belgii*. 'Climax', 1.2 m (4 ft) tall, has pale lavender-blue flowers; 'Fellowship', 1 m (3 ft) tall, has double, deep pink flowers; 'Kristina', 30 cm (12 in) tall, has semi-double, white flowers; and 'Lady in Blue', 30 cm (12 in) tall, has lavender flowers.

Choose cultivars that have been developed to resist mildew. The flowers are valuable for attracting late-season pollinators, including butterflies, beetles, moths and flies, and the seeds are good food for finches and siskins.

KEY FEATURES
• Annual, biennial or perennial
• Late-season flowers
• Attracts beneficial insects

PLANT
In sun or partial shade in moisture-retentive soil

PROPAGATE
Seed in autumn or spring; divide in autumn or spring

HARDINESS
Hardy to frost tender; zones 5–8

PESTS AND DISEASES
Aphids, eelworms, slugs, grey mould, powdery mildew

Astilbes are grown for their attractive, ferny foliage and plumes of colourful flowers. There are dozens of cultivars and they do best in moist soil, even in bog gardens, in light shade. Most cultivars have been developed from *Astilbe* x *arendsii* and produce erect plumes of tiny flowers. 'Amethyst', 1 m (3 ft) high and across, has lilac-pink flowers in early summer; 'Brautschleier', 75 cm (30 in) high and across, has bright green leaves and white flowers in midsummer; 'Fanal', 60 x 45 cm (24 x 18 in), has dark leaves and crimson flowers in early summer; 'Hyazinth', 1 m x 45 in (36 x 18 in), has bright green leaves and rich pink flowers in mid- to late summer; 'Irrlicht', 50 cm (20 in) high and across, has dark leaves and white flowers from late spring; and 'Venus' 1 m x 45 cm (36 x 18 in), has bright green leaves and pale pink flowers in early summer.

Other striking cultivars are *A.* 'Bronce Elegans' ('Bronze Elegance'), 45 cm (18 in) high and across, which has plumes of pink-red flowers in late summer and bronze foliage, and 'Deutschland', 50 x 30 cm (20 x 12 in), with bright green leaves and pure white flowers in late spring.

KEY FEATURES
• Perennial
• Plumes of colourful flowers
• Attractive foliage
• For woodland or bog gardens

PLANT
In sun or partial shade in moisture-retentive soil

PROPAGATE
Divide in spring or winter

HARDINESS
Hardy; zone 6

PESTS AND DISEASES
Leaf spot, powdery mildew

Athyrium
LADY FERN

Aucuba

▲ *Athyrium filix-femina*

▲ *Aucuba japonica* 'Variegata'

These deciduous ferns are highly variable, but all have pretty fronds that do well in moist, lightly shady places.

Athyrium filix-femina, usually 50 x 30 cm (20 x 12 in) although it can grow large in ideal conditions, is a pretty fern, with light green fronds with dark red stalks. 'Fieldii', 90 x 30 cm (3 x 1 ft), has long, narrow fronds. The compact 'Frizeliiae', 20 x 30 cm (8 x 12 in), has massed pinnae, which are contracted into tiny balls along the midribs and look like a necklace of green beads. Ferns in the Plumosum Group, 1.2 x 1 m (4 x 3 ft), have finely cut fronds; those in the Cristatum Group, 1 m (3 ft) high and across, have flat, fan-like crests.

A. niponicum (Japanese painted fern), 30 cm (12 in) high, has silver-green fronds and spreads indefinitely in the right conditions. *A. niponicum* var. *pictum*, 45 x 60 cm (18 x 24 in), is an especially beautiful form with triangular fronds with wine red stalks and silver-grey segments.

The recently introduced *A*. 'Ursula's Red' has dark reddish central areas and white-grey tips in its second year.

KEY FEATURES
• Deciduous fern
• Attractive foliage
• Good groundcover
• Good for woodland gardens

PLANT
In shade in fertile, neutral or acid soil

PROPAGATE
Ripe spores; divide in spring

HARDINESS
Hardy to frost tender; zones 4–9

PESTS AND DISEASES
Trouble free

The only species in the genus to be widely grown is *Aucuba japonica* (spotted laurel), which will get to 3 m (10 ft) high and across and which has glossy but rather unexciting dark leaves. Small red-purple flowers are borne in spring, and female plants have bright red berries in autumn.

The cultivars that have been developed have more interesting foliage. 'Crassifolia', which is a male form, has large, dark green leaves, to 25 cm (10 in) long. Both female forms, 'Crotonifolia' and 'Gold Dust', have dark green leaves covered with golden-yellow speckles. The medium-sized 'Golden King' has bold yellow blotches on the leaves. The leaves of 'Picturata' have golden-yellow markings in the centre. 'Variegata' (formerly known as 'Maculata') is a medium shrub with densely, yellow-spotted foliage; both male and female forms are available.

These shrubs do not need regular pruning, but cut out completely any shoots that begin to bear all-green leaves. These will be more vigorous than the variegated shoots and will gradually cause the whole plant to revert.

KEY FEATURES
• Evergreen shrub
• Tolerant of a range of situations and conditions
• Autumn berries
• Year-round interest

PLANT
In sun or partial shade in well-drained soil

PROPAGATE
Semi-ripe cuttings in summer

HARDINESS
Hardy; zones 7–10

PESTS AND DISEASES
Trouble free

Begonia

Bellis
DAISY

▲ *Begonia 'Sandra'*

▲ *Bellis perennis*

This enormous genus is the source of many garden and houseplants. Tuberous begonias are bushy perennials, grown for their handsome foliage and showy flowers. They are tender plants with a winter dormancy. Lift tubers before the first frosts and allow to dry off before storing in a dry place with a minimum temperature of 5°C (41°F).

Many reliable named cultivars are available so if you want a plant for a particular purpose it is worth searching for specific plants. 'Billie Langdon', 60 x 45 cm (24 x 18 in), flowers from summer to early autumn, bearing pure white flowers, each to 18 cm (7 in) across. 'Champagne', 20 cm (8 in) high and across, has cream-white, double flowers, each to 8 cm (3 in) across, which cascade around the plant; this is ideal for a windowbox or hanging basket.

Semperflorens begonias, usually 15–20 cm (6–8 in) high, are covered with pink, red, white or bicoloured flowers all summer long. They flower in sun or shade.

KEY FEATURES
- Annual, perennial or evergreen shrub
- Colourful, showy flowers
- Good in containers
- Useful summer bedding

PLANT
In sun or partial shade in well-drained, neutral to acid soil

PROPAGATE
Seed in early spring; divide rhizomes in summer

HARDINESS
Half-hardy to frost tender; zone 10

PESTS AND DISEASES
Aphids, mealybugs, vine weevils; grey mould, powdery mildew

The ornamental forms of *Bellis perennis* (daisy), 20 cm (8 in), are compact plants with colourful flowerheads, borne on erect stems. These relatives of the common lawn daisy are useful for edging, spring bedding and containers. Flowers diminish in quality and quantity after the first year, so it's best to treat them as annuals or biennials and replace them regularly. New colours and flower forms are being developed all the time, so look out for new shades. If you want to include a particular colour in your scheme, buy plants on which one or two flowers are just beginning to open. Otherwise, buy small plants, which will grow away quickly and will flower in early summer.

Among the best cultivars are 'Alba Plena', which has double white flowers; 'Dresden China', which has tiny, double pink flowers; 'Parkinson's Great White'; and 'Prolifera' (hen and chickens), which has double white flowers spotted with pink and tiny 'daughter' flowers hanging from the 'mother' bloom. The widely available Pomponette Series has early, semi-double flowers in white, pink or red. Tasso Series plants have large double flowers, to 6 cm (2½ in) across, in white, pink or red.

KEY FEATURES
- Perennial
- Colourful pompons

PLANT
In sun or partial shade in well-drained soil

PROPAGATE
Seed in early summer; divide in spring or after flowering

HARDINESS
Hardy; zones 4–8

PESTS AND DISEASES
Trouble free

Berberis

Bergenia
ELEPHANT'S EARS

▲ *Berberis thunbergii* 'Rose Glow'

▲ *Bergenia* 'Morgenröte'

These useful shrubs can be grown as specimen plants, included in mixed borders and used for hedging. When they are used for hedging, trim plants after flowering.

Berberis thunbergii, 1 x 2.4 m (3 x 8 ft), is one of the deciduous species. It is a dense, round shrub covered with small oval leaves, which turn vivid red and orange in autumn. Pale yellow flowers, borne in spring, are followed by red berries. The cultivar 'Rose Glow' has red-purple leaves variegated with white. The leaves of the slow-growing 'Silver Beauty' are variegated with cream-white.

The evergreen *B. darwinii*, 3 m (10 ft) high and across, has small, glossy leaves. In spring it produces a mass of orange flowers (sometimes with a second flush later) and in autumn blue-black fruits. This makes a good hedge.

The slow-growing evergreen *B.* 'Goldilocks', 4 x 3 m (12 x 10 ft), has glossy leaves and, in mid- to late spring, clusters of yellow-orange flowers (sometimes with a second display in midsummer), followed by blue-black fruit.

KEY FEATURES
• Deciduous, semi-evergreen or evergreen shrub
• Spring to early summer flowers
• Autumn berries and leaf colour
• Tolerant and easy to grow

PLANT
In sun or partial shade in well-drained soil

PROPAGATE
Softwood or semi-ripe cuttings in summer

HARDINESS
Hardy to frost hardy; zones 7–9

PESTS AND DISEASES
Aphids, powdery mildew

These clump-forming perennials are excellent for edging and woodland gardens. They have large, leathery leaves and clusters of small flowers on upright stems, borne in late winter to early spring. In autumn the leaves often become flushed with red and purple. Although hardy, plants will benefit from a winter mulch.

Bergenia cordifolia, 30 cm (12 in) high and across, has pink flowers and heart-shaped, slightly puckered leaves. *B. cordifolia* 'Purpurea' has dark purple flowers in spring, often with a second flush later in the year, and in autumn the leaves turn purplish.

'Baby Doll', 30 x 60 cm (12 x 24 in), has pale pink flowers and green leaves. 'Bressingham White', 45 x 60 cm (18 x 24 in), has white flowers and dark leaves. 'Morgenröte', 45 x 60 cm (18 x 24 in), has bright red-pink flowers on red stems; the large, oval leaves are dark green and up to 15 cm (6 in) long. 'Wintermärchen', 45 x 60 cm (18 x 24 in), has deep pink flowers and dark green leaves that turn red in autumn.

KEY FEATURES
• Evergreen perennial
• Good groundcover
• Spring flowers
• Coloured foliage

PLANT
In sun or partial shade in fertile, well-drained soil

PROPAGATE
Divide in autumn or spring

HARDINESS
Hardy to frost hardy; zones 4–8

PESTS AND DISEASES
Slugs and snails, vine weevils, leaf spot

Betula
BIRCH

Blechnum
HARD FERN

▲ *Betula pendula* 'Youngii'

▲ *Blechnum spicant*

These graceful trees have attractive bark and often good autumn colour. Many forms are suitable for small gardens, and they are usually easy to grow and quick to establish.

Betula pendula (silver birch), 25 x 10 m (80 x 30 ft), has slightly drooping branches and grey-white bark. The mid-green leaves turn yellow in autumn, and in early spring trees bear yellowish catkins. *B. pendula* 'Youngii' (Young's weeping birch) has a pleasing, dome-shaped form, to about 8 m (25 ft) tall, and it is ideal for a small garden. 'Purpurea', 10 x 3 m (30 x 10 ft), has purple leaves.

B. utilis (Himalayan birch), 18 x 10 m (60 x 30 ft), has coppery brown peeling bark. The naturally occurring form *B. utilis* var. *jacquemontii*, which eventually grows as high as the species, has white bark, which is outstanding in the winter garden. The leaves turn yellow in autumn. Cultivars include 'Grayswood Ghost', which has glossy foliage and white bark; 'Jermyns', which has particularly long catkins; and 'Silver Shadow', with large, dark leaves.

KEY FEATURES
• Deciduous tree
• Catkins in autumn
• Attractive bark
• Good for hole-nesting birds

PLANT
In full sun or light shade in well-drained soil

PROPAGATE
Softwood cuttings in summer; graft in winter

HARDINESS
Hardy; zones 3–8

PESTS AND DISEASES
Downy mildew but largely trouble free

These are useful evergreen ferns for shade, where some forms can be used as groundcover. *Blechnum spicant* is one of the low-growing species, to 50 cm (20 in) high and spreading to 60 cm (2 ft) or more by means of rhizomes. Dark green, glossy evergreen fronds form rosettes around upright central, deciduous fronds. There are forms with crested and serrated segments.

B. gibbum, 1 m (3 ft) high and across, has lance-shaped, bright green fronds, which form a neat shuttlecock.

The low-growing, carpeting *B. penna-marina*, 20 cm (8 in) high, will spread almost indefinitely in the right conditions. It has small, ladder-shaped fronds, tinged with bronze in spring, which form dense tufts.

B. tabulare, 1 x 1.2 m (3 x 4 ft), has dark green, sterile fronds. Young fronds are tinged with bronze and emerge throughout the growing season.

KEY FEATURES
• Evergreen fern
• Good for woodland gardens
• Good groundcover

PLANT
In partial shade in moist, fertile, acid soil

PROPAGATE
Spores in late summer; divide in spring

HARDINESS
Hardy to frost tender; zones 4–8

PESTS AND DISEASES
Trouble free

Briza
QUAKING GRASS

Buddleja
BUDDLEIA, BUTTERFLY BUSH

▲ *Briza maxima*

▲ *Buddleja davidii* 'Dartmoor'

These annual and perennial grasses have linear leaves, and the flowers take the form of little purple-brown spikelets, which hang from slender stalks and tremble in breezes. They are easy to grow and can be invasive.

In spring to late summer the annual *Briza maxima* (greater quaking grass, puffed wheat), 60 x 25 cm (24 x 10 in), produces panicles of green, heart-shaped spikelets, which age to pale yellow-brown. The leaves are pale green, and make a loose clump. *B. minor* (lesser quaking grass), 45 x 25 cm (18 x 10 in), is also annual. The inflorescences are at first pale green, then purplish then yellow-brown.

B. media (common quaking grass), 90 x 30 cm (3 x 1 ft), is an evergreen perennial. The branched inflorescences appear in early spring. These are tipped with pendent spikelets, which will persist through summer. The spikelets are green, then reddish-purple, maturing to light brown-yellow. The leaves form a dense clump. Use shears to remove the inflorescences in late summer to encourage a second flush of growth in autumn.

KEY FEATURES
• Annual or perennial grass
• Pretty seedheads
• Good in dried-flower arrangements

PLANT
In sun in well-drained soil

PROPAGATE
Seed in spring; divide in late spring

HARDINESS
Hardy; zones 5–8

PESTS AND DISEASES
Trouble free

Buddleias are grown for their fragrant flowers, which attract butterflies. Most have dark green, lance-shaped to ovate leaves. *Buddleja davidii* (butterfly bush), 3 x 5 m (10 x 15 ft), has green to grey-green leaves 25 cm (10 in) long. From summer to autumn it has long panicles of pale mauve flowers. The species has given rise to several fine cultivars, all with long panicles of scented flowers in late summer to autumn, including 'Black Knight' (dark purple), 'Dartmoor' (magenta), 'Nanho Blue' (pale lilac-blue) and 'White Profusion' (white, yellow-eyed).

B. davidii 'Harlequin' has yellow-edged leaves and dark red-purple flowers; 'White Harlequin' has cream-edged leaves and white flowers. *B.* 'Lochinch', 2.4 x 3 m (8 x 10 ft), has purple-blue, yellow-eyed flowers from late summer.

B. globosa (orange ball tree), 5 m (15 ft) high and across, has dark green leaves and fragrant yellow and orange flowers borne in round clusters in early summer.

Birds will be drawn to the insect life and caterpillars that are associated with buddleias.

KEY FEATURES
• Deciduous, evergreen or semi-evergreen shrub
• Sweetly scented flowers
• Easy to grow
• Attracts butterflies

PLANT
In sun in well-drained soil

PROPAGATE
Semi-ripe cuttings in summer; hardwood cuttings in autumn

HARDINESS
Hardy to frost tender; zones 7–9

PESTS AND DISEASES
Capsid bugs, mullein moth

Calamagrostis

REED GRASS, SMALLWEED

Calendula

MARIGOLD, POT MARIGOLD

▲ *Calamagrostis* x *acutiflora* 'Karl Foerster'

▲ *Calendula officinalis* 'Indian Prince'

This is a large genus of perennial grasses which have branching inflorescences. They can be grown in a moist, shady woodland garden or at the back of a mixed border.

Calamagrostis x *acutiflora* (feather reed grass), 1.8 x 1.2 m (6 x 4 ft), is a clump-forming plant, with arching green leaves. In mid- to late summer it produces long, feathery panicles of bronze to purple-brown inflorescences. The widely available *C.* x *acutiflora* 'Karl Foerster' grows to about 1.8 m (6 ft) high, with clumps growing to 60 cm (24 in) across. When they are young, the inflorescences are pink-brown, but they turn cream-brown as they age. The mid-green leaves are glossy and upright. *C.* x *acutiflora* 'Overdam', 1.2 m (4 ft) tall, has green leaves that are edged and striped with white; this form does not show such good colour in hot, humid weather.

C. brachytricha (Korean feather grass), 1.2 m (4 ft) tall, is a variable, clump-forming plant. The inflorescences are tinged with purple-red and last into winter. The glossy green leaves fade to yellow in autumn and should be cut back before winter.

KEY FEATURES
• Perennial grass
• Attractive flowerheads
• Good feature plant

PLANT
In sun or partial shade in moist soil

PROPAGATE
Divide in spring

HARDINESS
Hardy; zones 5–9

PESTS AND DISEASES
Trouble free

The fast-growing and sturdy *Calendula officinalis*, 70 x 45 cm (28 x 18 in), produces daisy-like flowers in every shade of yellow and orange. Sometimes the centres are darker, sometimes lighter. Sow seed in spring where you want the plants to grow. There are several cultivars, making compact plants as high as they are wide. Plants in the Art Shades Mixed Series, 60 cm (24 in), have semi-double, orange, apricot or cream flowers. 'Fiesta Gitana', 30 cm (12 in), has orange or yellow, sometimes bicolored, often double flowers. 'Indian Prince', 75 cm (30 in), has dark orange flowers, tinged with brown. Plants in the Kablouna Series, 60 cm (24 in), have double flowers in orange, gold and yellow. 'Lemon Queen', 45 cm (18 in), has double, pale yellow flowers. 'Orange King', 45 cm (18 in), has double, deep orange flowers. 'Pacific Apricot', 30 cm (12 in), has pale apricot flowers with darker edges.

Make space for this easy-going plant in a wildlife garden. They attract all manner of insects, which in turn attract birds. Those seeds that don't self-seed and germinate will be eaten by seed-eating birds.

KEY FEATURES
• Annual or evergreen perennial
• Attracts beneficial insects
• Easy to grow
• Good for cutting

PLANT
In sun or partial shade in well-drained soil

PROPAGATE
Seed in spring

HARDINESS
Hardy to half-hardy; zone 6

PESTS AND DISEASES
Aphids, powdery mildew

Callicarpa

BEAUTY BERRY

Calluna

HEATHER, LING

▲ *Callicarpa bodinieri* var. *giraldii*

▲ *Calluna vulgaris* 'Peter Sparkes'

These attractive shrubs are grown for their autumn fruits and summer flowers. In cold areas plant against a sunny wall. *Callicarpa bodinieri* var. *giraldii*, to about 3 x 2.4 m (10 x 8 ft), has small lilac-pink flowers in summer followed by purple-blue berries. The young leaves of 'Profusion' are bronze-purple, the flowers pink and fruits violet.

C. dichotoma, 1.2 m (4 ft) high and across, has an upright habit. The deciduous pale green leaves are 10 cm (4 in) long, and pale pink flowers appear in the leaf axils in summer. These are followed by dark purple fruits.

The compact and deciduous *C. japonica* 'Leucocarpa', 1.5 m (5 ft) high and across, has oval, pale green leaves. The flowers are borne in late summer and are white to pale pink; the berries that follow are white.

The evergreen or semi-evergreen *C. rubella*, 3 x 1.8 m (10 x 6 ft), is tender and should be grown in a container that can be moved into a greenhouse in winter. It has yellow-green leaves, purple-pink flowers and purple fruits.

Although there is only one species in the genus, there are hundreds of cultivars, with new introductions every year. Most are fairly compact shrubs between 10 cm (4 in) and 50 cm (20 in) tall. Clip plants after flowering.

Grow in groups in heather beds or combine with conifers for year-round colour. They can also be grown in containers. Among the most colourful are: 'Alba Rigida', 15 x 30 cm (6 x 12 in), white flowers in late summer to early autumn; 'Annemarie', 50 x 60 cm (20 x 24 in), double, rose-pink flowers in autumn and dark foliage; 'Darkness', 25 x 35 cm (10 x 14 in), dark red flowers in late summer and dark foliage; 'Elsie Purnell', 40 x 75 cm (16 x 30 in), pink flowers in autumn and grey-green foliage; 'Mullion', 20 x 50 cm (8 x 20 in), lilac-pink flowers in late summer and dark foliage; 'My Dream', 45 x 75 cm (18 x 30 in), white flowers; 'Peter Sparkes', 25 x 55 cm (10 x 22 in), double pink flowers in late autumn; 'Wickwar Flame', 50 x 60 cm (20 x 24 in), mauve-pink flowers in late summer and gold-orange foliage, turning orange red in winter.

KEY FEATURES
• Evergreen or deciduous shrub
• White, pink or purple flowers
• Colourful fruits

PLANT
In sun or light shade in well-drained soil

PROPAGATE
Seed in autumn; softwood cuttings in spring; semi-ripe cuttings in summer

HARDINESS
Hardy to frost tender; zones 9–10

PESTS AND DISEASES
Trouble free

KEY FEATURES
• Evergreen shrub
• Colourful flowers
• Year-round interest
• Attracts bees

PLANT
In sun in well-drained, fertile, acid soil

PROPAGATE
Semi-ripe cuttings in summer; layer in spring

HARDINESS
Hardy; zones 5–7

PESTS AND DISEASES
Grey mould, root rot

Caltha

KING CUP, MARSH MARIGOLD

Calycanthus

ALLSPICE, SPICEBUSH

▲ *Caltha palustris* var. *palustris*

▲ *Calycanthus floridus*

Caltha palustris, 40 x 45 cm (16 x 18 in), is a rather variable plant, often grown as a marginal in the shallow water at the edge of a natural pond. It has dark green, long-stalked leaves and, in early spring, glistening yellow flowers, each to 4 cm (1½ in) across. There is a white form, *C. palustris* var. *alba*, 23 x 30 cm (9 x 12 in), which sometimes flowers before the leaves appear. The double-flowered 'Flore Pleno', 25 cm (10 in) high and across, bears a mass of yellow flowers in spring and a second flush in summer.

C. palustris var. *palustris* (giant marsh marigold) is larger than the species in every respect. The beautiful saucer-shaped, yellow flowers, which appear in early summer, are to 8 cm (3 in) across and plants will get to 60 cm (24 in) high and to 75 cm (30 in) across. It, too, will grow happily in the moist soil of a bog garden.

Beneficial flies and beetles will be attracted to the flowers, and the dense foliage is useful cover in shallow water for amphibians and water insects.

KEY FEATURES
• Perennial
• Yellow flowers in early spring
• Neat mound of foliage

PLANT
In sun in boggy ground or water
to 15 cm (6 in) deep

PROPAGATE
Ripe seed; divide in early spring
or late summer

HARDINESS
Hardy to frost hardy; zones 4–9

PESTS AND DISEASES
Mildew

In summer the vigorous *C. occidentalis* (Californian allspice), 3 x 4 m (10 x 12 ft), has attractive dark red flowers, to about 5 cm (2 in) across, which consist of many narrow petals. The dark leaves give off a pleasant, spicy odour if they are crushed.

C. floridus (Carolina allspice) has aromatic, glossy, dark green leaves and many-petalled, dark red flowers over a long period in late summer. It is slightly more compact than *C. occidentalis*, getting to about 2.4 x 3 m (8 x 10 ft).

Although these plants are classified as hardy, they will do best in a sheltered corner or against a south-facing fence or wall. Remember, they are native to southern parts of the United States. Prolonged cold weather, especially cold, piercing winds, may cause damage, although this should not be terminal on an established plant.

KEY FEATURES
• Deciduous shrub
• Fragrant flowers
• Aromatic foliage
• Autumn colour

PLANT
In sun in fertile, moisture-
retentive soil

PROPAGATE
Ripe seed; softwood cuttings in
summer; layer in autumn

HARDINESS
Hardy; zones 5–8

PESTS AND DISEASES
Trouble free

Camellia

Not only are there some 250 species of beautiful shrubs in this large genus, but there are now hundreds of cultivars, all grown for their glossy foliage and wonderful flowers, which range in colour from pure white through cream and pink to the deepest of reds.

If you have acid soil, you are certain to find a camellia that fits into the colour scheme in your garden. Many camellias can be grown in containers, so even if your garden soil is unsuitable, you can still enjoy one of these lovely plants.

The flowers of *Camellia japonica* and its cultivars are borne from early spring. Those of *C.* x *williamsii* are borne from mid- to late spring. *C. reticulata* flowers in late winter to spring, and *C. sasanqua* flowers in autumn.

C. japonica (common camellia) is the parent plant of a host of hardy, beautiful plants. 'Adolphe Audusson', 5 x 4 m (15 x 12 ft), has semi-double, dark red flowers in early to mid-spring. 'Apollo', 3 m (10 ft) high and across, has semi-double red flowers in spring. 'Janet Waterhouse', 3 m (10 ft) high and across, has semi-double or formal double, white flowers in mid- to late spring. 'Nuccio's Gem', 3 m (10 ft) high and across, has formal double, white flowers from late winter to mid-spring.

C. reticulata is a half-hardy species, which can be trained as a wall shrub. Among the cultivars developed from it are 'Captain Rawes', 10 m (30 ft) high and across, which has large, semi-double to peony-form, carmine-rose flowers in mid- to late spring, and 'Mandalay Queen', also 10 m (30 ft) high and across, which has semi-double, dark rose-pink flowers in mid-spring.

The hardy *C. sasanqua*, 6 x 3 m (20 x 10 ft), has fragrant flowers from late autumn to late winter. In very cold areas, grow it and its cultivars in a container so that the flowers can be protected from the worst of the winter weather. The compact 'Cleopatra' has semi-double, rose-pink flowers. 'Narumigata' has single, pink-tinged white flowers.

Many hybrids have been developed from *C.* x *williamsii.* 'Anticipation', 4 x 1.8 m (12 x 6 ft), has large, peony-form, deep rose-pink flowers from late winter to early spring. 'Golden Spangles', 2.4 x 1.8 m (8 x 6 ft), has single,

pink-red flowers from mid- to late spring. 'Jury's Yellow', 2.4 x 1.8 m (8 x 6 ft), has anemone to peony-form, creamy-white flowers in mid- to late spring.

Do not plant camellias where the flower buds will be warmed by winter sun first thing in the morning. Against a south- or west-facing wall is ideal so that frost within plant tissue has time to melt before it is warmed by the sun. These are long-lived plants, but they have shallow roots, so take care when weeding around them. They appreciate an annual mulch of leafmould or shredded bark, and in prolonged dry spells water all camellias, even established plants. If necessary, prune after flowering to remove dead or damaged shoots or to cut back overlong shoots.

▼ *Camellia sasanqua* 'Crimson King'

▲ *Camellia japonica* 'Nuccio's Gem'

▲ *Camellia* x *williamsii* 'Anticipation'

◄ *Camellia* 'Cornish Snow'

KEY FEATURES
- Evergreen shrub
- Winter and spring flowers
- Vast range of flower colour and shape
- Glossy foliage
- Year-round interest

PLANT
In shade or partial shade in fertile, well-drained, acid soil

PROPAGATE
Semi-ripe cuttings in late summer or late winter; graft in late winter

HARDINESS
Hardy to frost hardy; zones 7–9

PESTS AND DISEASES
Aphids, scale insects, honey fungus, leaf spot,

TOP 10 CAMELLIAS
'Cornish Snow'
Single white flowers, midwinter to late spring, 3 x 1.5 m (10 x 5 ft)
'Dr Clifford Parks'
Semi-double to peony- or anemone-form, dark red flowers, mid-spring, 4 x 2.4 m (12 x 8 ft)
Camellia japonica **'Alba Simplex'**
Single white flowers, mid- to late spring, 2.4 x 1.8 m (8 x 6 ft)
Camellia japonica **'Bob Hope'**
Semi-double to peony-form, very dark red flowers, mid- to late spring, 3 x 1.8 m (10 x 6 ft)
Camellia japonica **'Ave Maria'**
Formal double, pale pink flowers, early to late spring, 3 x 3 m (10 x 10 ft)
Camellia sasanqua **'Crimson King'**
Single, dark red flowers, late autumn to late winter, 2.4 x 3 m (8 x 10 ft)
'Shiro-wabisuke'
Single, fragrant, white flowers, midwinter to early spring, 1.3 x 1.3 m (4 ft 6 in x 4 ft 6 in)
'Spring Festival'
Formal double, pink flowers, mid- to late spring, 4 x 1.8 m (12 x 6 ft)
Camellia x *williamsii* **'Donation'**
Semi-double, pink flowers, late winter to late spring, 5 x 2.4 m (15 x 8 ft)
Camellia x *williamsii* **'George Blandford'**
Semi-double to peony-form, carmine flowers, early to mid-spring, 4 x 4 m (12 x 12 ft)

Campanula
BELLFLOWER

Canna
INDIAN SHOT PLANT

▲ *Campanula 'Birch Hybrid'*

▲ *Canna 'Richard Wallace'*

This is a large genus and there can be few gardens that don't have space for at least one campanula, whether in a rock garden or a perennial border.

The reliable *Campanula* 'Birch Hybrid' is a low-growing evergreen perennial, rarely getting more than 10 cm (4 in) high but spreading to 50 cm (20 in) or more. Deep blue-mauve flowers appear in summer. This is a good choice for a raised bed or wall, where it will thrive in well-drained, moisture-retentive soil in sun or partial shade. In a white garden the low-growing *C. carpatica* 'Bressingham White' can be used for edging.

In a border the upright *C. lactiflora*, 1.2 m x 60 cm (4 x 2 ft), has variable flowers. 'Loddon Anna', 90 x 45 cm (36 x 18 in), has lilac-pink flowers. 'Prichard's Variety', 1.5 m x 60 cm (5 x 2 ft) has violet-blue flowers. These plants need neutral to alkaline, well-drained soil and a position in sun or partial shade.

KEY FEATURES
- Annual, biennial or perennial
- Some evergreen forms
- Beautiful bell-shaped flowers
- Range of sizes and growth habits
- Easy to grow

PLANT
Different species have different requirements but avoid waterlogged soil

PROPAGATE
Seed in spring; divide in spring or autumn; cuttings in autumn

HARDINESS
Hardy to frost tender; zones 4–8

PESTS AND DISEASES
Slugs and snails, mildew

These colourful plants are best grown in containers that can be moved to a frost-free place in winter; alternatively, lift the rhizomes in autumn and replant after the last frosts in spring. Despite this, the large, showy summer flowers and handsome foliage are worth the trouble. The trumpet flowers, in vivid shades of yellow, orange and red, are borne from summer to autumn on erect stems.

An old favourite, *Canna* 'Richard Wallace', 1.5 m x 50 cm (5 ft x 20 in), has rich yellow flowers above dark leaves. 'Black Knight', 1.8 m x 50 cm (6 ft x 20 in), has very dark red flowers and bronze foliage. 'Lucifer', 60 x 50 cm (24 x 20 in), has brilliant red flowers edged with yellow. 'Monet', 90 x 50 cm (36 x 20 in), has salmon flowers and blue-green leaves. 'Rosemond Coles', 1.5 m x 50 cm (5 ft x 20 in), has red flowers, the petals edged and spotted with yellow.

Among the newer cultivars are 'Pretoria' (orange flowers and striped leaves), 'Golden Vine' (dark, variegated leaves), 'Stuttgart' (cream and green foliage), and 'Black Forest' (black, glossy flowers).

KEY FEATURES
- Perennial
- Large, colourful flowers
- Handsome foliage
- Good in containers

PLANT
In full sun in well-drained soil

PROPAGATE
Seed in spring or autumn; divide rhizomes in spring

HARDINESS
Half-hardy to frost hardy; zones 7–10

PESTS AND DISEASES
Slugs and snails

Carex
SEDGE

Carpenteria

▲ *Carex elata 'Aurea'*

▲ *Carpenteria californica*

This is a large genus from a wide range of habitats, but only a few are grown in gardens. One of the most popular and reliable is the deciduous *Carex elata* 'Aurea' (Bowles's golden sedge), 70 x 45 cm (28 x 18 in), which will form a dense clump of gracefully arching, yellow leaves. Erect flower spikes appear in early summer. This is useful for providing contrast in both form and colour in a mixed border. Plant in reliably moist soil.

Another popular sedge is the evergreen *C. hachijoensis* 'Evergold', 30 x 35 cm (12 x 14 in), which has dark green leaves that are so broadly striped with yellow that from a distance the clump appears to be yellow-green. Plant in moisture-retentive but well-drained, fertile soil.

From late spring to summer the attractive *C. pendula* (weeping sedge), 1.2 m (4 ft) or more high and 1.5 m (5 ft) across, bears dark brown, pendulous flower spikes, rather like catkins, on arching stems. The evergreen leaves are dark brown. Plant in reliably moist soil.

Do not cut down deciduous plants in autumn. The seedheads of *C. elata* (tufted sedge) are valuable winter food for birds, which can shelter in the tufts of growth.

KEY FEATURES
• Deciduous or evergreen
• Colourful foliage
• Attractive flowerheads

PLANT
In sun or partial shade

PROPAGATE
Seed in spring; divide from mid-spring to early summer

HARDINESS
Hardy; zones 5–9

PESTS AND DISEASES
Aphids

The species *Carpenteria californica* is an attractive shrub, producing large, fragrant, white flowers, to 6 cm (2^1/$_2$ in) across, in early to midsummer. Each flower has a prominent boss of bright yellow stamens. The glossy leaves are dark green and to 12 cm (5 in) long, and they are whitish on the undersides. This is a good choice for training as a wall shrub, but left to its own devices it will eventually grow to about 1.8 m (6 ft) high and across.

A few cultivars have been developed. 'Ladham's Variety' is a strongly growing, free-flowering shrub, with flowers to 8 cm (3 in) across. Look out for the compact form 'Elizabeth', which has flowers to 2.5 cm (1 in) across. 'Bodnant' is a vigorous cultivar with large flowers.

These are largely trouble-free shrubs, but they do need a sheltered site, especially in exposed gardens where strong cold winds will cause damage. For this reason they are often grown successfully as wall shrubs as long as they have plenty of space to develop.

KEY FEATURES
• Evergreen shrub
• Fragrant flowers
• Glossy foliage
• Can be grown as a wall shrub

PLANT
In full sun in well-drained soil

PROPAGATE
Seed in autumn; semi-ripe cuttings in summer

HARDINESS
Frost hardy; zone 8

PESTS AND DISEASES
Fungal leaf spot

Caryopteris

Ceanothus
CALIFORNIA LILAC

▲ *Caryopteris* x *clandonensis* 'Ferndown'

▲ *Ceanothus arboreus* 'Trewithen Blue'

Most available cultivars have been developed from the rather variable *Caryopteris* x *clandonensis*. They are small, deciduous shrubs, no more than 1 x 1.5 m (3 x 5 ft), which bear clusters of small flowers in shades of blue from late summer to early autumn. Cut back plants in spring.

Among the cultivars of *C.* x *clandonensis* are 'Ferndown', which has lovely deep violet-blue flowers. 'Arthur Simmons' has purplish-blue flowers. The compact and widely available 'Heavenly Blue', which gets to about 75 cm (30 in) high and across, has rich blue flowers. 'Kew Blue' has dark blue flowers. The leaves of most forms are dark green with a distinct silver-grey on the undersides, although 'Worcester Gold', which bears pale lavender-blue flowers, has yellow foliage.

C. incana, 1.2 x 1.5 m (4 x 5 ft), has long, grey-green leaves and bright blue flowers in late summer to autumn.

KEY FEATURES
- Perennial or deciduous shrub
- Blue flowers
- Easy to grow
- Tolerant

PLANT
In sun in well-drained soil

PROPAGATE
Seed in autumn; softwood cuttings in late spring

HARDINESS
Hardy; zones 6–8

PESTS AND DISEASES
Capsid bugs

These shrubs are grown for their beautiful blue flowers, which are borne in large clusters in late spring or in late summer to early autumn. The large evergreen *Ceanothus arboreus* 'Trewithen Blue', 6 x 8 m (20 x 25 ft), has dark green leaves. In spring to early summer it bears large panicles of deep blue flowers. Not completely hardy, this is an excellent wall shrub, benefiting from the protection.

The evergreen *C.* 'Italian Skies', 1.5 x 3 m (5 x 10 ft), has glossy mid-green leaves and, in late spring, dense cymes of bright blue flowers. *C.* 'Autumnal Blue', 3 m (10 ft) high and across, is a hardy evergreen form, bearing pale blue flowers in late summer to autumn.

Although these plants are best known for their lovely blue flowers, purple, pink and white forms are available. The evergreen *C. incanus* (coast whitethorn), 3 x 4 m (10 x 12 ft), has grey-green leaves and in spring panicles of white flowers. The deciduous *C.* x *pallidus* 'Perle Rose', 1.5 m (5 ft) tall and across, has panicles of pink flowers from late summer to autumn. Prune deciduous plants in spring and evergreen plants after flowering.

KEY FEATURES
- Deciduous or evergreen shrub
- Blue flowers
- Good wall shrub

PLANT
In full sun in well-drained soil

PROPAGATE
Seed in autumn; greenwood cuttings (deciduous) or semi-ripe cuttings (evergreen) in autumn

HARDINESS
Hardy to frost hardy; zones 7–9

PESTS AND DISEASES
Honey fungus

Centaurea
KNAPWEED, HARDHEADS

Centranthus
VALERIAN

▲ *Centaurea montana*

▲ *Centranthus ruber*

This is a large genus of about 450 species of annuals and perennials, many of which are invaluable in wildflower and cottage gardens.

The hardy perennial *Centaurea montana*, 45 x 60 cm (18 x 24 in), has blue flowers, 5 cm (2 in) across. *C. montana* 'Alba' has white flowers; 'Rosea' (syn. 'Carnea') has deep pink flowers; 'Parham' has striking deep violet flowers. These mat-forming plants have mid-green leaves and hairy stems. In exposed areas they will need staking.

C. macrocephala, to 1 m (3 ft) high, is a good middle-of-the-border plant, producing large yellow, thistle-like flowerheads, which make very popular subjects for dried-flower arrangements.

The blue, pink, purple or white flowers of the annual *C. cyanus* (cornflower) attract a wide range of insects, which bring birds in their wake. The seedheads are useful for tits and finches. *C. nigra* (common knapweed) is host to a range of insects, which will attract birds, and the seedheads will attract finches in winter.

KEY FEATURES
• Annual or perennial
• Colourful flowers
• Good for cutting
• Good for wildflower gardens
• Attracts beneficial insects

PLANT
In full sun in well-drained soil

PROPAGATE
Seed in spring; divide perennials in autumn

HARDINESS
Hardy to frost hardy; zone 7

PESTS AND DISEASES
Mildew

Although the genus contains annuals, perennials and subshrubs, only the perennial *Centranthus ruber* (red valerian) is widely grown. This is a rather lax, spreading plant, to 1 m (3 ft) high and across, which bears dense clusters of small, star-shaped flowers from spring to late summer. It is often seen growing in the wild in sheltered, mild areas, appearing on apparently inhospitable waste land or between gaps in stone walls. In the garden this is an ideal plant for growing on a rocky wall or in well-drained soil at the front of a sunny border. It does best in fairly poor soil, and when it is grown in good garden soil it will get leggy and not flower well; plants should be replaced every two or three years. In mild areas cut plants hard back after flowering – they will sometimes produce a second flush of flowers.

The flowers of the species vary from pale pink, to pinkish-red to dark red. *C. ruber* 'Albus' has white flowers, and *C. ruber* var. *coccineus* has deep pink flowers; both grow to 60 cm (24 in) high and across.

KEY FEATURES
• Annual or perennial
• Flowers over a long period
• Self-seeds
• Attracts bees and other beneficial insects

PLANT
In full sun in well-drained soil

PROPAGATE
Seed in spring; divide in spring

HARDINESS
Hardy to half-hardy; zones 4–8

PESTS AND DISEASES
Trouble free

Ceratostigma

Cercis

▲ *Ceratostigma willmottianum*

▲ *Cercis siliquastrum*

The deciduous shrub *Ceratostigma willmottianum*, 1 x 1.5 m (3 x 5 ft), is grown for its pale blue flowers, to 2.5 cm (1 in) across, which are borne in late summer and early autumn. The attractive leaves, which are edged with purple, turn red in autumn. This plant will do best in a sheltered, sunny position, perhaps grown as a wall shrub against a south-facing wall. In a cold garden treat it as a hardy perennial and cut it back to ground level in late autumn and apply a good winter mulch.

The compact, red-stemmed *C. plumbaginoides*, 45 x 30 cm (18 x 12 in), is a hardy, woody-based perennial with an upright habit. In late summer it bears clusters of blue flowers. The leaves, which have wavy edges, turn a bright red in autumn. The evergreen or semi-evergreen *C. griffithii*, 1 x 1.5 m (3 x 5 ft), has purple-edged green leaves and, in late summer to autumn, bright blue flowers.

KEY FEATURES
• Deciduous or evergreen perennial or subshrub
• Blue flowers
• Autumn colour
• Good groundcover

PLANT
In sun in moisture-retentive, well-drained soil

PROPAGATE
Softwood cuttings in spring; semi-ripe cuttings in summer; layer in autumn

HARDINESS
Hardy to frost tender; zones 7–10

PESTS AND DISEASES
Mildew

The small trees and shrubs in this genus are grown for their attractive heart-shaped leaves, which take on good autumn colours, but especially for the flowers that appear in early spring, often before the leaves emerge.

Cercis siliquastrum (Judas tree), 10 m (30 ft) high and across, is remarkable for its bright pink, sometimes white, flowers that appear in spring before the foliage. The leaves are an attractive glaucous green, turning rich yellow in autumn. This is a fine feature tree in a lawn. *C. siliquastrum* f. *albida* has white flowers and pale green leaves. The cultivar 'Bodnant' has dark purplish-pink flowers.

C. canadensis (eastern redbud), also 10 m (30 ft) high and across, has red, pink or white flowers in clusters in spring, before the leaves. The heart-shaped leaves are tinged with bronze when they first emerge and turn yellow before they fall in autumn. The cultivar 'Forest Pansy' has bronze, reddish-purple leaves.

KEY FEATURES
• Deciduous shrub or tree
• Early spring flowers
• Attractive foliage
• Excellent autumn colour

PLANT
In sun or partial shade in deep, moisture-retentive and well-drained soil

PROPAGATE
Seed in autumn; semi-ripe cuttings in summer

HARDINESS
Hardy; zones 8–9

PESTS AND DISEASES
Scale insects, canker, coral spot

Chaenomeles

FLOWERING QUINCE, JAPANESE QUINCE, JAPONICA

Chamaecyparis

CYPRESS

▲ *Chaenomeles speciosa* 'Rubra Grandiflora'

▲ *Chamaecyparis lawsoniana* 'Aurea Densa'

These useful shrubs can be grown as specimens in a lawn, in a shrub border, in an informal hedge or trained against a wall. All bear colourful flowers, which may be single or double, and the flowers are followed by yellow-green or purple-green fruits.

The vigorous *Chaenomeles speciosa*, 2.4 x 5 m (8 x 15 ft), has spiny stems and in spring scarlet flowers, followed by green-yellow fruits. Several attractive cultivars have been developed: 'Nivalis' and 'Winter Snow' have white flowers; 'Geisha Girl' has unusual double, apricot-pink flowers; 'Rubra Grandiflora' has large red flowers.

C. x *superba*, a rounded shrub to 1.5 x 1.8 m (5 x 6 ft), has spiny branches and mid-green leaves. In spring to summer it bears pink, dark red, orange or orange-red single flowers, which are followed by green fruits, which ripen to yellow. The cultivar 'Crimson and Gold' has lovely deep red flowers with glowing yellow stamens. 'Knap Hill Scarlet' has large, orange-scarlet flowers. The low-growing 'Rowallane' has eye-catching scarlet flowers.

KEY FEATURES
- Deciduous shrub
- Colourful flowers
- Useful informal hedge
- Spiny stems

PLANT
In sun or partial shade in well-drained soil

PROPAGATE
Semi-ripe cuttings in summer; layer in autumn

HARDINESS
Hardy; zones 7–8

PESTS AND DISEASES
Aphids, scale insects, canker

Although this is a small genus of only seven species, an enormous number of cultivars has been developed, providing trees and shrubs of every size and habit, ranging from small plants for rock gardens to magnificent specimen trees that attain heights of 40 m (130 ft).

The best-known cultivars have been developed from *Chamaecyparis lawsoniana* (Lawson cypress). The slow-growing 'Aurea Densa' will get to only about 1.8 m (6 ft) high. The golden-yellow foliage is dense and stiff, making this ideal for a hedge or a focal point. In a small garden the fastigiate 'Columnaris', to 10 m (30 ft) tall, will provide useful height and structure with its blue-grey foliage. The popular 'Ellwoodii' makes a dense column of blue-grey foliage, eventually to 3 m (10 ft) tall.

C. nootkatensis (nootka cypress) has a pleasing conical shape, but the cultivar 'Pendula' is even more attractive, producing gracefully hanging foliage and eventually growing to about 30 x 8 m (100 x 25 ft).

KEY FEATURES
- Evergreen conifer
- Suitable for containers
- Slow-growing and versatile
- Suitable for hedging
- Cover for nesting birds

PLANT
In sun in neutral to slightly acid soil

PROPAGATE
Cuttings in late summer

HARDINESS
Hardy; zones 6–9

PESTS AND DISEASES
Aphids, canker, honey fungus, root rot

Chelone

TURTLEHEAD

Chimonanthus

WINTERSWEET

▲ *Chelone obliqua*

▲ *Chimonanthus praecox* 'Grandiflorus'

Chelones are grown for their tubular flowers, which are borne on erect stems and which, as the common name suggests, resemble the heads of turtles looking up to the sky. These are clump-forming plants, tolerant of a range of conditions, which spread by underground runners, so they can be used for groundcover where the soil is moist.

From late summer to mid-autumn *Chelone obliqua*, 60 x 30 cm (24 x 12 in), bears dark pink to mauve-purple, tubular flowers with a yellow beard on red-tinged stems. The flowers are followed by round seedheads. The leaves are dark green with noticeable veins.

C. glabra (syn. *C. obliqua* var. *alba*), 60 x 45 cm (24 x 18 in), has white flowers that are flushed with pink; they have a white beard. The mid-green leaves are up to 8 cm (3 in) long.

KEY FEATURES
• Perennial
• Colourful flowers
• Good groundcover

PLANT
In sun or partial shade in moisture-retentive soil

PROPAGATE
Seed in early spring; divide in spring; tip cuttings in late spring or early summer

HARDINESS
Hardy; zones 3–7

PESTS AND DISEASES
Slugs and snails

The genus contains six species, but there is only one, *Chimonanthus praecox*, that is widely grown. It is a vigorous, upright, deciduous shrub, 4 x 3 m (12 x 10 ft), which is grown for its fragrant, bowl-shaped, lemon-yellow flowers, to 2.5 cm (1 in) across. The flowers are borne on bare stems in winter, before the long, lance-shaped, glossy, mid-green leaves appear.

A few cultivars have been developed, although they are not as strongly scented as the species. 'Grandiflorus' has deep yellow flowers, to 4.5 cm (1³/₄ in) long, with bold, dark red markings at the centre. 'Parviflorus' has pale yellow flowers, to 1 cm (¹/₂ in) across. The later flowering 'Luteus' (syn. 'Concolor') has clear yellow flowers.

Wintersweet can be grown as a specimen plant in a lawn, although it is rather uninteresting once the flowers are over, or in a mixed border. It has sufficiently flexible stems to be trained as a wall shrub. If necessary, prune plants in spring, after flowering.

KEY FEATURES
• Deciduous or evergreen shrub
• Fragrant winter flowers
• Good wall shrub

PLANT
In full sun in well-drained soil

PROPAGATE
Softwood cuttings in summer

HARDINESS
Hardy; zone 7

PESTS AND DISEASES
Trouble free

Chionodoxa
GLORY OF THE SNOW

Choisya
MEXICAN ORANGE BLOSSOM

▲ *Chionodoxa luciliae*

▲ *Choisya ternata 'Sundance'*

These attractive spring-flowering bulbs are easy to grow and will self-seed and naturalize, providing large patches of colour early in the year. They are also dainty enough for raised beds and rock gardens.

In spring *Chionodoxa luciliae* bears clusters of, usually, three star-shaped, blue flowers with white centres. The mid-green leaves are to 20 cm (8 in) long, and the flowers are held on erect stems at about 15 cm (6 in) high. 'Alba' is similar but has all-white flowers.

C. forbesii is slightly larger, with leaves to 28 cm (11 in) long and flower stems to 20 cm (8 in) high. In spring it bears clusters of up to 12 star-shaped, blue flowers with white centres, which are loved by early-flying insects. *C. forbesii* 'Blue Giant', to 15 cm (6 in) tall, has bold flower clusters, a deep, clear blue, which are produced a little later than those of the species.

The species *C. sardensis* bears clusters of up to 12 star-shaped, deep blue flowers with lighter blue centres. The flower stems are to 20 cm (8 in) high. The cultivar *C.* 'Pink Giant' has pale pink flowers, about 1 cm ($1/2$ in) across, with white centres.

KEY FEATURES
• Bulb
• Early-spring flowers
• Will self-seed
• Suitable for rock gardens

PLANT
In full sun in well-drained soil

PROPAGATE
Offsets in summer

HARDINESS
Hardy; zones 3–9

PESTS AND DISEASES
Trouble free

Choisya ternata, one of the most attractive and reliable of all evergreen shrubs, is suitable for a mixed border or for growing as a feature plant. The small, glossy, dark green leaves are formed of three oval leaflets; they are aromatic when crushed. In spring to early summer sweetly scented white flowers are borne in clusters amid the leaves; a second flush of flowers may follow in autumn. Plants will eventually get to 2.4 m (8 ft) high and across. The cultivar *C. ternata* 'Sundance' has bright yellow-green leaves and is therefore often planted to brighten dark corners (when the leaves darken), but it rarely produces flowers. It looks most striking when it is planted in front of plants with dark green foliage.

C. 'Aztec Pearl' has narrower leaves than the species, although they are also aromatic, and it bears larger flowers, lightly tinged with pink, in profuse clusters. It, too, will get to about 2.4 m (8 ft) high and across.

Choisyas can also be trained as wall shrubs. Pruning is not usually necessary on free-standing plants, but over-long shoots can be cut back in spring.

KEY FEATURES
• Evergreen shrub
• Aromatic leaves
• Scented flowers

PLANT
In sun in well-drained soil

PROPAGATE
Semi-ripe cuttings in summer

HARDINESS
Hardy; zone 7

PESTS AND DISEASES
Trouble free

Chrysanthemum

Chusquea

▲ *Chrysanthemum 'Allouise'*

▲ *Chusquea culeou*

Unless you grow chrysanthemums with the intention of showing them, you will be more interested in their colour, height and shape than in the intricacies of the 30 divisions and many subdivisions of the flower shape and size: reflexed, anemone, single and so on. These are useful plants for cut flowers, especially as many have long, sturdy stems. Taller plants need staking.

There is a vast range of cultivars. 'Allouise', 1.2 m x 75 cm (4 ft x 30 in), is classified as an early-flowering outdoor intermediate, medium-flowered plant. It is a fine plant for the mixed border but will need staking. 'Beacon', 1.2 m x 60 cm (4 x 2 ft), has bronze-red flowers. The hardy 'Emperor of China', 1.2 m x 60 cm (4 x 2 ft), has double, silver-pink flowers and autumn red-tinged foliage. 'George Griffiths', 1.5 m x 75 cm (5 ft x 30 in), has dark red, fully reflexed flowers. The hardy 'Pennine Oriel', 1.2 m x 75 cm (4 ft x 30 in), has anemone-centred white flowers. 'Silver Gigantic', 1.2 m x 30 cm (4 x 1 ft), has incurved or loosely reflexed silver-white flowers.

KEY FEATURES
• Annual
• Vast range of flower colour and shape
• Late-season flowers

PLANT
In full sun in well-drained soil

PROPAGATE
Seed in spring; divide in autumn or spring

HARDINESS
Hardy to frost tender; zones 4–9

PESTS AND DISEASES
Aphids, capsid bugs, earwigs, grey mould, mildew, viruses

This is a large genus containing almost a hundred species, but only a few are available to gardeners. Unlike most bamboos, chusqueas are native to South and Central America, where they are found in upland woodlands. They can be grown in woodland gardens or as feature plants. The thick, solid canes are filled with pith.

Chusquea culeou, 6 x 2.4 m (20 x 8 ft), is the most often grown species. The upright canes, which are pale olive green at first, turning darker as they age, bear clusters of short, leafy branches from the nodes. The leaves are 8 cm (3 in) long, and tall canes often bend gracefully at the top. *C. culeou* 'Tenuis' (syn. 'Breviglumis) has longer leaves and a more spreading habit of growth than the species. The thin culms get to 2.1 m (7 ft) long.

The clump-forming *C. coronalis*, to 2.4 m (8 ft) high, can be grown well in a container.

KEY FEATURES
• Evergreen bamboo
• Good feature plant
• Good for cutting
• Forms dense clumps

PLANT
In sun or partial shade in fertile, moisture-retentive but well-drained soil

PROPAGATE
Divide in spring

HARDINESS
Hardy to frost tender; zones 6–9

PESTS AND DISEASES
Slugs and snails

Cimicifuga
BUGBANE, COHOSH

Cistus
ROCK ROSE, SUN ROSE

▲ *Cimicifuga simplex*

▲ *Cistus x purpureus*

The clump-forming *Cimicifuga simplex*, 1.2 m x 60 cm (4 x 2 ft), is ideal in a woodland garden. It has pale green to purplish leaves and from these in autumn arise spires of white flowers. There are several attractive cultivars. The eye-catching 'Atropurpurea' has large spikes of scented white flowers, which are borne on erect purple-green stems. The leaves are dark maroon with bright green undersides. 'Brunette' has dark brown-purple leaves above which the purplish flower stems emerge, with racemes of purple-tinged, white flowers. 'Elstead', which gets to 1 m (3 ft) high, has purplish stems and cream-white flowers. 'Prichard's Giant' (syn. *C. ramosa*) grows to 1.8 m (6 ft) tall. The compact 'White Pearl', 60 cm (2 ft) high and across, has pure white flowers and pale green leaves.

Good for the back of the border, *C. racemosa* (black snake root), 2.1 m (7 ft) high, has dark green, ferny leaves and, in summer, upright stems with fluffy racemes of white, unpleasantly scented flowers.

KEY FEATURES
- Perennial
- Erect spires of flowers in autumn
- Suitable for bog gardens

PLANT
In partial shade in fertile, moisture-retentive soil

PROPAGATE
Divide in spring

HARDINESS
Hardy; zones 3–8

PESTS AND DISEASES
Trouble free

These evergreen shrubs are grown for their colourful flowers, which, although short lived, are borne in profusion from early to late summer. They need a well-drained position in full sun and deep, fertile soil. Deadhead regularly to ensure a succession of blooms. The plants are not long lived but can be quickly and easily replaced when they get straggly and leggy. There are about 20 species in the genus, but these have been widely hybridized, and many attractive cultivars are available.

In summer *Cistus ladanifer* (gum cistus), 2.4 x 1 m (8 x 3 ft), has large white flowers, each petal with a distinctive maroon spot at the base. In summer *Cistus x purpureus*, 1 m (3 ft) high and across, produces dark pink flowers, each to 8 cm (3 in) across and with a reddish blotch at the base of each petal and a bright yellow centre. The dark green leaves have wavy edges. *C.* 'Peggy Sammons', 1 m (3 ft) high and across, has grey-green leaves and pale purple-pink flowers in early summer. 'Silver Pink', 75 x 90 cm (30 x 36 in), has dark green leaves and pale pink flowers with golden stamens. The hybrid *C. x pulverulentus*, 60 cm (2 ft) high and across, has pink-purple flowers.

KEY FEATURES
- Evergreen shrub
- Colourful flowers
- Ideal for containers

PLANT
In sun in well-drained soil

PROPAGATE
Seed in spring; softwood cuttings in summer

HARDINESS
Frost hardy; zones 7–9

PESTS AND DISEASES
Trouble free

Clematis

Sometimes known as the queen of climbers, clematis are perhaps the most useful and beautiful of all climbing plants.

▲ *Clematis 'Duchess of Edinburgh'*

▲ *Clematis 'Nelly Moser'*

The large-flowered clematis hybrids need no introduction, but there are many less well-known but wonderful species and cultivars, including some evergreen and herbaceous forms – so many, in fact, that it is possible to have clematis flowers almost all year round.

Early-flowering species, such as *Clematis alpina* and *C. macropetala*, have nodding, bell-shaped blue or soft mauve-pink flowers in mid- and late spring. *C. montana*, which has masses of small white or pink flowers in early summer, is one of the most vigorous and spectacular of all clematis, but it can be kept in check by shortening the side growths in early autumn.

Early large-flowered hybrids, blooming in early and midsummer, are grown for the size and beauty of the flowers. The group includes 'Nelly Moser', 'The President' and 'Lasurstern'. They flower on shoots produced the previous year so are pruned only when necessary and not severely in spring.

Late-flowering species and hybrids, such as *C. viticella* and *C.* 'Jackmanii', bloom in late summer and into autumn on shoots produced in the current year. These are pruned in spring to encourage flowers on new stems.

The evergreen *Clematis cirrhosa* has fern-like leaves and white, bell-shaped flowers between midwinter and early spring. Plant *C. armandii*, with clusters of fragrant white flowers, to follow in early and mid-spring. These species are not as hardy as the others described and do best when protected by a sheltered wall.

Herbaceous perennials, such as *C. heracleifolia*, are a largely overlooked group but are useful in gardens with no suitable surface to train one of the climbing forms.

The evergreen, early-flowering *C. alpina* has the additional advantage that seed-eating birds are attracted to the silvery seedheads. The foliage is useful cover for birds when other plants are still leafless.

The key to success is to make sure that the roots are planted in a shady position in a deep hole with plenty of well-rotted compost. The topgrowth can then be trained up into the sun, where the flowers will be seen at their best. Don't be put off by their reputation for being difficult to prune. In general, prune after flowering, and if you aren't sure, don't prune for a year or two to see what happens.

KEY FEATURES
- Deciduous or evergreen climber or herbaceous perennial
- Wide range of flower colour and shape
- Long flowering period
- Attractive seedheads
- Suitable for containers

PLANT
With roots in shade and top-growth in sun in fertile, well-drained soil

PROPAGATE
Seed in autumn; cuttings in spring or early summer; layer in late winter or early spring

HARDINESS
Hardy to half-hardy; zones 4–8

PESTS AND DISEASES
Aphids, clematis wilt, powdery mildew

▲ *Clematis* 'Ville de Lyon'

TOP 10 CLEMATIS CULTIVARS
'Beauty of Worcester'
Violet-blue flowers, double in late spring, single in late summer
'Belle of Woking'
Double mauve flowers, summer
'Duchess of Edinburgh'
Double white flowers, summer
'Ernest Markham'
Petunia red flowers, summer
'Henryi'
White flowers, summer

'Jackmanii Superba'
Deep violet-purple flowers, midsummer
'Lasurstern'
Purple-blue flowers, summer
'Nelly Moser'
Mauve and carmine flowers, early summer
'Ville de Lyon'
Carmine red flowers, midsummer
'White Moth'
Double white flowers, late spring

▲ *Clematis macropetala*

◄ *Clematis* 'White Moth'

Clerodendron

▲ *Clerodendron thomsoniae*

These plants are grown for their colourful, sometimes fragrant flowers. The hardier forms are suitable for a sunny, sheltered border, but they are often grown in conservatories and greenhouses, where larger plants should be pruned after flowering to keep them in check.

The deciduous half-hardy shrub *Clerondendron bungei* (glory flower), 1.8 m (6 ft) high and across, has large, dark green leaves, to 20 cm (8 in) long. In late summer and autumn it bears clusters of fragrant, dark pink flowers.

C. thomsoniae (bleeding heart vine, glory bower) is a tender, evergreen, twining climber, with large, oval to heart-shaped leaves, 20 cm (8 in) or more long, and clusters, to 15 cm (6 in) across, of bell-shaped flowers that have pure white calyces and startling red petals.

C. trichotomum var. *fargesii*, eventually to 6 m (20 ft) high and across, is a hardy vigorous deciduous shrub. The leaves are bronze as they emerge in spring, and the fragrant white flowers are followed by blue berries.

KEY FEATURES
- Deciduous or evergreen climber, shrub or tree
- Good in containers

PLANT
In sun in fertile, moisture-retentive, well-drained soil

PROPAGATE
Seed in spring; semi-ripe cuttings in summer; root cuttings in winter

HARDINESS
Hardy to frost tender; zone 4

PESTS AND DISEASES
Under glass: mealybugs, red spider mites, whitefly

Colchicum
AUTUMN CROCUS, NAKED LADIES

▲ *Colchicum agrippinum*

Large-flowered colchicums look attractive planted under trees and shrubs. The flowers emerge in autumn, before the long, strappy leaves. Plant individual corms 10 cm (4 in) deep and 20 cm (8 in) apart, and lift and divide clumps when they become congested after the leaves have died back. The flowers do not withstand heavy rain or strong winds so they do best in sheltered corners. The large leaves persist into spring and can overpower some spring-flowering bulbs, so position these plants carefully.

In autumn *Colchicum autumnale* (meadow saffron), 15 cm (6 in) high and across, produces goblet-shaped, lavender-pink flowers, which are followed by the long leaves, which last until spring. The lovely *C. speciosum* 'Album' has large, goblet-shaped white flowers, which are surprisingly weather resistant. The large, glossy leaves follow and last through winter into early spring.

Among the most popular cultivars are *C.* 'The Giant', to 20 cm (8 in) high, which bears up to five purple-violet flowers in succession. 'Waterlily', to 15 cm (6 in) high, has double pinkish-lilac flowers. The dainty *C. agrippinum*, 10 cm (4 in) high, flowers in early autumn, producing pretty pink flowers that are heavily chequered with purple.

KEY FEATURES
- Autumn-flowering corms
- Suitable for rock gardens

PLANT
In sun in well-drained soil

PROPAGATE
Separate corms in summer

HARDINESS
Hardy to half-hardy; zones 4–9

PESTS AND DISEASES
Slugs and snails, grey mould

Convolvulus

Cordyline
CABBAGE PALM, CABBAGE TREE

▲ *Convolvulus sabatius*

▲ *Cordyline australis* 'Torbay Dazzler'

Don't be put off growing convolvulus by their cousins, the well-known invasive garden weeds.

The perennial *Convolvulus sabatius* has trailing stems, which can be trained to climb. It bears the typically shaped flowers in summer and autumn. The flowers, each to 2.5 cm (1 in) across, are a beautiful rich blue.

C. tricolor, 40 x 30 cm (16 x 12 in), is a short-lived perennial, usually grown as an annual, which is an ideal plant for a hanging basket. It has a succession of funnel-shaped blue flowers throughout summer. The cultivar 'Royal Ensign', 50 cm (20 in) high and across, has deep blue, trumpet-shaped flowers, with striking white and yellow centres.

C. cneorum is a neat, rounded shrub, up to about 60 x 90 cm (2 x 3 ft), with small, narrow, silver-grey leaves and large white flowers, which open from pink buds in summer. This is not reliably hardy and needs a sheltered corner in full sun.

KEY FEATURES
• Annual or perennial climber or
  evergreen shrub
• Beautiful flowers

PLANT
In full sun in well-drained soil

PROPAGATE
Seed in spring; divide in spring;
softwood cuttings in summer

HARDINESS
Hardy to frost tender; zone 8

PESTS AND DISEASES
Trouble free

Cordyline australis and its cultivars are upright plants, resembling palm trees as they mature and develop a thick, woody stem topped by a mass of long, lance-shaped leaves. Established trees sometimes form branches and may produce large panicles of small white flowers. These plants are not reliably hardy, although in favoured areas they might reach a height of 10 m (30 ft). They are often grown in containers on patios or even in conservatories.

The species has yellow-green leaves, which emerge from a central point, which means that they take up more space than can perhaps be spared in a border where there are more interesting plants competing for space. Several cultivars have been developed with strikingly coloured leaves. The leaves of 'Torbay Dazzler', for example, are strongly striped with cream, and those of 'Torbay Plum' are deep red. The mid-green leaves of 'Alberti' have red centres, cream stripes and pink edges. Plants in the Purpurea Group have dark purple or bronze leaves.

KEY FEATURES
• Evergreen woody-stemmed
  perennials
• Good feature plant
• Striking flower panicles
• Attractive foliage
• Good in containers

PLANT
In sun or partial shade in
well-drained soil

PROPAGATE
Remove suckers in spring

HARDINESS
Half-hardy to tender; zones 3–4

PESTS AND DISEASES
Trouble free

Coreopsis
TICKSEED

Cornus
CORNEL, DOGWOOD

▲ *Coreopsis verticillata*

▲ *Cornus kousa*

These annuals and perennials are grown for their bright yellow, daisy-like flowers. The perennials are not long-lived, and they are often treated as summer bedding.

Coreopsis verticillata is a spreading perennial, 80 x 45 cm (32 x 18 in), with mid-green leaves. Over a long period from early summer it bears clusters of bright yellow flowers, each 5 cm (2 in) across. The cultivars vary only in size and the intensity of yellow displayed by their flowers: 'Grandiflora' (sometimes sold as 'Golden Shower') has dark yellow flowers; 'Moonbeam' has lemon yellow flowers on bronzed stems and is a good front-of-border choice at 50 cm (20 in) high; 'Zagreb', which is neat and compact at 30 cm (12 in) high and across, has deep yellow flowers.

In late spring to late summer the clump-forming *C. grandiflora*, 90 x 45 cm (36 x 18 in), bears large yellow daisy flowers with darker yellow centres. 'Early Sunrise', 45 x 38 cm (18 x 15 in), has semi-double yellow flowers. 'Mayfield Giant', 1 m x 45 cm (36 x 18 in), has large yellow flowers, each to 8 cm (3 in) across.

KEY FEATURES
- Annual or perennial
- Bright yellow, freely borne flowers
- Good cut flowers
- Attracts beneficial insects

PLANT
In sun or partial shade in fertile, well-drained soil

PROPAGATE
Seed in spring; divide in spring

HARDINESS
Hardy to frost tender; zones 4–9

PESTS AND DISEASES
Slugs and snails

This genus contains a large number of interesting plants with winter stem or bark colour, fruits, delicate flowers or a striking habit of growth. *Cornus kousa*, a deciduous shrub to 7 x 5 m (22 x 15 ft), produces tiny green flowers with striking white bracts. In autumn the leaves turn red-purple. The bracts of *C. kousa* var. *chinensis* turn pink as they age. The beautiful *C. alternifolia*, to 6 m (20 ft) high and across, has spreading branches and autumn colour.

C. sericea 'Kelseyi', 75 cm x 1.5 m (30 in x 5 ft), is widely available but rather dull. Far more interesting are the dogwoods that have vividly coloured winter stems. *C. sericea* 'Flaviramea', to 1.8 m (6 ft) high and across, has bright greenish-yellow winter stems and the leaves turn golden in autumn. *Cornus alba* 'Sibirica' (red-barked dogwood), which grows to about 2.4 m (8 ft) high, has vivid red winter shoots and the leaves turn red in autumn. *C. alba* 'Kesselringii', to 1.8 m (6 ft) high and across, has black-purple winter shoots and good autumn colour.

KEY FEATURES
- Deciduous shrub or small tree
- Good autumn/winter interest
- Attractive flowers

PLANT
Different species have different requirements

PROPAGATE
Greenwood cuttings in summer; hardwood cuttings in autumn; graft in winter

HARDINESS
Hardy to frost hardy; zones 2–7

PESTS AND DISEASES
Anthracnose but largely trouble free

Cortaderia

PAMPAS GRASS, TUSSOCK GRASS

Corydalis

▲ *Cortaderia selloana*

▲ *Corydalis lutea*

Not long ago cortaderias were a common sight used as feature plants in the centres of lawns, the tall, stately plumes of flowers swaying in the breeze. The species, *Cortaderia selloana*, 3 x 1.5 m (10 x 5 ft), is less often seen these days, although it can still be a handsome and imposing plant in a large garden. Its long, arching, mid-green leaves make a dense clump, from which arise the erect stems of silvery flowerheads in autumn, and the plant is a striking feature of the winter garden.

Several smaller and more manageable cultivars are available. 'Pumila', for instance, grows to 1.5 x 1.2 m (5 x 4 ft); it has mid-green leaves and silver-yellow plumes. 'Aureolinata' (also known as 'Gold Band'), to 2.1 m (7 ft) tall, has yellow-green leaves that mature to golden-yellow. 'Sunningdale Silver', one the most attractive cultivars, has dense silver-white plumes borne on sturdy, erect stems; it will grow to 3 m (10 ft) tall and spread to 2.4 m (8 ft) or more across. Remove dead leaves in early winter or early spring. Wear strong gloves when you do this because the leaves have sharp edges.

KEY FEATURES
• Evergreen grass
• Good feature plant
• Striking flower panicles
• Easy to grow

PLANT
In sun in fertile, well-drained soil

PROPAGATE
Divide in spring

HARDINESS
Hardy to frost hardy; zones 7–9

PESTS AND DISEASES
Trouble free

The hardy evergreen perennial *Corydalis lutea* bears yellow flowers in clusters from spring to late summer. The ferny, pale green leaves have a glaucous appearance on the underside. This species, which will grow in sun or partial shade, will self-seed.

The blue flowers of *C. flexuosa* appear in late spring, amid the pale green leaves, which are often tinged with purple. This erect, hardy perennial, up to 30 x 20 cm (12 x 10 in), undergoes a summer dormancy. It needs a position in partial shade and fertile, moisture-retentive but well-drained soil.

The rather variable spring-flowering *C. solida* (fumewort), 18 x 10 cm (7 x 4 in), does best in full sun, when it bears dense clusters of pale mauve-pink or reddish-purple or white flowers, each to 8 cm (3 in) long, above the grey-green foliage. *C. solida* 'George Baker' has dark reddish-pink flowers.

KEY FEATURES
• Annual, biennial or perennial
• Attractive, ferny foliage
• Dainty flowers
• Self-seeds

PLANT
Species have different requirements but all need well-drained soil

PROPAGATE
Divide in autumn (spring-flowering forms) or spring (summer-flowering forms)

HARDINESS
Hardy to frost hardy; zones 6–8

PESTS AND DISEASES
Slugs and snails

Cosmos

Cotinus

▲ *Cosmos sulphureus* 'Bright Lights'

▲ *Cotinus* 'Grace'

The annual *Cosmos bipinnatus*, which can grow to 1.5 m (5 ft) tall, bears white, pink or dark red flowers, 8 cm (3 in) across, in summer. If you want a specific colour in a themed border, look for the cultivars. Plants in the Sonata Series are much dwarfer than the species, growing to about 45 cm (18 in) tall: 'Sonata White' has lovely white flowers, 'Sonata Pink' has delicate pink blooms. The Sensation Series cosmos are rather taller, to about 90 cm (36 in), and are similarly available as named colours. The flowers of 'Sea Shells' are white, pink or red.

Also annual, *C. sulphureus* and its cultivars, 60 x 30 cm (2 x 1 ft), bear yellow or orange flowers with black centres from midsummer to early autumn.

The tender perennial *C. atrosanguineus* (chocolate cosmos), 75 x 45 cm (30 x 18 in) has velvety maroon flowers on erect stems. They have a true scent of chocolate and are borne in late summer, lasting until the first really cold nights. Resist the temptation to tidy up the dead stems and simply cover the crown with a thick mulch; you should find that new shoots appear the following spring.

KEY FEATURES
• Annual or perennial
• Good for cut flowers
• Easy to grow

PLANT
In full sun in well-drained soil

PROPAGATE
Seed in late spring; basal cuttings in early spring

HARDINESS
Frost hardy to frost tender; zones 1–10

PESTS AND DISEASES
Slugs and snails, grey mould

These deciduous plants are grown for their glorious leaf colour, which is intensified in autumn. *Cotinus coggygria* (smoke bush, Venetian sumach), 4 m (12 ft) high and across, has oval green leaves. In summer large panicles of tiny flowers are borne in dense clouds, and in autumn the leaves turn vivid shades of orange, yellow and red. The smaller cultivar 'Royal Purple' has dark purplish-red leaves, which turn deeper in autumn.

C. 'Grace' becomes a rather sprawling plant, which benefits from pruning early in the year to keep it under control. It has the potential to grow to 6 x 5 m (20 x 15 ft). It has the most wonderfully translucent, large, oval, red-purple leaves, which turn eye-catching shades of orange, purple and gold in autumn. The sprays of tiny flowers appear in summer. The large *C.* 'Flame', 6 x 5 m (20 x 15 ft), has light green leaves that turn reddish-orange in autumn.

Purple-leaved forms have the best foliage colour when they are planted in full sun. Pruning in spring will encourage larger leaves.

KEY FEATURES
• Deciduous shrub or tree
• Good foliage colour
• Unusual flowers

PLANT
In sun or partial shade in fertile, moisture-retentive but well-drained soil

PROPAGATE
Softwood cuttings in summer; layer in spring

HARDINESS
Hardy; zones 5–9

PESTS AND DISEASES
Mildew, verticillium wilt

Cotoneaster

Crambe

▲ *Cotoneaster frigidus* 'Cornubia'

▲ *Crambe cordifolia*

These shrubs can be used for hedging, as specimen plants, as wall shrubs or groundcover. All are tolerant, and many put up with dry conditions. Among the evergreen plants are *C. lacteus*, 4 m (12 ft) high and wide, which has white flowers and red berries. *C. dammeri*, which grows only 20 cm (8 in) high but spreads to 1.8 m (6 ft), is useful groundcover. Its white flowers are followed by red berries.

Deciduous species include *C. frigidus*, which makes a large shrub or small tree, 10 m (30 ft) high and across. In summer it bears large clusters of white flowers, followed by red berries. *C. frigidus* 'Cornubia', 6 m (20 ft) high and across, is semi-evergreen; it, too has white flowers and bright red berries. The spreading stems of the deciduous *C. horizontalis* (herringbone cotoneaster), 1 x 1.5 m (3 x 5 ft), are excellent cover for birds, which feed on the nutritious berries. The small leaves turn red in autumn.

KEY FEATURES
- Deciduous, evergreen or semi-evergreen shrub
- Autumn and winter berries
- Good for hedging
- Easy to grow

PLANT
In sun in well-drained soil

PROPAGATE
Semi-ripe cuttings (evergreen and semi-evergreen) in late summer; greenwood cuttings (deciduous) in early summer

HARDINESS
Hardy; zones 5–8

PESTS AND DISEASES
Aphids, scale insects, fireblight, honey fungus

These large stately perennials are often found in coastal areas, growing in sand dunes. They are also tolerant of quite poor soil in gardens.

The clump-forming perennial *Crambe cordifolia* has large, fleshy, puckered, dark green leaves, each to 35 cm (14 in) across. From spring to midsummer large, airy panicles of tiny white flowers are borne on sturdy stems, to 1.5 m (5 ft) tall. The flowers have a strong scent that is not entirely pleasant. This is one of the mainstays of a white garden, and if the flowerheads are not cut back, the crambe can be used to support an annual climber.

The smaller *C. maritima* (sea kale) has blue-green leaves, to 30 cm (12 in) long, and cloudy clusters of tiny white, honey-scented flowers on stems to 75 cm (30 in) tall. The young stems are edible and can be forced or blanched, like rhubarb, to provide a spring vegetable.

KEY FEATURES
- Perennial
- Attractive foliage
- Masses of tiny flowers
- Attracts beneficial insects

PLANT
In sun in well-drained soil

PROPAGATE
Seed in spring or autumn; divide in spring

HARDINESS
Hardy; zones 6–9

PESTS AND DISEASES
Black rot, clubfoot

▲ *Crataegus orientalis*

▲ *Crinodendron hookerianum*

The shrubs and small trees in this genus have spines, which makes them ideal for hedging, when they make a dense, impenetrable barrier. Because they are tolerant of pollution, they are useful in city gardens and can also be used as windbreaks in coastal areas.

Crataegus laevigata (may, Midland hawthorn) is a neat, small tree, striking in late spring when it is covered with white-pink blossom and in autumn when the red berries appear. The cultivar 'Paul's Scarlet' has double red-pink flowers and dark red berries.

C. orientalis (syn. *C. lacinata*) is a deciduous, spreading tree, 6 m (20 ft) high and across. It has dark green leaves and, in spring, clusters of white flowers. These are followed by red or orange-red fruits.

When used for hedging, prune in autumn, after flowering, unless you prefer to leave the berries for birds.

KEY FEATURES
- Deciduous or semi-evergreen shrub or tree
- Fragrant flowers
- Autumn and early winter fruits
- Attracts birds
- Good cover for roosting and nesting birds

PLANT
In sun or partial shade in well-drained soil

PROPAGATE
Seed in spring; graft in autumn

HARDINESS
Hardy; zones 5–8

PESTS AND DISEASES
Aphids, fireblight, honey fungus, mildew, rust

The two species in this genus come from Chile, and although they will survive in most gardens, a late spring frost can damage tender shoots and early flower buds. Both species need fertile, moisture-retentive, well-drained, acid soil. They will not do well in alkaline conditions.

Crinodendron hookerianum (lantern tree) is an upright shrub, with narrow, glossy, dark green leaves. In a sheltered position it will grow to 6 x 5 m (20 x 15 ft), although it is fairly slow growing and in most temperate gardens will rarely grow to more than 4 m (12 ft) high. It is planted for its attractive flowers, which appear in late spring and last until late summer. They take the form of clusters of lantern-shaped, dark red-pink, pendent blooms, which open from white buds.

The other species, *C. patagua*, which grows to 8 x 5 m (25 x 15 ft), bears white, bell-shaped, scented flowers in summer. It benefits from the protection of a sunny wall.

Prune crinodendrons only when absolutely necessary after flowering, by removing dead and damaged shoots.

KEY FEATURES
- Evergreen shrub
- Unusual flowers
- Neat habit of growth

PLANT
In sun or partial shade in well-drained, acid soil

PROPAGATE
Greenwood cuttings in early summer; semi-ripe cuttings in late summer

HARDINESS
Borderline hardy; zones 8–9

PESTS AND DISEASES
Trouble free

Crinum

Crocosmia
MONTBRETIA

▲ *Crinum powellii 'Album'*

▲ *Crocosmia* x *crocosmiiflora* 'Emily McKenzie'

The large, showy, lily-like flowers of crinums are borne on erect, sturdy stems, making them useful additions to a mixed border. They are also ideal for containers that can stand on a sunny patio in summer but be moved to a warm conservatory or greenhouse in winter.

From late summer to autumn the hardy *Crinum* x *powellii* bears clusters of fragrant, pale pink flowers, each 10 cm (4 in) long, on erect stems that may reach 1.5 m (5 ft) high. The strappy, mid-green leaves may also grow to 1.5 m (5 ft) long. *C.* x *powellii* 'Album' has up to ten beautiful, pure white, bell-shaped flowers, each to 10 cm (4 in) long, also borne on erect stems.

The tender *C. americanum* (Florida swamp lily) and *C. asiaticum* should be grown in tubs and stood outside only when night-time temperatures won't fall below 10°C (50°F). Both flower in spring to summer, *C. americanum*, 50 x 15 cm (20 x 6 in), with white flowers with dark brown backs and *C. asiaticum* with fragrant white flowers.

KEY FEATURES
• Bulb
• Striking flowers
• Scented flowers
• Good in containers

PLANT
In full sun in fertile, moisture-retentive but well-drained soil

PROPAGATE
Offsets in spring

HARDINESS
Hardy to frost tender; zones 6–10

PESTS AND DISEASES
Trouble free

The vivid red, orange and yellow flowers of crocosmias are borne on tall, arching stems above bright green, lance-shaped leaves. Many cultivars have been developed from the hardy hybrid *Crocosmia* x *crocosmiiflora*, 60 cm (24 in) tall, which bears yellow-orange flowers in summer. 'Emily McKenzie', also 60 cm (24 in), has large bright orange flowers; 'Solfatare', 70 cm (28 in), has handsome bronze-green leaves and soft orange-yellow flowers; 'Gerbe d'Or' (syn. *C.* 'Golden Fleece'), 75 x 20 cm (30 x 8 in), has beautiful pale yellow flowers in late summer.

One of the most eye-catching is *C.* 'Lucifer', 1.2 m (4 ft) tall, with bright red flowers in summer. *C.* 'Bressingham Blaze', 90 x 20 cm (36 x 8 in), has orange-red flowers with yellow throats and pleated mid-green leaves. The marginally hardy *C. masoniorum*, 1.2 m (4 ft) tall, produces upward-facing, orange-red flowers in midsummer.

Crocosmias will spread and naturalize. Clumps that muscle in on less robust neighbours can be lifted and divided in spring.

KEY FEATURES
• Corm
• Late-summer flowers
• Easy to grow
• Good for cut flowers

PLANT
In sun or partial shade in moisture-retentive but well-drained soil

PROPAGATE
Divide in spring

HARDINESS
Hardy to frost hardy; zones 5–9

PESTS AND DISEASES
Trouble free

Crocus

Cryptomeria

▲ *Crocus tommasinianus*

▲ *Cryptomeria japonica*

Crocuses are among the most reliable and obliging of all spring bulbs. Planted under deciduous trees and shrubs or even in grass, they will flower year after year, spreading steadily to carpet areas with welcome colour.

The species *Crocus tommasinianus*, 8–10 cm (3–4 in) high, is good for naturalizing, with pale lilac flowers. As well as the pure white *C. tommasinianus* f. *albus*, the species has several fine cultivars such as 'Ruby Giant', with deep violet flowers, and 'Whitewell Purple', with purple flowers.

Flowering from late winter, *C. chrysanthus* 'Blue Pearl' has pale blue outer petals, white on the inside with yellow throats. 'E.A. Bowles', another Chrysanthus hybrid, has cream-yellow flowers, and 'Zwanenburg Bronze' has pale yellow flowers with a bronze sheen on the outside.

C. vernus (Dutch crocus) has several cultivars that flower in spring to early summer: 'Pickwick' has large white flowers striped with lilac and purple; 'Jeanne d'Arc' has white flowers faintly streaked with purple; 'Remembrance' has glossy, violet flowers.

KEY FEATURES
• Corm
• Late-winter to spring or autumn flowers
• Good for naturalizing
• Easy to grow

PLANT
In sun in well-drained soil

PROPAGATE
Separate cormlets in summer; many forms self-seed

HARDINESS
Hardy to frost hardy; zones 3–8

PESTS AND DISEASES
Mice and squirrels

The species *Cryptomeria japonica* can grow to 25 m (80 ft) high and has a broadly columnar habit, to 6 m (20 ft) wide. It is a handsome tree, with shedding, reddish-brown bark and downward-sweeping branches, covered in needle-like leaves, which darken to deep green. It is the parent of numerous plants that are compact enough for small gardens. Plants in the Elegans Group have a columnar habit and grow to about 20 m (70 ft) high. They have blue-green foliage that turns green as it matures and bronze-red in autumn. The slow-growing 'Elegans Compacta', 4 m (12 ft) high, has feathery foliage that turns purple in winter. 'Bandai-sugi', 1.8 m (6 ft) high and across, is slow growing and has blue-green foliage, turning bronze in cold weather. 'Cristata' (syn. 'Sekka-sugi') has leaves that are fused together so that they resemble coral; the cream-yellow leaves turn almost white in winter. The dwarf 'Vilmoriniana', 1 m (3 ft) high and across, has dense, light green foliage, which turns red-brown in winter; 'Compressa' is similar.

KEY FEATURES
• Evergreen conifer
• Year-round colour and shape
• Specimen trees

PLANT
In sun or partial shade in fertile, well-drained soil

PROPAGATE
Seed in spring; ripewood cuttings in late summer or early autumn

HARDINESS
Hardy; zones 6–9

PESTS AND DISEASES
Trouble free

Cyclamen

▲ *Cyclamen hederifolium*

Cytisus

BROOM

▲ *Cytisus battandieri*

Cyclamen will self-seed, forming large colonies under deciduous trees and shrubs, where their pretty leaves are useful groundcover from autumn to spring.

The autumn-flowering *Cyclamen cilicium*, 12 x 8 cm (5 x 3 in), has pink or white flowers with maroon staining. The round or heart-shaped leaves are often prettily patterned and last through winter into spring.

C. coum, 8 x 10 cm (3 x 4 in), flowers in late winter to early spring. The flowers are white, pale pink or pink-purple with darker marks. *C. coum* subsp. *caucasicum* 'Album' has white flowers with the distinctive pink mark around the mouth. Plants in *C. coum* subsp. *coum* Pewter Group have pewter leaves with bold dark green midribs; the flowers are pink.

C. hederifolium, 10 x 8 cm (4 x 3 in), flowers in autumn. The heart- or ivy-shaped leaves are prettily marked and usually follow the pink flowers. *C. hederifolium* var. *hederifolium* 'Album' is a white form.

KEY FEATURES
• Tuberous perennial
• Attractive foliage
• Pretty flowers
• Easy to grow
• Good groundcover

PLANT
Different species have different requirements but plant in well-drained soil

PROPAGATE
Ripe seed

HARDINESS
Hardy to frost tender; zones 5–9

PESTS AND DISEASES
Mice and squirrels, vine weevils

Although the genus contains some evergreen shrubs, many of the best garden plants are deciduous. These are not longlived, especially on thin soil, but are worthwhile for their profuse, fragrant flowers, usually yellow, which are followed by green seedpods. If pruning is needed, do it after flowering but do not cut into old wood.

The deciduous *C. battandieri* (pineapple broom), 4 m (12 ft) high and across, is an initially upright plant, spreading as it ages. The silver-grey leaves are 10 cm (4 in) long, and the golden-yellow, pineapple-scented flowers are borne from late spring to midsummer.

C. x *beanii*, 60 cm x 1 m (2 x 3 ft), is a deciduous, almost prostrate plant, producing rich yellow flowers in spring.

The compact and deciduous *C.* x *praecox*, 1.2 x 1.5 m (4 x 5 ft), has arching shoots and pale yellow flowers. The cultivar 'Allgold' has very dark flowers, and 'Warminster' (Warminster broom) has cream-yellow flowers.

KEY FEATURES
• Deciduous shrub
• Fragrant pea-like flowers
  in spring
• Good wall shrub
• Good groundcover

PLANT
In sun in well-drained soil

PROPAGATE
Seed in spring or autumn; ripewood cuttings in midsummer; semi-ripe cuttings in late summer

HARDINESS
Hardy to frost tender; zones 7–9

PESTS AND DISEASES
Gall mites

Dahlia

Although the genus contains only about 30 species, approximately 20,000 cultivars have been developed over the years, and these are now classified by flower type and size.

▲ *Dahlia* 'Bishop of Llandaff'

KEY FEATURES
- Tuberous perennial
- Showy flowers
- Good for display or bedding
- Good for cutting

PLANT
In full sun in fertile, moisture-retentive but well-drained soil

PROPAGATE
Seed in early spring; basal cuttings in spring; divide tubers

HARDINESS
Frost hardy to frost tender; all zones

PESTS AND DISEASES
Aphids, capsid bugs, earwigs, slugs and snails, mildew, viruses

TOP 10 DAHLIAS
'Arabian Night'
Decorative-type, small velvet-red flowers, 1 m (3 ft)
'Clair de Lune'
Collerette-type, lemon-yellow and cream flowers, 1.1 m (3 ft 6 in) tall
'Cryfield Rosie'
Ball-type, small red-tinged, yellow flowers, 1 m (3 ft)
'Dark Desire'
Single flowers, dark chocolate petals, yellow centre, 1 m (3 ft)
'Doris Day'
Cactus-type, small dark red flowers, 1 m (3 ft)
'Gerrie Hoek'
Waterlily-type, small pale pink flowers, 1.2 m (4 ft)
'Jescot Julie'
Miscellaneous (orchid-type), orange and dark orange flowers, 1 m (3 ft)
'Kenora Sunset'
Semi-cactus-type, small red and yellow flowers, 1.2 m (4 ft)
'Scarlet Comet'
Anemone-type, bright red flowers, 1.2 m (4 ft)
'Small World'
Pompon-type, pure white flowers, 1 m (3 ft)

Unless you are tempted by the show bench, you are more likely to choose dahlias because of their impact in the garden, and there is a wonderful range of colours to suit every type of planting scheme, from pale cream-yellow to dark, vibrant red. Some forms have flowers of more than one colour. The flowers vary in size from the pompons, which can be no more than 5 cm (2 in) across, to the giant decorative forms, which produce flowers that are 25 cm (10 in) across. Taller plants and those with large, heavy flowerheads will need staking.

Dahlias are not hardy. In warm, reliably frost-free areas tubers can be left in the ground, protected by a thick winter mulch, but in most gardens tubers should be lifted after the first autumn frost has blackened the topgrowth, and allowed to dry off. They should then be cleaned and stored, with a dusting of fungicide, in dry, frost-free conditions, until they can be started into growth again in spring and planted out after the last spring frost.

Dahlias flower from summer into autumn, until the first frosts. As well as the tall border dahlias, there is a group of bedding dahlias, often grown from seed and treated as half-hardy annuals. These, too, are available in a range of flower types and colours: 'Bednall Beauty', to 60 cm (24 in) tall, has double, dark red flowers; 'Longwood Dainty', 40 cm (16 in) tall, has apricot flowers; 'Diabalo', 35 cm (14 in) tall, has double and semi-double flowers that may be orange, yellow, lavender, lilac or white above bronze-green foliage.

Among the vast range of border dahlias, 'Moor Place', 1.1 m x 60 cm (3 ft 6 in x 2 ft), has dark red pompon-type flowers. 'Porcelain', 1.2 m x 60 cm (4 x 2 ft), is a small-flowered, waterlily-type, with beautiful white flowers tinged with lilac. 'Daleko Jupiter', 1.3 m x 60 cm (4 ft 6 in x 2 ft), has giant, spiky semi-cactus-type flowers that shade from deep pink-red to pink-yellow in the centre.

▲ *Dahlia* 'Porcelain'

◀ *Dahlia* 'Moor Place'

▼ *Dahlia* 'Gerrie Hoek'

Some dahlias also have attractive foliage. The bedding dahlia 'Ellen Houston', 30 cm (12 in) high and across, for example, has single orange-red flowers which contrast with the purple-tinged foliage. The popular dahlia 'Bishop of Llandaff', 85 x 90 cm (2 ft 10 in x 3 ft), has scarlet flowers with dark centres and yellow anthers; the leaves are dark bronze-green. 'David Howard', 75 cm (30 in) high and across, is a miniature decorative cultivar with golden-orange flowers and bronze foliage.

Daphne

Delphinium

▲ *Daphne odora* 'Aureomarginata'

▲ *Delphinium* Elatum Group

This genus provides a range of shrubs for rock gardens, mixed borders or woodland gardens. The evergreen *Daphne laureola* (spurge laurel), 1 x 1.5 m (3 x 5 ft), has glossy leaves and, in late winter, clusters of lightly scented yellow-green flowers. It will tolerate deep shade.

The deciduous *D. mezereum* (mezereon), 1.2 x 1 m (4 x 3 ft), is grown for its fragrant, pink-purplish flowers, borne in late winter to early spring, before the leaves appear.

From late winter to spring the evergreen *D. odora*, 1.5 m (5 ft) high and across, bears fragrant deep pink to white flowers. *D. odora* 'Aureomarginata', 1.3 m (4 ft 6 in) high and across, has beautifully fragrant, white, pink-edged flowers; the rather leathery leaves are edged with cream.

The low-growing, evergreen *D. cneorum*, 15 cm x 1.8 m (6 in x 6 ft), has trailing stems covered with dark green leaves. In late spring it produces abundant clusters of fragrant, pale purplish-pink or white flowers.

KEY FEATURES
• Deciduous or evergreen shrub
• Winter to spring flowers
• Wonderful fragrance

PLANT
In sun or partial shade in fertile, moisture-retentive but well-drained soil

PROPAGATE
Ripe seed; softwood cuttings in summer; semi-ripe or evergreen cuttings in late summer

HARDINESS
Hardy to frost hardy; zones 5–8

PESTS AND DISEASES
Aphids, grey mould, leaf spot, viruses

Delphiniums add height and colour to beds and borders. Some forms, such as the New Zealand Hybrids, are resistant to powdery mildew and blackspot.

There is a vast range of cultivars. Belladonna Group plants, 1.2 m x 45 cm (4 ft x 18 in), are upright, branching perennials with single flowers. 'Casablanca' has pure white flowers with a yellow centre and 'Cliveden Beauty' sky blue flowers. Elatum Group delphiniums, 1.2–1.8 m (4–6 ft) are clump-forming perennials with a single, tall flower spike. 'Blue Nile' has pale blue flowers with a white eye, 'Fenella' has semi-double blue flowers with a black eye, 'Rosemary Brock' has semi-double, deep pink flowers and a brown eye, 'Finsteraahorn' has rich purple flowers with a black eye and 'Sandpiper' has white flowers with a brown eye.

Pacific Hybrids, 1.5 m (5 ft), are grown as annuals or biennials. They have large, semi-double flowers. 'Astolat' has pink-lilac flowers with a black eye, 'Black Knight' has violet flowers with a black eye, and 'Summer Skies' has blue flowers with a white eye.

KEY FEATURES
• Annual, biennial or perennial
• Tall flower spikes

PLANT
In full sun in fertile, moisture-retentive but well-drained, alkaline soil

PROPAGATE
Seed in spring; basal cuttings in early spring

HARDINESS
Hardy; zones 2–7

PESTS AND DISEASES
Leaf moth, slugs and snails, blackspot, mildew, viruses

Deschampsia
HAIR GRASS

Deutzia

▲ *Deschampsia flexuosa* 'Tatra Gold'

▲ *Deutzia* x *rosea* 'Carminea'

These grasses can be grown in borders or wildflower gardens. Trim off the inflorescences before new growth begins in spring. *D. cespitosa* (tufted hair grass), 1.8 x 1.2 m (6 x 4 ft), is an evergreen plant, forming dense mounds of mid-green leaves. The silver-green panicles are borne from early to late summer. 'Bronzeschleier' ('Bronze Veil'), 1.2 m (4 ft) high and across, produces on tall green stems inflorescences that are silvery at first but that turn bronze as they age. 'Goldschleier' ('Golden Veil'), 1.2 m (4 ft) high and across, has dark green leaves and spikelets that age to bright silver-yellow.

The evergreen *D. flexuosa* (wavy hair grass), 60 x 30 cm (24 x 12 in), has fine, blue-green leaves, each to about 20 cm (8 in) long. In early to midsummer erect panicles, to 12 cm (5 in) long, of silver-brown spikelets are borne on wavy stalks. The cultivar 'Tatra Gold', 50 cm (20 in) high, has fine, bright yellow leaves and bronze inflorescences from late spring to midsummer.

KEY FEATURES
• Evergreen perennial grass
• Elegant inflorescence
• Grows in shade
• Good for cutting

PLANT
In sun or partial shade in moisture-retentive, neutral to acid soil

PROPAGATE
Seed in spring or autumn; divide in spring or early summer

HARDINESS
Hardy; zones 4–7

PESTS AND DISEASES
Trouble free

These useful shrubs can be grown in borders or trained as wall shrubs. They bear masses of purple, pink or white flowers from late spring to early summer. Prune in midsummer, after flowering, if necessary.

Deutzia x *rosea* is a compact hybrid, growing to about 1.2 m (4 ft) high and across. In early summer it bears white, star-shaped flowers, which are pinkish on the outside. The cultivar 'Carminea' has rose-carmine flowers, tinged with paler pink. 'Campanulata' has white, bell-shaped flowers.

D. x *elegantissima*, 1.5 m (5 ft) high and across has fragrant pink flowers. The compact 'Roselind', 1.2 x 1.5 m (4 x 5 ft), has star-shaped, white, pink-flushed flowers in late spring and early summer. 'Rosea Plena' has double flowers that open pink and mature to white.

D. longifolia, 1.8 x 3 m (6 x 10 ft), is a spreading shrub with greyish leaves. In summer it bears white flowers, pink on the undersides. 'Veitchii' has large, lilac-pink flowers.

D. 'Mont Rose', 1.2 m (4 ft) high and across, bears star-shaped, deep pink flowers in early summer.

KEY FEATURES
• Deciduous shrub
• Plentiful spring flowers
• Good wall shrub

PLANT
In sun in fertile, moisture-retentive soil

PROPAGATE
Seed in autumn; softwood cuttings in summer; hardwood cuttings in autumn

HARDINESS
Hardy to frost hardy; zones 5–9

PESTS AND DISEASES
Trouble free

Dianthus

CARNATION, PINK

Diascia

▲ *Dianthus 'Diane'*

▲ *Diascia fetcaniensis*

This large genus contains carnations, pinks and sweet williams. There are plants for containers, gravel gardens or borders. Garden pinks, 45 x 30 cm (18 x 12 in), are usually divided into the old-fashioned forms, which flower in early summer and are usually clove scented, and modern pinks, which have a longer flowering period (from early summer to autumn) and which may or may not be scented.

Old-fashioned pinks include 'Brympton Red' (single, bright red); 'Dad's Favourite' (semi-double, white, red-edged); 'Excelsior' (double, pink, fringed petals); 'Mrs Sinkins' (double, white, fringed petals); and 'Musgrave's Pink' (single, white, green eye). Modern pinks include 'Bovey Belle' (double, purple flowers); 'Devon Dove' (scented, double white flowers); 'Diane' (deep salmon red); 'Gran's Favourite' (scented, white, laced with maroon); 'Tropic Butterfly' (deep pink, edged in white).

Among the so-called patio pinks are the fragrant *D.* 'Mendlesham Minx', which has double, dark red flowers, splashed with silver, and 'Mendlesham Sweetheart', which has large, double white flowers with a dark red centre.

KEY FEATURES
• Annual or perennial subshrub
• Fragrant flowers
• Good for cutting

PLANT
In sun in well-drained, neutral to alkaline soil

PROPAGATE
Seed in autumn; cuttings in summer

HARDINESS
Hardy; zones 4–8

PESTS AND DISEASES
Aphids, slugs and snails, viruses

These colourful summer-flowering plants are good at the front of a border or in a container. Deadheading regularly will encourage new blooms to form.

Diascia barberae is the parent of several attractive cultivars. 'Blackthorn Apricot', 25 x 50 cm (10 x 20 in), has loose spires of apricot-pink flowers, each to 2 cm ($^3/_4$ in) across, from summer to autumn. The mat-forming 'Ruby Field', 25 x 60 cm (10 x 24 in), has pale green leaves and dark pink flowers; it is a good choice for a hanging basket.

D. fetcaniensis, 25 x 50 cm (10 x 20 in), has heart-shaped leaves and spikes of rose-pink, tubular flowers from summer to early autumn.

The versatile *D. rigescens*, 30 x 50 cm (12 x 20 in), bears dense spikes of coppery-pink flowers from early to late summer. It is a trailing plant but with stiff stems, which is useful in containers and at the front of borders.

D. vigilis, 30 x 60 cm (12 x 24 in), is a creeping, prostrate form, with fleshy leaves, to 4 cm ($1^1/_2$ in) long, and spikes of clear pink flowers.

KEY FEATURES
• Annual or semi-evergreen perennial
• Colourful flowers
• Good in containers

PLANT
In full sun in moisture-retentive but well-drained soil

PROPAGATE
Seed in spring; divide in spring; softwood cuttings in spring

HARDINESS
Borderline hardy; zones 7–9

PESTS AND DISEASES
Slugs and snails

Dicentra

Digitalis
FOXGLOVE

▲ *Dicentra spectabilis*

▲ *Digitalis purpurea*

In late spring and early summer the familiar clump-forming *Dicentra spectabilis* (bleeding heart, Dutchman's breeches), 60 x 45 cm (24 x 18 in), bears lobed, mid-green leaves above which arching stems emerge, bearing racemes of rose-pink, locket-like flowers with white inner petals. *D. spectabilis* 'Alba' has pure white flowers.

D. formosa (wild bleeding heart), 45 x 90 cm (18 x 36 in), forms a dense clump of ferny, mid-green leaves. Clusters of deep rose-pink flowers are borne on reddish stems from late spring to early summer. This plant will self-seed. *D. formosa* var. *alba* has pale green foliage and white flowers. *D. formosa* subsp. *oregana* has grey-green leaves and blue-pink flowers.

The clump-forming cultivar 'Adrian Bloom', 35 x 45 cm (14 x 18 in), has grey-green leaves and racemes of dark red flowers in late spring to early autumn. 'Stuart Boothman', 30 x 40 cm (12 x 16 in), has bluish-grey leaves and delicate pink flowers on arching stems.

KEY FEATURES
- Perennial
- Spring flowers
- Good for rock gardens

PLANT
In partial shade in fertile, moisture-retentive, neutral to alkaline soil

PROPAGATE
Ripe seed; divide in early spring; root cuttings in winter

HARDINESS
Hardy; zones 4–8

PESTS AND DISEASES
Slugs and snails

These typical woodland plants are useful in a mixed border, especially in cottage gardens. Although they will tolerate full sun, they do best in partial shade.

Digitalis purpurea (common foxglove), 1–1.8 m x 60 cm (3–6 x 2 ft), produces rosettes of soft, grey-green leaves, often flushed purple at the base. The bell-shaped, variable flowers are usually pink, red or purple, spotted with darker purple, and they are borne on one side of erect stems in early summer. The white form, *D. purpurea* f. *albiflora*, is especially lovely. If you have a clump of white foxgloves as well as some purple-flowered plants, keep them apart, because the purple flowers will eventually take over.

The short-lived *D. ferruginea* (rusty foxglove), 1–1.2 m (3–4 ft) high, is a rosette-forming plant. The dark yellow, bell-shaped flowers, marked with darker stripes inside, are borne on erect stems in summer.

Resist the temptation to cut back the seedheads of foxgloves in autumn. Many types of bird will appreciate the food in the cold winter weather.

KEY FEATURES
- Biennial or perennial
- Tall flower spikes
- Self-seeds
- Attracts beneficial insects

PLANT
In partial shade in moisture-retentive but well-drained soil

PROPAGATE
Seed in late spring

HARDINESS
Hardy; zones 5–9

PESTS AND DISEASES
Leaf spot, mildew

Dipsacus
TEASEL

Doronicum
LEOPARD'S BANE

▲ *Dipsacus fullonum*

▲ *Doronicum orientale* 'Magnificum'

Although there are 15 species in the genus, only one, *Dipsacus fullonum* (common teasel), is widely grown. This is a large perennial, 1.8 m x 80 cm (6 ft x 32 in), that produces narrow, lance-shaped, toothed, dark green leaves, which may be 30 cm (12 in) or more long. The leaves are borne in pairs, forming a cup around the stem. The flowerhead consists of a mass of tiny, purple-pink, occasionally white, flowers, which create an oval, thistle-like head, 8 cm (3 in) long. Stiff, curved bracts form a collar around the base of the flowerhead, which appears in mid- and late summer.

D. *sativus*, 1.8 m x 60 cm (6 x 2 ft), bears large, pale purple flowerheads, to 11 cm ($4^{1}/_{4}$ in) long.

Pollinating insects, especially bees, will be attracted to the heads of tiny purple flowers, and in late summer and autumn sparrows, goldfinches and buntings will flock around the seedheads.

KEY FEATURES
• Biennial or perennial
• Autumn seedheads
• Food for seed-eating birds
• Ideal for wildlife gardens

PLANT
In sun or partial shade in any soil

PROPAGATE
Seed in spring or autumn

HARDINESS
Hardy; zones 5–9

PESTS AND DISEASES
Aphids

Doronicum orientale, 60 x 90 cm (2 x 3 ft), is a rhizomatous perennial, which can be invasive in a shady border. It has scalloped leaves and single, golden-yellow flowers, 5 cm (2 in) across, in mid-spring to early summer. The cultivar 'Frühlingspract' ('Spring Beauty'), to 40 cm (16 in) tall, has double, golden-yellow flowers. The bright yellow flowers of 'Miss Mason', 45 x 60 cm (18 x 24 in), are 8 cm (3 in) across and are borne well above the heart-shaped leaves. 'Magnificum' grows to 50 cm (20 in) tall and has large yellow flowers.

D. x *excelsum* 'Harpur Crewe', 60 cm (24 in) high and across, has toothed leaves, heart-shaped at the base, and in spring three or four golden-yellow flowers, with darker centres, on each stem.

D. *pardalianches* (great leopard's bane), 1 m x 60 cm (3 x 2 ft), will colonize areas of light woodland and is useful for colour under trees and shrubs. The yellow, daisy-like flowers are produced in mid- to late spring.

KEY FEATURES
• Perennial
• Good for cutting
• Easy to grow

PLANT
In partial shade in fertile, moisture-retentive soil

PROPAGATE
Seed in spring; divide in autumn

HARDINESS
Hardy; zones 4–8

PESTS AND DISEASES
Leaf spot, mildew, root rot

Dryopteris
BUCKLER FERN

Echinops
GLOBE THISTLE

▲ *Dryopteris filix-mas*

▲ *Echinops ritro*

These deciduous ferns are robust and vigorous, providing large clumps of greenery in the garden. In mild winters they may be semi-evergreen.

Dryopteris affinis (golden male fern), 1 m (3 ft) high and across, has a shuttlecock of lance-shaped, pale green fronds, which darken as they mature. 'Cristata' (king fern) is an especially handsome form, producing large, symmetrical, crested fronds.

D. dilatata (broad buckler fern), 1 x 1.2 m (3 x 4 ft), is useful for naturalizing in a woodland garden or near a pool. It forms a shuttlecock of dark green, broad fronds on long, bright green stalks.

D. filix-mas (male fern), 1 m (3 ft) or more high and across, has tall, upright, light green, rather feathery fronds, with brownish scales on the stems. It is not entirely deciduous: the fronds do not die back but lie prostrate in winter. This is a good plant for a natural garden.

KEY FEATURES
- Deciduous fern
- Easy to grow
- Good in woodland and bog gardens

PLANT
In partial shade in fertile, moisture-retentive soil

PROPAGATE
Ripe spores; divide in spring or autumn

HARDINESS
Hardy; zones 4–9

PESTS AND DISEASES
Trouble free

The spiky, thistle-like leaves of these perennials are dark green to grey-green and are topped by architectural, almost spherical flowerheads.

The clump-forming *Echinops ritro*, 60 x 45 cm (24 x 18 in), has spiny leaves 20 cm (8 in) long and grey underneath. The round flowerhead, 4 cm (1½ in) across, is packed with steely blue flowers, opening to bright blue, in late summer. *E. ritro* subsp. *ruthenicus*, 90 x 50 cm (36 x 20 in), has bright blue flowers and dark green, glossy leaves, which are white on the undersides. The cultivar 'Veitch's Blue', 1 m (3 ft) tall, has dark blue flowerheads.

E. bannaticus, 1.2 m x 38 cm (4 ft x 15 in), has dark green leaves. The grey-blue flowerheads are borne on branching stems. 'Blue Gold', 1 m (3 ft) tall, has dark blue flowerheads.

The large and vigorous *E. sphaerocephalus*, 1.8 x 1 m (6 x 3 ft), will make an imposing clump if left undisturbed at the back of the border. The greyish-white flowerheads are 6 cm (2½ in) across.

KEY FEATURES
- Perennial or biennial
- Unusual flowers
- Attracts butterflies and bees
- Easy to grow

PLANT
In full sun in well-drained soil

PROPAGATE
Seed in mid-spring; divide in spring or autumn

HARDINESS
Hardy to frost hardy; zone 3

PESTS AND DISEASES
Aphids

Elaeagnus

Epimedium
BARRENWORT, BISHOP'S MITRE

▲ *Elaeagnus pungens* 'Maculata'

▲ *Epimedium perralderianum*

These useful and adaptable shrubs can be grown almost anywhere in the garden as long as the soil is not shallow and chalky. The evergreen *Elaeagnus pungens*, 4 x 5 m (12 x 15 ft), has dark glossy leaves, the scaly undersides tinged with white. In autumn it bears pendent white flowers, followed by brown fruit that ripen to red. The cultivar 'Maculata' has leaves with bold yellow markings.

    E. angustifolia (oleaster), 6 m (20 ft) high and across, is a spiny deciduous plant, with grey leaves and fragrant flowers in early summer. Oval, amber-coloured berries are borne in autumn. The cultivar 'Quicksilver', 4 m (12 ft) high and across, has silvery leaves and yellow flowers.

    Several handsome evergreen cultivars have been developed from the hybrid *E.* x *ebbingei*, which grows to 4 m (12 ft) high and across. 'Gilt Edge' has dark green leaves with broad golden-yellow margins. The light green leaves of 'Limelight' have bold yellow markings and are silvery beneath.

KEY FEATURES
- Deciduous or evergreen shrub
- Variegated foliage
- Fragrant flowers
- Easy to grow

PLANT
In sun in fertile, well-drained soil

PROPAGATE
Seed in autumn; greenwood cuttings in spring; semi-ripe cuttings (deciduous forms) in midsummer

HARDINESS
Hardy; zones 7–9

PESTS AND DISEASES
Coral spot

These useful perennials are ideal for growing around trees and shrubs. The leaves of deciduous forms often persist through winter, providing year-round cover, and disappear only when the new leaves begin to appear in spring. The flowers are borne on wiry stems above the foliage.

    Epimedium perralderianum, 30 x 60 cm (12 x 24 in), an evergreen or semi-evergreen form, has glossy green leaves, which are bronze when they first emerge and copper-bronze in winter. The yellow, short-spurred flowers appear in mid- to late spring. The deciduous *E. alpinum*, 15 x 30 cm (6 x 12 in), is a clump-forming perennial. The bright green leaves are bronze in early spring and turn red-bronze in autumn. The yellow flowers have red spurs. This is a good groundcover plant.

    E. x *perralchicum*, 40 x 60 cm (16 x 24 in), is a clump-forming evergreen. The new leaves are bronze or red, turning dark green as they mature. The yellow flowers have short spurs. The cultivar 'Fröhnleiten' has prettily marbled young leaves and golden-yellow flowers.

KEY FEATURES
- Deciduous, semi-evergreen or evergreen perennial
- Good groundcover
- Spring flowers

PLANT
In partial shade in fertile, moisture-retentive soil

PROPAGATE
Ripe seed; divide after flowering or in autumn

HARDINESS
Hardy; zones 3–7

PESTS AND DISEASES
Vine weevils, viruses

Eremurus
DESERT CANDLE, FOXTAIL LILY

Erica
HEATHER

▲ *Eremurus robustus*

▲ *Erica carnea* 'Challenger'

These plants are characterized by tall flower spikes, which emerge in summer above rosettes of strappy leaves. Once established they are easy to grow, but they need staking in exposed areas, and do not respond well to being disturbed, so take care when you are weeding.

Among the best garden plants are the cultivars of *Eremurus* x *isabellinus*. The perennial Ruiter hybrids are 1.5 x 1 m (5 x 3 ft) with long racemes of orange, copper and pink flowers. 'Cleopatra' has apricot-orange flowers; 'Sahara' has coppery flowers; 'Image' has yellow flowers; and 'Parade' has pink flowers.

E. 'Oase' is a shorter form, to 1.2 m (4 ft) high. The handsome racemes of yellow flowers fade to brownish-orange. A good plant for the back of a border, *E. robustus* grows to 2.4 x 1 m (8 x 3 ft). It has blue-green leaves and the flower spikes are a mass of pale pink flowers.

E. stenophyllus is a shorter form, to 1 m (3 ft), bearing dark golden flowers, turning coppery as they age. *E. stenophyllus* subsp. *stenophyllus* is another tall plant, 1.5 m x 75 cm (5 ft x 2 ft 6 in), with long, narrow leaves and long racemes of yellow flowers, which fade to brownish-orange.

KEY FEATURES
• Perennial
• Tall flower spikes
• Easy to grow

PLANT
In full sun in well-drained soil

PROPAGATE
Seed in autumn; divide in autumn

HARDINESS
Hardy; zones 5–8

PESTS AND DISEASES
Slugs and snails

This is a large genus of some 700 species, and there are now hundreds of cultivars offering a huge range of plant size and shape and flower and foliage colour.

The best plants for carpeting are cultivars of *Erica carnea* (alpine heath, winter heath), which is a low, spreading shrub. Flowers are borne from late autumn to mid-spring. 'Ann Sparkes', 15 x 25 cm (6 x 10 in), has pink flowers late winter to spring and bronze-tipped foliage, turning red in winter. 'Challenger', 15 x 45 cm (6 x 18 in), has dark red flowers and dark foliage. The trailing 'Springwood White', 15 x 45 cm (6 x 18 in), has white flowers and bright foliage.

E. cinerea (bell heather) is the parent of summer-flowering heathers. 'Hookstone White', 35 x 65 cm (14 x 26 in), has white flowers. 'Pink Ice', 20 x 38 cm (8 x 14 in), has rose flowers and dark green foliage, bronze in winter.

Plants derived from *E.* x *darleyensis* (Darley Dale heath) flower from midwinter until late spring. 'Archie Graham', 50 x 60 cm (20 x 24 in), has lilac-pink flowers. 'Kramer's Rote', 35 x 60 cm (14 x 24 in), has magenta flowers and bronze-green foliage.

KEY FEATURES
• Evergreen shrub
• Colourful flowers
• Flowers in all seasons
• Good groundcover

PLANT
In sun in well-drained soil; most forms need acid soil

PROPAGATE
Semi-ripe cuttings in midsummer

HARDINESS
Hardy; zones 5–8

PESTS AND DISEASES
Root rot

Erigeron

FLEABANE

Escallonia

▲ *Erigeron karvinskianus*

▲ *Escallonia 'Iveyi'*

These colourful flowers, which are borne in long periods in summer, are useful in mixed borders, in cottage gardens and in wild gardens. They have daisy-like flowers in a range of colours with yellow centres. Many of the taller hybrids need staking. Deadhead regularly to encourage new flowers.

Erigeron karvinskianus (wall daisy), 30 x 90 cm (1 x 3 ft), has grey-green leaves to 4 cm (1¹/₂ in) long and masses of white, daisy-like flowers with yellow centres, which age to shades of pink and purple. This is a useful plant for paving and sunny walls.

Many of the most colourful erigerons are hybrids. 'Azurfee' ('Azure Fairy'), 45 cm (18 in) high and across, has semi-double, lavender-blue flowers. 'Dignity', 50 x 45 cm (20 x 18 in), has violet-blue flowers. 'Dunkelste Aller' ('Darkest of All'), 60 x 45 cm (24 x 18 in), has deep purple flowers. 'Prosperity', 45 cm (18 in) high and across, has double, mauve-blue flowers.

KEY FEATURES
- Annual, biennial or perennial
- Colourful daisy-like flowers
- Good cut flowers

PLANT
In full sun in well-drained soil

PROPAGATE
Seed in spring; divide in spring

HARDINESS
Hardy; zones 8–9

PESTS AND DISEASES
Powdery mildew

These useful shrubs can be used for hedging, grown in a mixed border, trained as wall shrubs or planted as a windbreak in coastal gardens. The flowers are borne over a long period in summer and early autumn. Unless they are grown as a hedge, escallonias do not need pruning. When necessary, cut back straggly stems after flowering.

Most of the plants grown today are cultivars, selected for their profuse and colourful flowers. They have small, glossy, dark green leaves.

'Apple Blossom', 2.4 m (8 ft) high and across, has pale pink flowers in early to midsummer. 'Donard Seedling', one of the most widely grown escallonias, is a vigorous plant, 2.4 m (8 ft) high and across, with pink-tinted white flowers in early to midsummer. The upright 'Iveyi', 3 m (10 ft) high and across, has fragrant, white flowers, 1 cm (¹/₂ in) across, from mid- to late summer. The compact 'Red Elf', 2.4 x 4 m (8 x 12 ft), has dark red flowers, each to 1 cm (¹/₂ in) long, which appear in early to midsummer.

KEY FEATURES
- Evergreen shrub
- Attractive flowers
- Useful hedging
- Wall shrub

PLANT
In sun in fertile, well-drained soil

PROPAGATE
Softwood cuttings in early summer; semi-ripe cuttings in late summer; hardwood cuttings in autumn

HARDINESS
Hardy; zone 9

PESTS AND DISEASES
Trouble free

Eucalyptus
GUM, IRONBARK

Euonymus
SPINDLE TREE

▲ *Eucalyptus gunnii*

▲ *Euonymus europaeus*

These plants are grown mostly for their attractive foliage and peeling bark. Although most of the trees will grow large, they respond well to pruning and can be kept small enough for most gardens. The juvenile leaves are usually more attractive than the mature foliage.

When it is allowed to develop, *Eucalyptus gunnii* (cider gum), 25 x 15 m (80 x 50 ft), grows into a dense single or multi-stemmed tree. It can, however, be pruned hard and grown as a shrub in a mixed border. The regular pruning has the advantage of encouraging the production of juvenile leaves, which are like small silver-grey coins.

E. pauciflora (cabbage gum), 20 x 15 m (70 x 50 ft), is a dense, spreading tree. The whitish bark sheds to reveal brown or green patches, and cream flowers are borne from late spring to summer. The slow-growing *E. pauciflora* subsp. *niphophila* (snow gum) has blue-grey, oval juvenile leaves, and sickle-shaped mature leaves.

KEY FEATURES
- Evergreen shrub or tree
- Handsome silvery foliage
- Tolerates pollution

PLANT
In full sun in moisture-retentive, neutral to acid soil; protect from cold winds

PROPAGATE
Seed in spring or summer

HARDINESS
Hardy to frost tender; zones 8–10

PESTS AND DISEASES
Silver leaf

This is a large genus containing a wide range of plant types. Among the best-known and most useful garden plants are the cultivars of the shrub *Euonymus fortunei*. These often have variegated foliage and can be grown as feature shrubs and in borders. The compact 'Emerald Gaiety', 1 x 1.5 m (3 x 5 ft), has dark green leaves with broad white margins; in autumn they are tinged with red. The leaves of 'Silver Queen', 1.5 m (5 ft) high and across, are broadly edged with cream-white.

E. europaeus, 1.8 x 3 m (6 x 10 ft), is a deciduous shrub or small tree. In autumn the leaves turn rich shades of red and yellow, and purplish-pink fruits open to reveal the bright orange seeds. 'Red Cascade', 3 x 2.4 m (10 x 8 ft), has dark green leaves that turn red in autumn and bears a mass of red fruits.

The deciduous *E. latifolius*, 3 m (10 ft) high and across, has dark green leaves, to 12 cm (5 in) long, which turn red in autumn. The red fruits open to reveal orange seeds.

KEY FEATURES
- Deciduous or evergreen climber, shrub or tree
- Variegated foliage
- Useful hedging

PLANT
In sun or partial shade in well-drained soil

PROPAGATE
Ripe seed; greenwood cuttings and semi-ripe cuttings in summer

HARDINESS
Hardy to frost hardy; zones 4–9

PESTS AND DISEASES
Scale insects, leaf spot, mildew

Eupatorium

HEMP AGRIMONY

Euphorbia

▲ *Eupatorium purpureum* subsp. *maculatum* 'Atropurpureum'

▲ *Euphorbia griffithii*

The hardy, clump-forming perennial *Eupatorium purpureum* (Joe Pye weed), 2.1 x 1 m (7 x 3 ft), is an imposing plant for a mixed border. It has large, rough, mid-green leaves, each to 25 cm (10 in) long and borne on purplish stems. The cream-white, pink or pink-purple flowers are borne in clusters to 15 cm (6 in) across from midsummer to early autumn. *E. purpureum* subsp. *maculatum* 'Atropurpureum', 1.8 x 1 m (6 x 3 ft), has purple-flushed stems and leaves and pale purple flowers.

E. cannabinum (hemp agrimony), 1.5 x 1.2 m (5 x 4 ft), is also a clump-forming perennial, with red-tinged stems and large, dark green leaves, each to 12 cm (5 in) across. Flat-topped clusters, to 10 cm (4 in) across, of pink, purple or white flowers are borne from summer to early autumn.

The smaller *E. album*, 90 x 45 cm (36 x 18 in), has clusters of white flowers in late summer, and its cultivar 'Braunlaub' has brownish flowers and leaves.

KEY FEATURES
• Perennial
• Good for wild gardens
• Attracts butterflies and bees

PLANT
In sun or partial shade in moisture-retentive soil

PROPAGATE
Seed in spring; divide in spring; softwood cuttings in spring

HARDINESS
Hardy to frost tender; zones 3–8

PESTS AND DISEASES
Aphids, slugs and snails

This is a large genus with some 2,000 species, providing a wide range of plant types, from the popular houseplant poinsettia to hardy, evergreen shrubs. The flowers are insignificant but usually surrounded by colourful bracts.

One of the best perennials is *Euphorbia griffithii*, 90 x 60 cm (3 x 2 ft), which grows in sun or light shade. The dark green leaves have red ribs and in summer red, yellow or orange flowerheads. 'Fireglow', 75 cm x 1 m (30 in x 36 in), has orange-red flowerheads.

E. characias, 1.2 m (4 ft) high and across, is an evergreen shrub for sun or shade. The grey-green leaves are borne on purplish stems, and yellow-green flowerheads appear from early spring to early summer. *E. characias* subsp. *wulfenii* has especially bright flowerheads.

In a shady position or in poor soil plant the evergreen perennial *E. amygdaloides* var. *robbiae* (Mrs Robb's bonnet), 80 x 60 cm (32 x 24 in), which has dark green leaves and good green flowers in spring.

KEY FEATURES
• Annual, biennial, perennial or shrub
• Wide range of size and habit
• Evergreen foliage
• Groundcover

PLANT
In sun or shade in well-drained soil

PROPAGATE
Seed in spring; divide in early spring; basal cuttings in spring

HARDINESS
Hardy to frost tender; zones 5–9

PESTS AND DISEASES
Aphids, grey mould

Fargesia

Festuca
FESCUE

▲ *Fargesia nitida*

▲ *Festuca glauca*

These useful clump-forming, evergreen bamboos can be used as feature plants or grown for hedging or screening. They are useful in wildlife gardens, providing welcome shelter for birds. *Fargesia nitida* (syn. *Arundinaria nitida*, *Sinarundinaria nitida*; fountain bamboo) is a good hedging plant, growing to about 4 m (12 ft) high and making dense clumps about 1 m (3 ft) across. It is slow-growing, does best in partial shade and needs to be protected from cold wind. The dark purplish-green canes, which arch gracefully, are clothed with green leaves on purple stems.

F. murieliae (syn. *Arundinaria murieliae*, *Sinarundinaria murieliae*; umbrella bamboo), 4 x 1.5 m (12 x 5 ft), will tolerate a position in full sun, and it stands up to strong winds better than *F. nitida* does. It has yellow-green canes, which often branch and arch. They are covered with narrow, bright green leaves, each to 15 cm (6 in) long.

KEY FEATURES
- Evergreen bamboo
- Year-round colour and structure
- Good feature plant
- Good for hedging
- Good in containers

PLANT
In sun or partial shade in fertile, moisture-retentive soil

PROPAGATE
Divide in spring; divide rhizomes in spring

HARDINESS
Hardy; zones 4–9

PESTS AND DISEASES
Slugs and snails

The evergreen *Festuca glauca* (blue fescue), 30 x 25 cm (12 x 10 in), is one of the grasses that has benefited from the recent trend for gravel and container gardening. It makes a dense, neat clump of narrow, blue-grey leaves, above which inflorescences are borne on erect stems in early to midsummer. Several cultivars are available, differing mainly in the intensity of the blue of the leaves. 'Blaufuchs' ('Blue Fox') has bright blue leaves; 'Elijah Blue' has vivid blue leaves; 'Harz' has blue-green leaves tipped with purple'. The cultivar 'Golden Toupee' has bright yellow-green leaves. These aren't long-lived plants, and it is often better to replace congested and overgrown clumps every two or three years, especially as new and improved cultivars keep on appearing.

F. amethystina (large blue fescue), 45 x 25 cm (18 x 10 in), is also evergreen. It has fine, grey-green leaves and, in late spring to early summer, green-purple inflorescences on rather lax stems.

Leave seedheads in place until the spring to provide food for birds, which will also find insects and snails overwintering in the tufted thickets.

KEY FEATURES
- Perennial or evergreen grass
- Good edging
- Neat habit

PLANT
In full sun in well-drained soil

PROPAGATE
Seed in spring; divide in spring

HARDINESS
Hardy; zones 4–8

PESTS AND DISEASES
Trouble free

Filipendula

Forsythia

▲ *Filipendula rubra* 'Venusta'

▲ *Forsythia* x *intermedia* 'Lynwood Variety'

The genus is often represented in gardens by the moisture-loving *Filipendula ulmaria* (meadowsweet, queen of the meadow), which is a clump-forming perennial growing to 90 x 60 cm (3 x 2 ft). The leaves, which may get to 30 cm (12 in) long, are strongly veined. In summer dense clusters of fragrant, cream-white flowers are borne on branching stems. The cultivar 'Aurea' has yellow then yellow-green leaves and needs some shelter from direct sun to protect the foliage from scorching.

The large, spreading *F. rubra* (queen of the prairies), 2.4 x 1.2 m (8 x 4 ft), has dark green, lobed leaves and, in early to midsummer, fragrant deep pink flowers on erect, branching stems. The cultivar 'Venusta' (sometimes sold as 'Venusta Magnifica') has deep rose-pink flowers.

Similar to *F. rubra* but better suited to a small garden is *F. purpurea*, 1.2 m x 60 cm (4 x 2 ft), which has deeply lobed leaves. In mid- to late summer branched purplish stems carry clusters of red-pink flowers, fading to pink as they age. *F. purpurea* f. *albiflora* has white flowers.

KEY FEATURES
• Perennial
• Fragrant flowers
• Good in bog gardens
• Suitable for wild gardens

PLANT
In sun or partial shade in moisture-retentive soil

PROPAGATE
Seed in spring; divide in spring or autumn

HARDINESS
Hardy; zone 4

PESTS AND DISEASES
Mildew

Although forsythias seem to have fallen from favour in recent years, they are still seen in dozens of gardens with their bright yellow spring flowers, which are borne before the leaves appear. Sadly, for the remainder of the year forsythias have little to offer, and although they can be grown as specimen plants, they are better suited to a mixed border. Neglected plants can be cut hard back, although you might not have flowers the following spring.

Among the most widely grown is *Forsythia* x *intermedia* 'Lynwood Variety' (or simply 'Lynwood'), which will grow to 3 m (10 ft) high and across and which bears masses of large yellow flowers on arching stems in early to mid-spring. 'Arnold Giant' has fewer but larger flowers.

There are other forsythias. *F. suspensa* (golden bell), 3 m (10 ft) high and across, has dark leaves and clusters of yellow spring flowers. The cultivar 'Nymans' has attractive bronze-green young shoots and pale yellow flowers.

KEY FEATURES
• Deciduous shrub
• Spring flowers
• Good wall shrub
• Suitable for hedging

PLANT
In sun or partial shade in moisture-retentive but well-drained soil

PROPAGATE
Greenwood cuttings in late spring; semi-ripe cuttings in late summer

HARDINESS
Hardy; zones 5–9

PESTS AND DISEASES
Honey fungus

Freesia

Fritillaria
FRITILLARY

▲ Freesia 'Everett'

▲ Fritillaria imperialis

The genus contains six species, but there are hundreds of cultivars, all with beautiful funnel-shaped, usually fragrant flowers on gracefully arching stems. Freesias are often grown as conservatory plants, although there are specially prepared corms that can be grown outdoors in summer. Treat as annuals and plant 8 cm (3 in) deep in a warm, sheltered place, when they will flower in late summer.

Freesia corms are usually available in mixed colours of white, mauve, pink, red, yellow, orange and pink-blue; many double flowers are available. The species and a few named cultivars are available from specialist suppliers. Most cultivars reach heights of about 30 cm (12 in) with a spread of 20 cm (8 in). 'Ballerina' has white flowers; 'Corona' has yellow flowers; 'Everett' has pinkish-red flowers; 'Royal Blue' has lilac-blue flowers; 'Winter Gold' has golden-yellow flowers. 'Blue Heaven', 40 x 20 cm (16 x 8 in), has blue-mauve flowers with a yellow throat, and the shorter 'Wintergold', 25 x 10 cm (10 x 4 in), has yellow flowers, which last well when cut.

KEY FEATURES
• Corm
• Fragrant flowers
• Good in containers
• Good cut flowers

PLANT
In sun in well-drained soil

PROPAGATE
Seed in winter; remove offsets in autumn

HARDINESS
Half-hardy; zones 9–10

PESTS AND DISEASES
Aphids, red spider mites, dry rot, wilt

The genus contains about 100 species which have a wide range of flower types, from the dainty *Fritillaria meleagris* (snakeshead fritillary) to the large and colourful *F. imperialis* (crown imperial). When you plant the bulbs, add some grit in the planting hole to guard against rot.

F. meleagris, 23 x 8 cm (9 x 3 in), which flowers in mid-spring, bears bell-shaped, white, pink or purple flowers, all with checkerboard markings. These fritillaries need fertile, well-drained soil and do best in full sun. They naturalize well in grass or will grow happily in a border or a container.

In late spring to early summer *F. imperialis*, 1.5 m x 30 cm (5 x 1 ft), produces stout stems with six to eight bell-shaped, yellow-orange flowers, topped by a tuft of green bracts.

In spring *F. michailovskyi*, 20 x 5 cm (8 x 2 in), bears clusters of bell-shaped, brown-purple flowers, tinged with green and edged with yellow. These bulbs need very sharply drained soil and are suited to raised beds or containers.

Plant *F. persica* 'Adiyaman' at the back of a sunny border. This striking bulb grows to 1.5 m (5 ft) tall and in late spring bears dark purple, bell-shaped flowers.

KEY FEATURES
• Bulb
• Striking flowers
• Easy to grow
• Good in containers

PLANT
In well-drained soil

PROPAGATE
Seed in autumn; offsets in late summer

HARDINESS
Hardy to frost hardy; zones 5–9

PESTS AND DISEASES
Lily beetle, slugs and snails

Fuchsia

The 100 or so species that make up the *Fuchsia* genus have given rise to thousands of hardy and tender hybrids. These eye-catching plants are primarily grown for their showy, usually two-colour flowers with their distinctive pendent shape.

Some of the larger fuchsias can be used in borders or trained as wall shrubs or specimen plants, while the smaller ones are often used as edging plants or even in rock gardens. The tender forms are often the mainstay of summer bedding arrangements, where they are treated as half-hardy perennials. The trailing forms are especially useful in hanging baskets or windowboxes. Even tender plants can usually be overwintered if they are allowed to dry off at the end of summer and stored in frost-free conditions. Hardy fuchsias can be left in the ground in winter: cut back to ground level and apply a thick mulch.

The shrub *Fuchsia magellanica* (lady's eardrops) is the hardiest of the species but is nevertheless only borderline hardy. It has lots of small red and blue-purple flowers from early summer to autumn, carried on arching stems. Individual plants grow to about 3 m (10 ft) in height and 1.8 m (6 ft) across, and in sheltered gardens they will make a good flowering hedge. The black fruits that follow

the flowers are eaten by birds when other food is scarce. The daintier *F. magellanica* var. *gracilis* has attractive leaves that are finely edged in cream.

Frost-hardy hybrids flower in summer, and the group includes a wide range of flower colour and shape as well as plant size and habit. 'Alice Hoffman', 60 cm (24 in) high and across, has bronze- and purple-green foliage and semi-double flowers, deep pink and pink-veined white. 'Display', 75 x 60 cm (30 x 24 in), has single, red and rose-pink flowers. 'Hawkshead', 60 x 45 cm (24 x 18 in), has single, pink-white, green-tinged flowers. 'Mrs Popple' 1 m (3 ft) high and across, has single, deep violet and scarlet flowers. 'Phyllis', 1.2 x 1 m (4 x 3 ft), has semi-double, reddish-pink and deep pink flowers. The smaller 'Tom Thumb', 50 cm (20 in) in height and width, has mauve-purple and rich red flowers.

The tender hybrids, which are half-hardy to frost tender, are some of the showiest of all fuchsias. 'Annabel', 60 cm

▼ *Fuchsia* 'Display'

◄ *Fuchsia* 'Joy Patmore'

▼ *Fuchsia* 'Phyllis'

(2 ft) high and across, upright and free flowering, has double flowers, white and pink-flushed white. 'Golden Eden Lady', 90 x 75 cm (36 x 30 in), has yellow-green leaves and single, violet and pink flowers. 'Golden Marinka', 30 x 45 cm (12 x 18 in), has variegated green and yellow foliage and single red flowers. 'Joy Patmore', 45 x 60 cm (18 x 24 in), has single white and dark red flowers. 'La Campanella', 30 x 45 cm (12 x 18 in), has small semi-double, pale pink and pink-tinged white flowers.

Among the most spectacular but also the least hardy are the Triphylla hybrids, which have been developed from *F. triphylla*, a species that is native to Hispaniola. It bears clusters of long-tubed, orange-scarlet flowers with small sepals at the end of arching stems. 'Billy Green', 60 x 45 cm (24 x 18 in), has light green leaves and small, long-tubed, bright pink flowers. 'Thalia', 45 cm x 1 m (18 in x 36 in), has dark green leaves, tinged with bronze-red, and long-tubed, orange-red flowers.

▲ *Fuchsia* 'Dollar Princess'

KEY FEATURES
- Deciduous or evergreen shrub
- Colourful flowers
- Suitable for containers and hanging baskets
- Easy to grow

PLANT
In sun or partial shade in fertile, moisture-retentive but well-drained soil

PROPAGATE
Softwood cuttings in spring; semi-ripe cuttings in autumn

HARDINESS
Hardy to frost tender; 7–9

PESTS AND DISEASES
Aphids, capsid bugs, vine weevils, grey mould, rust

TOP 10 FUCHSIAS
'Caspar Hauser'
Double, clear red and mahogany red, tender
'Dark Eyes'
Double, deep red and violet-blue, tender
'Dollar Princess'
Double, cerise and rich purple to deep pink, half-hardy
'Gartenmeister Bonstedt'
Triphylla type, brick-red, tender
'Hawkshead'
Single, greenish-white, frost hardy
'Igloo Maid'
Double, white and pink-tinged white, tender
'Prosperity'
Double, pale pink and crimson, hardy
'Riccartonii' (syn. *F. magellanica* 'Riccartonii')
Single, scarlet and dark purple, borderline hardy
'Roesse Blacky'
Double, bright pink and black-purple, tender
'Winston Churchill'
Double, green-tipped pink and lavender-blue, tender

◄ *Fuchsia* 'La Campanella'

Galanthus
SNOWDROP

Galega
GOAT'S RUE

▲ *Galanthus nivalis*

▲ *Galega officinalis* 'Alba'

There are, perhaps surprisingly, 19 species and dozens of cultivars of snowdrop, but all have the dainty drooping heads, variously marked with green. *G. nivalis* (common snowdrop), 10 cm (4 in) tall, bears pure white flowers, the inner petals with a V-shaped green mark, which have a faint scent of honey. The dark green leaves are strap shaped. *G. nivalis* 'Flore Pleno' has double flowers, and although it is sterile, it readily multiplies from offsets.

G. elwesii, 23 cm (9 in) tall, flowers in late winter. It is an altogether larger plant than the common snowdrop and has broad, rather glaucous leaves and bolder green markings on the inner petals.

Among the best of the cultivars is *G.* 'Atkinsii', to 20 cm (8 in) tall, a vigorous, strongly scented snowdrop with green markings at the tip of the inner petals. 'S. Arnott', also to 20 cm (8 in) tall, flowers in late winter to early spring. Leaves are grey-green and the flowers rounded.

Rather than buying bulbs in autumn, plant snowdrops 'in the green' in spring with leaves still attached.

KEY FEATURES
- Bulb
- Spring flowers
- Good in containers
- Easy to grow

PLANT
In sun or partial shade in moisture-retentive but well-drained soil

PROPAGATE
Divide after flowering

HARDINESS
Hardy to frost hardy; zones 3–9

PESTS AND DISEASES
Narcissus bulb fly, grey mould

Galega officinalis, 1.5 x 1 m (5 x 3 ft), is a clump-forming perennial that looks like a giant vetch. The green leaves are made up of narrow leaflets, each to 5 cm (2 in) long, and the pea-like white or mauve flowers are borne in long racemes from early summer to early autumn. *G. officinalis* 'Alba' has white flowers.

Several hybrids have been developed from *G.* x *hartlandii*. They grow to 1.5 x 1 m (5 x 3 ft) and have white, lilac, lavender, pink or pink-mauve flowers from early summer to early autumn. 'His Majesty' (syn. 'Her Majesty') has bicoloured white and mauve-pink flowers, borne in racemes to 15 cm (6 in) long. 'Lady Wilson' has white and mauve-blue flowers, and 'Candida' has pure white flowers.

KEY FEATURES
- Perennial
- Summer flowers
- Easy to grow
- Good for cutting

PLANT
In sun or partial shade in moisture-retentive soil

PROPAGATE
Seed in spring; divide in early spring

HARDINESS
Hardy; zones 3–8

PESTS AND DISEASES
Trouble free

Galtonia

Garrya

▲ *Galtonia candicans*

▲ *Garrya elliptica*

This is a small genus of only four species. They are useful in the mixed border, providing flowers in late summer. These plants should survive over winter in most temperate areas if left in the ground, although a thick mulch is beneficial. In areas where the ground freezes, the bulbs should be lifted and stored in a frost-free place. Plants grown in containers should be moved to a greenhouse or conservatory. When you are planting the bulbs in early spring, add a handful of grit to the bottom of the planting hole to improve the drainage.

The most widely grown species is *Galtonia candicans* (Cape hyacinth, summer hyacinth). In late summer it produces 30–40 cream-white, bell-shaped flowers, each to 5 cm (2 in) long, on sturdy, erect stems to 1.2 m (4 ft) tall. The long, grey-green leaves are lance shaped. The flowers are faintly scented.

G. viridiflora, to 1 m (3 ft) in height, produces elegant spikes of 15–30 greenish-white, bell-shaped flowers, also in late summer.

KEY FEATURES
- Bulb
- Flowers in late summer
- Good in containers

PLANT
In full sun in moisture-retentive but well-drained soil

PROPAGATE
Seed in spring; remove offsets in spring

HARDINESS
Hardy to frost tender; zones 7–10

PESTS AND DISEASES
Trouble free

These shrubs are useful in hedges and shrub borders or they can be grown as windbreaks in coastal areas. They are useful in towns because they tolerate pollution. They are often grown as wall shrubs as they benefit from the support and protection. Although they will grow in a shady position, plants grown in full sun produce the best catkins.

The most widely grown species is *Garrya elliptica* (silk tassel bush), 4 m (12 ft) high and across, which has rather dull, oval to rounded, grey-green leaves. The shrubs are not grown for their foliage, however, but for the catkins. Male plants bear grey-green catkins, to 15 cm (6 in) long, from midwinter to early spring. Female plants produce clusters of spherical, purple-brown berries in autumn.

The cultivar *G.* 'James Roof', a male form, is a vigorous plant, with dark green-blue leaves and long, silver-grey catkins, which are said to grow to 20 cm (8 in).

These plants rarely need pruning. Dead wood can be cut out immediately after flowering because the catkins are produced on the previous season's growth.

KEY FEATURES
- Evergreen shrub
- Useful hedge
- Attractive catkins
- Good windbreak in coastal areas

PLANT
In sun or partial shade in well-drained soil

PROPAGATE
Semi-ripe cuttings in summer

HARDINESS
Frost hardy to half-hardy; zone 9

PESTS AND DISEASES
Leaf spot

Gaultheria

Gazania
TREASURE FLOWER

▲ *Gaultheria mucronata*

▲ *Gazania* Chansonette Series

These evergreen shrubs, formerly classified as *Pernettya*, can be used as groundcover in woodland gardens or rock gardens. They need a peaty, acid soil.

The compact *Gaultheria mucronata*, 1.2 m (4 ft) high and across, has glossy, spiny, dark green leaves. From late spring to early summer it bears white, pink-tinged flowers, and these are followed by round berries, which may be white, pink, lilac, purple or red. To ensure a good display of berries, you need to plant both male (non-fruiting) and female plants together. Several reliable cultivars are available. 'Bell's Seedling' (self-fertile) has deep red berries. 'Cherry Ripe' (female) has bright pink-red berries. 'Crimsonia' (female) has carmine-red berries. 'Mulberry Wine' (female) has magenta berries that ripen to dark purple. 'Parelmoer' ('Mother of Pearl'; female) has pale pink berries. 'Sneeuwwitje' ('Snow White'; female) has white berries.

G. cuneata, 30 x 90 cm (1 x 3 ft), has mid-green leaves. In late spring to early summer it bears racemes of white flowers, and these are followed by white berries.

KEY FEATURES
• Evergreen shrub
• Spring and summer flowers
• Colourful autumn berries

PLANT
In partial shade in moisture-retentive, acid to neutral soil

PROPAGATE
Seed in autumn; semi-ripe cuttings in summer

HARDINESS
Hardy to half-hardy; zone 9

PESTS AND DISEASES
Trouble free

These colourful daisy-like flowers are usually treated as half-hardy annuals and included in summer bedding schemes. They do best in a sunny position because the flowers open fully only in sunshine. The cultivars are compact plants, rarely more than 20 x 25 cm (8 x 10 in), suitable for the front of a border.

Plants in the Chansonette Series produce flowers in shades of yellow, apricot, orange, bronze, lavender-pink or dark red, all zoned with a contrasting colour. Those in the Daybreak Series have bronze, orange, pink, yellow or white flowers, usually with a contrasting central zone.

Mini-star Series has plants with orange, white, yellow, cream-yellow, bronze or bright pink flowers, some zoned with a contrasting colour. Single colour selections, with self-explanatory names such as 'Mini-star Tangerine' and 'Mini-star Yellow', are available.

'Tiger Stripes', which gets to 30 cm (12 in) high and across, has yellow petals with a bold orange-brown stripe down the centre of each petal and bright yellow centres.

KEY FEATURES
• Annual or evergreen perennial
• Ideal for bedding
• Good in containers
• Good for cutting

PLANT
In full sun in well-drained soil

PROPAGATE
Seed in early spring

HARDINESS
Half-hardy to frost tender; zones 8–10

PESTS AND DISEASES
Trouble free

Genista
BROOM

Gentiana
GENTIAN

▲ *Genista hispanica*

▲ *Gentiana sino-ornata*

Brooms are grown for the showy pea-like flowers, which are borne in spring or summer. They can be grown as specimen plants or in a mixed border. They are not long-lived plants but can be grown from seed. They grow especially well in gravel gardens, which most closely resemble the conditions they favour in the wild.

At 6 m (20 ft) or more high and across, *Genista aetnensis* (Mt Etna broom) may be too large for many gardens. It has slender, arching branches, which are covered with bright yellow flowers from mid- to late summer. These are followed by seedpods.

G. hispanica (Spanish gorse), 75 cm x 1.5 m (30 in x 5 ft), is a low, rounded shrub, which grows especially well in dry, sunny places. The small leaves are borne only on flowering shoots, and the golden-yellow flowers are borne in late spring to early summer.

G. lydia, 30 x 90 cm (1 x 3 ft), produces a mass of twiggy branches that are completely covered by yellow flowers in early summer. The leaves are blue-green.

KEY FEATURES
• Deciduous shrub
• Bright yellow flowers
• Seedpods in autumn
• Attracts birds

PLANT
In full sun in well-drained soil

PROPAGATE
Seed in spring or autumn; semi-ripe cuttings in summer

HARDINESS
Hardy to half-hardy; zones 9–10

PESTS AND DISEASES
Aphids

This is a large genus with about 400 species. Some flower in spring, others in autumn. Some are small enough for a rock garden, others are at home in a mixed border or a woodland garden. Although the genus is best known for its vivid blue flowers, some have white, yellow, purple or red blooms. Some species need acid soil.

Gentiana sino-ornata (autumn gentian), 8 x 40 cm (3 x 16 in), is a semi-evergreen perennial, which needs neutral to acid soil. It has dark green leaves and, in autumn, stalkless, dark blue, trumpet-shaped flowers to 6 cm ($2^1/_2$ in) long. The flowers are striped with darker blue and have green-yellow stripes on the outside.

G. lutea (yellow gentian), 1.2 m x 60 cm (4 x 2 ft), is a clump-forming herbaceous perennial, which bears whorls of yellow flowers, each 3 cm ($1^1/_4$ in) long, on tall spikes in summer. The basal leaves grow to 30 cm (12 in) long.

G. verna (spring gentian, star gentian), 4 x 10 cm ($1^1/_2$ x 4 in), is a mat-forming evergreen perennial. The rich blue flowers, about 2.5 cm (1 in) long, have white centres and are borne above rosettes of small, grey-green leaves.

KEY FEATURES
• Perennial
• Blue flowers
• Suitable for rock gardens and bog gardens

PLANT
In sun in moisture-retentive but well-drained soil

PROPAGATE
Ripe seed; divide in spring

HARDINESS
Hardy; zones 3–8

PESTS AND DISEASES
Aphids, slugs and snails, rust

Geranium
CRANESBILL

Geum
AVENS

▲ *Geranium ibericum*

▲ *Geum rivale*

Geraniums are valuable in gardens of all types. They combine well in a cottage garden or wild garden, they are useful filling plants in a mixed border, and they can be used for groundcover. Most flower in early to midsummer. After the first flush the clumps can be sheared back to ground level to encourage new leaves and flowers.

Among the herbaceous perennials, the clump-forming *Geranium ibericum*, 50 x 60 cm (20 x 24 in), has cup-shaped, violet-blue flowers, each to 5 cm (2 in) across. *G. clarkei*, 50 cm (20 in) high, will spread indefinitely, but selected forms are more compact. 'Kashmir Blue', 60 cm high, has pale blue flowers in early to midsummer. 'Kashmir White', 45 cm (18 in), has white flowers, veined with pale lilac.

G. phaeum (mourning widow), 60 cm (24 in) high and across, has dark purple flowers in mid-spring. 'Album' has pure white flowers, and 'Lily Lovell' has large mauve ones.

In summer *G. sanguineum* var. *striatum*, 15 x 30 cm (6 x 12 in), produces dark green foliage and pale pink flowers with crimson veins; plant in sun or partial shade.

G. sylvaticum (wood cranesbill) attracts pollinating insects and butterflies to the garden.

KEY FEATURES
• Perennial
• Good groundcover
• Easy to grow

PLANT
In sun or shade in fertile, well-drained soil

PROPAGATE
Seed in spring; divide in spring

HARDINESS
Hardy to half-hardy; zones 4–8

PESTS AND DISEASES
Slugs and snails, vine weevils

These perennials are useful border plants, providing colour over a long period in early summer. They are easy-to-grow plants, tolerant of a wide range of conditions, but they will not thrive in waterlogged soils.

Many of the plants grown are cultivars of *Geum rivale*, which is an upright perennial. 'Coppertone', 30 cm (12 in) high and across, has copper-apricot flowers. 'Leonard's Variety', 45 x 60 cm (18 x 24 in), has orange-tinged, copper-pink flowers. 'Tangerine', 30 cm (12 in) high and across, has bright orange flowers.

Other summer-flowering hybrids have been developed from *G. chiloense*. 'Lady Stratheden' (syn. 'Goldball'), 45 x 30 cm (18 x 12 in), has semi-double, yellow flowers, each to 4 cm ($1^{1}/_{2}$ in) or more across. 'Georgenberg', 25 x 30 cm (10 x 12 in) has large orange-yellow flowers. 'Mrs J. Bradshaw' (syn. 'Feuerball'), 60 cm (24 in) high and across, has semi-double, copper-red flowers.

KEY FEATURES
• Perennial
• Colourful flowers
• Long-lasting flowers

PLANT
In full sun in fertile, well-drained soil

PROPAGATE
Seed in spring or autumn

HARDINESS
Hardy; zones 4–9

PESTS AND DISEASES
Trouble free

Gladiolus

Gunnera

▲ *Gladiolus 'Peter Pears'*

▲ *Gunnera manicata*

Gladioli cultivars are ideal for mixed borders. After they flower, lift the corms and allow to dry. Remove new corms, discarding the old ones, and keep, dusted with fungicide, in a frost-free place until spring.

Grandiflorus gladioli have one flower spike in early to late summer. This group includes Butterfly gladioli, which have ruffled flowers, often with a splodge of contrasting colour. In early summer Nanus gladioli produce several flower spikes with loosely arranged flowers. Primulinus gladioli produce a single flowering stem with triangular flowers from early to late summer. The Grandiflorus hybrids include 'Amy Beth', 1.2 m (4 ft), lilac-pink and cream; 'Green Woodpecker', 1.5 m (5 ft), greenish-yellow; and 'Peter Pears', 1 m (3 ft), orange. Nanus gladioli include 'Charming Beauty', 60 cm (2 ft), rose-pink; and 'Nymph', 70 cm (28 in), red-edged white. Primulinus hybrids include 'Leonore', 1 m (3 ft), yellow; and 'White City', 1.1 m (3 ft 6 in), white. The hardy *Gladiolus communis* subsp. *byzantinus*, to 1 m (3 ft) tall, produces magenta-pink blooms on upright stems late summer to early autumn.

KEY FEATURES
• Corm
• Tall flower spikes

PLANT
In full sun in reliably moist soil

PROPAGATE
Seed in spring; remove cormlets during dormancy

HARDINESS
Hardy to frost tender; zones 6–10

PESTS AND DISEASES
Aphids, slugs and snails, thrips, grey mould, rot

Gunnera manicata is not a plant for a small garden. The ultimate height of 2.4 m (8 ft) or so may not be a problem, but before you buy, remember that each leaf will grow to 1.2 m (4 ft) or more long and will be borne on a sturdy, rather prickly stalk. Established plants will easily take up an area 4 m (12 ft) across. If you have space, however, and the soil is reliably moist, this is a handsome plant. It produces a mass of tiny, red-green flowers that form dense, erect panicles, to 1 m (3 ft) or more long. Although it will look rather messy, do not tidy up the dead leaves at the end of autumn. Use them to protect the crown, holding them in place with stones or mounds of soil.

If you really want a gunnera but have a small garden, plant *G. magellanica*, which grows to 15 cm (6 in) high and spreads to about 30 cm (12 in). It has the same scalloped, dark green leaves, but these are about 8 cm (3 in) across and are borne on upright stems that may get to 15 cm (6 in) long. The flower spike will rarely be longer than 12 cm (5 in). This is a useful plant for groundcover.

KEY FEATURES
• Perennial
• Dramatic foliage
• Good feature plant
• Unusual flowers

PLANT
In sun or partial shade in fertile, reliably moist soil

PROPAGATE
Ripe seed; basal cuttings of established plants in spring

HARDINESS
Borderline hardy; zones 7–10

PESTS AND DISEASES
Slugs and snails

Halesia

SILVER BELL, SNOWDROP TREE

x Halimiocistus

▲ *Halesia carolina*

▲ x *Halimiocistus wintonensis*

These shrubs and trees are grown for their bell-shaped, white flowers, borne in spring, and for their unusual fruits. They need woodland conditions and acid soil.

The spreading *Halesia carolina* (snowdrop tree), 8 x 10 m (25 x 30 ft), has mid-green leaves and, in spring, is covered with white, bell-shaped flowers, borne in clusters of up to six. The four-winged, green fruits are pear shaped.

H. diptera, 6 x 10 m (20 x 30 ft), is a wide-spreading shrub. The white spring flowers are followed by two-winged, green fruits. The leaves turn yellow in autumn. *H. diptera* var. *magniflora* has especially large flowers.

H. monticola (mountain snowdrop tree), 12 x 8 m (40 x 25 ft), has downy mid-green leaves, which become yellow in autumn. Like other species in the genus, it bears bell-shaped white flowers in late spring, sometimes before the leaves appear. The green fruits have four wings.

KEY FEATURES
- Deciduous tree or shrub
- Bell-shaped flowers
- Autumn colour
- Specimen tree
- Suitable for small gardens

PLANT
In sun or partial shade in fertile, moisture-retentive but well-drained neutral to acid soil

PROPAGATE
Seed in autumn; softwood cuttings in summer; layer in spring

HARDINESS
Hardy; zones 5–6

PESTS AND DISEASES
Trouble free

These usually evergreen plants are a cross between *Halimium* and *Cistus*. They have saucer-shaped, rather papery flowers and are ideal for a sunny, well-drained position. They do not need especially fertile soil and rarely need pruning.

One of the more popular plants is x *Halimiocistus wintonensis*, 60 x 90 cm (24 x 36 in), a compact shrub with grey-green leaves. The white flowers, to 5 cm (2 in) across, are boldly marked with yellow and maroon at the base of the petals and are borne in late spring to early summer.

Flowering in summer and sometimes into autumn, x *H. sahucii*, 45 x 90 cm (18 x 36 in), has dark green leaves and pure white flowers.

The cultivar x *H.* 'Ingwersenii', 45 x 90 cm (18 x 36 in), has dark green leaves, and from late spring to midsummer it bears clusters of saucer-shaped white flowers.

KEY FEATURES
- Evergreen shrub
- Large flowers
- Easy to grow
- Good in gravel gardens

PLANT
In full sun in well-drained soil

PROPAGATE
Semi-ripe cuttings in late summer

HARDINESS
Hardy to frost hardy; zones 7–9

PESTS AND DISEASES
Trouble free

Hamamelis

WITCH HAZEL

Hebe

▲ *Hamamelis* x *intermedia* 'Pallida'

▲ *Hebe* 'Great Orme'

Witch hazels are among the best of all winter-flowering shrubs and deserve to be more widely grown. Not only are the spidery flowers sweetly scented, but the leaves take on good autumn colours. The shrubs can be grown as specimen plants or in a woodland garden or mixed border. All forms eventually grow to about 4 m (12 ft) high and across. Pruning is not necessary.

The hybrid *Hamamelis* x *intermedia* is a slow-growing plant with bright green leaves and yellow, red or orange flowers on the bare stems in winter. 'Arnold Promise' has bright yellow flowers and good autumn leaf colour. 'Diane' has dark red flowers and red and orange autumn leaf colour. 'Pallida' has large, bright yellow flowers. 'Sunburst', a more upright form, has pale yellow flowers.

H. japonica (Japanese witch hazel) has glossy green leaves and yellow flowers in mid- to late winter. The more erect *H. mollis* (Chinese witch hazel) has mid-green leaves, which turn yellow in autumn, and golden-yellow flowers.

KEY FEATURES
- Deciduous shrub
- Fragrant flowers in winter to spring
- Autumn leaf colour

PLANT
In sun or partial shade in moisture-retentive but well-drained, acid to neutral soil

PROPAGATE
Ripe seed; graft in late winter

HARDINESS
Hardy; zones 5–9

PESTS AND DISEASES
Honey fungus

This large genus contains many attractive garden plants, which can be used as specimen plants, in hedges, in containers, in rock gardens and in mixed borders.

Hebe 'Great Orme', 1.2 m (4 ft) high and across, is one of the best hybrids. It has narrow leaves and pale pink flowers, which age to white, from summer to autumn. 'Blue Clouds', 1 x 1.2 m (3 x 4 ft), has spikes of blue-mauve flowers from early summer to autumn.

H. x *franciscana*, 1.2 m (4 ft) high and across, is a dense shrub, which bears pink-purple flowers in summer to autumn. The cultivar 'Blue Gem', 1.3 m (4 ft 6 in) high and across, has light mauve-blue flowers.

Whipcord hebes have small, scale-like leaves that lie flat against the stems, and they are excellent for containers and rock gardens. *H. cupressoides*, 1.2 m (4 ft) high and across, has grey-green leaves. In summer it bears small pale lilac-blue flowers. The domed 'Boughton Dome', 30 x 60 cm (12 x 24 in), looks like a conifer, its branches covered with small, scale-like green leaves. It rarely flowers.

KEY FEATURES
- Evergreen shrub
- Summer flowers
- Good in containers
- Attracts pollinating insects

PLANT
In sun or partial shade in well-drained, neutral to alkaline soil

PROPAGATE
Ripe seed; semi-ripe cuttings in late summer

HARDINESS
Hardy to half-hardy; zones 8–10

PESTS AND DISEASES
Aphids, leaf spot, mildew

Hedera
IVY

Helenium
SNEEZEWEED, HELEN'S FLOWER

▲ *Hedera canariensis* 'Gloire de Marengo'

▲ *Helenium autumnale* 'Septemberfuchs'

Ivies are among the most versatile of all climbing plants, with large forms happily covering walls and tree stumps and small ones growing in hanging baskets and containers. In a wildlife garden the flowers attract pollinating insects in late summer and autumn, and the winter berries are useful high-energy food for birds. Ivies with gold markings show their best colour in sun; *Hedera helix* 'Oro di Bogliasco' (syn. 'Goldheart') is the only gold form that will do well in shade. Other leaf colours grow well in sun or shade.

H. canariensis (Canary Island ivy) has glossy green leaves on red stalks. 'Gloire de Marengo' has dark green leaves with silver and cream edges. This is not reliably hardy.

Forms of *H. colchica* (Persian ivy) and *H. helix* (common ivy) are hardy. *H. colchica* has large, dark green leaves and is excellent for groundcover. 'Dentata' has bright green leaves, occasionally notched at the edges, and 'Dentata Variegata' has mid-green leaves with yellow variegation.

There are dozens of forms of *H. helix*. Some, such as 'Atropurpurea' have bronze-purple leaves in winter; others, such as 'Buttercup', yellow leaves in full sun.

KEY FEATURES
- Evergreen climber
- Attracts insects and birds
- Good for groundcover

PLANT
In sun or shade in fertile, well-drained, alkaline soil

PROPAGATE
Root cuttings in summer

HARDINESS
Hardy to half-hardy; zones 6–9

PESTS AND DISEASES
Aphids, red spider mites, leaf spot

Grown for their bright, daisy-like flowers, heleniums thrive in sunny borders, where they will flower over a long period in summer and into autumn. Taller forms will need staking.

Helenium autumnale, 1.5 m x 45 cm (5 ft x 18 in), flowers from late summer to mid-autumn. The red flowers, tinged with yellow, are borne in large clusters.

Many perennial hybrids are available, all flowering from late summer to mid-autumn and all growing to about 1 m x 60 cm (3 x 2 ft). 'Coppelia' has copper-orange flowers with brown centres; 'Gartensonne' has pale yellow flowers with dark centres; 'Indiansommer' has golden-yellow flowers. 'Moerheim Beauty' has reddish-brown flowers with dark brown centres. 'The Bishop' has yellow flowers with brown centres. Taller forms, growing up to 1.2 m (4 ft) high, include 'Bruno', which has dark red flowers with brown centres, and 'Rotgold' ('Red and Gold'), which has yellow flowers with brown centres. 'Septemberfuchs' grows to 1.5 m (5 ft) high and has orange-brown flowers with yellow and brown centres.

KEY FEATURES
- Annual, biennial or perennial
- Colourful summer flowers
- Good for cutting

PLANT
In full sun in moisture-retentive soil

PROPAGATE
Seed in spring; divide in spring or autumn

HARDINESS
Hardy to frost hardy; zones 3–8

PESTS AND DISEASES
Occasionally leaf spot but usually trouble free

Helianthus
SUNFLOWER

Helichrysum

▲ *Helianthus decapetalus*

▲ *Helichrysum petiolare*

The genus is best known for its fast-growing annual plants which grow to several metres and produce a single, huge flower at the top of a sturdy stem. These can be fun to grow.

The perennial sunflowers include *Helianthus decapetalus* (thin-leaved sunflower), which grows to 1.5 x 1 m (5 x 3 ft). Yellow flowers, each 8 cm (3 in) across with brown-yellow centres, are borne from late summer to mid-autumn.

The annuals are derived from *H. annuus*, which can get to 5 m (15 ft) tall, but it is possible to find many smaller plants. 'Sundials', which has bright yellow petals and brown centres, grows to about 1.2 m (4 ft) tall. 'Teddy Bear' has double, golden-yellow flowers and grows to only 45 x 30 cm (18 x 12 in).

Don't cut down plants when the flowers go over. The seedheads that follow will attract tits and finches, which balance precariously on the flat heads, prising out the individual seeds.

KEY FEATURES
• Annual or perennial
• Good cut flowers
• Autumn seeds
• Easy to grow
• Good source of autumn food for birds

PLANT
In full sun in fertile, moisture-retentive but well-drained neutral to alkaline soil

PROPAGATE
Seed in spring; divide in spring

HARDINESS
Hardy to frost hardy; zones 4–7

PESTS AND DISEASES
Slugs and snails

This large genus contains some of the most popular of garden plants, which can be grown in containers and hanging baskets as well as in beds and borders. The tiny, daisy-like flowers can be used in dried arrangements.

Helichrysum petiolare, 1 m (3 ft) high and across, is often included in hanging baskets for its trailing stems, which are covered with small grey-green leaves. This is an evergreen shrub, but is tender and usually treated as an annual. The leaves of 'Variegatum' are prettily variegated with cream, and 'Limelight' has bright lime-green leaves.

In a perennial border, hybrids such as *H*. 'Schweffellicht' ('Sulphur Light'), 40 x 30 cm (16 x 12 in), will provide long-lasting interest. This has white woolly foliage and clusters of tiny, orange, daisy-like flowers in mid- to late summer.

KEY FEATURES
• Annual or herbaceous or evergreen perennial or shrub
• Attractive foliage
• Good in containers
• Good dried flowers

PLANT
In full sun in well-drained, neutral to alkaline soil

PROPAGATE
Seed in spring; divide in spring; semi-ripe cuttings in summer

HARDINESS
Hardy to frost tender; zones 5–10

PESTS AND DISEASES
Mildew but usually trouble free

Helleborus
HELLEBORE

Hemerocallis
DAYLILY

▲ *Helleborus foetidus* Wester Flisk Group

▲ *Hemerocallis* 'Buzz Bomb'

These perennials are grown for their flowers, borne in late winter to mid-spring. They are ideal plants for woodland gardens or mixed borders. Some self-seed but cross-fertilization means that seedlings often do not come true to the parent.

Helleborus foetidus (stinking hellebore), 80 x 45 cm (32 x 18 in), has dark green foliage and in late winter to early spring clusters of bell-shaped green flowers, which are often edged with dark red. This is the parent plant of the Wester Flisk Group, 60 x 45 cm (24 x 18 in), which has leaves, stems and flowers flushed with red.

H. niger (Christmas rose), 30 x 45 cm (12 x 18 in), has dark green, leathery leaves and large white flowers in mid- to late winter. 'Potter's Wheel' has especially large flowers.

H. argutifolius (Corsican hellebore), 1 m (3 ft) high and across, has dark green leaves and clusters of bright green flowers in late winter to early spring. This will self-seed. Cut down old plants to make room for the new ones.

KEY FEATURES
• Perennial
• Beautiful winter flowers
• Evergreen foliage
• Suitable for shade

PLANT
In partial shade in neutral to alkaline soil

PROPAGATE
Ripe seed; divide in early spring or late summer

HARDINESS
Hardy to frost hardy; zones 4–7

PESTS AND DISEASES
Slugs and snails, black rot, leaf spot

Daylilies are grown for their flowers, which last for only a day but which are borne in profusion over a long period. Once established in the garden, plants make large clumps, and they are ideal in a mixed border or wild garden.

Many hybrids are available with different flower shapes and colours. 'Cartwheels', 75 cm (30 in) high and across, has star-shaped, yellow-orange flowers; 'Golden Chimes' 90 x 45 cm (36 x 18 in), has dark yellow flowers; 'Jake Russell', 90 x 45 cm (36 x 18 in) has golden-yellow flowers; 'Joan Senior', 60 x 75 cm (24 x 30 in) has pink-flushed white flowers; 'Prairie Blue Eyes', 70 x 75 cm (28 x 30 in), has lavender flowers; 'Root Beer', 1 m (3 ft) high and across, has red-black flowers; 'Stafford', 70 x 90 cm (28 x 36 in), has red flowers with yellow centres.

Some forms, such as 'Stella d'Oro', which has bright yellow flowers and grows to 30 x 45 cm (12 x 18 in), are suitable for containers.

KEY FEATURES
• Evergreen, semi-evergreen and herbaceous perennial
• Colourful flowers over a long period
• Good in wild gardens
• Suitable for containers

PLANT
In sun in fertile, moisture-retentive but well-drained soil

PROPAGATE
Seed in spring or autumn; divide in spring or autumn

HARDINESS
Hardy; zones 3–9

PESTS AND DISEASES
Aphids, thrips, slugs and snails, crown rot, rust

Heuchera

ALUM BELLS, CORAL BELLS

Hibiscus

ROSE MALLOW

▲ *Heuchera sanguinea*

▲ *Hibiscus syriacus* 'Oiseau Bleu'

Heucheras are often grown for their attractive foliage, which may be variegated or an unusual colour, from mahogany brown to lime green. The plants make good clumps, above which the flowers are borne on erect, wiry stems. They can be grown in herbaceous and shrub borders. The flowers attract bees.

Heuchera sanguinea, 30 cm (12 in) high and across, has rounded, dark green leaves, usually flushed with purple, above which sprays of red flowers are borne in summer. This is the parent plant of many hybrids, including 'Pearl Drops', which has pink-tinged white flowers, and 'Firebird', which has bright red flowers. Both grow to 60 x 30 cm (24 x 12 in).

One of the best-known forms is *H. micrantha* var. *diversifolia* 'Palace Purple', 60 cm (24 in) high and across, although some plants sold with this name are variable. The large, purple-bronze leaves, each to 15 cm (6 in) long, form a neat mound above which pink-white flowers are borne in airy sprays in midsummer. 'Chocolate Ruffles' is similar but has mahogany-red leaves.

KEY FEATURES
• Evergreen perennial
• Attractive foliage
• Good groundcover

PLANT
In sun or partial shade in well-drained neutral soil

PROPAGATE
Divide in autumn

HARDINESS
Hardy to frost hardy; zones 4–8

PESTS AND DISEASES
Usually trouble free

This genus is well known for annual and perennial species, especially *Hibiscus rosa-sinensis*, which need to be grown under glass to produce the showy, rather exotic flowers in early to midsummer. Outdoors, the hardy deciduous shrub *H. syriacus* and its many cultivars are grown for their beautiful summer flowers.

H. syriacus is a rather slow-growing, upright shrub, 2.4 x 1.8 m (8 x 6 ft), with dark green, three-lobed leaves. It is one of the last deciduous shrubs to come into leaf, and for this reason needs a sheltered position to protect the buds from late frosts. From late summer to early autumn it bears single, trumpet-shaped, lilac-blue flowers, to 6 cm ($2^{1}/_{2}$ in) across.

Among the cultivars, 'Oiseau Bleu' ('Blue Bird') is one of the best, producing violet-blue flowers with purple veins and dark red centres, each to 8 cm (3 in) across. 'Pink Giant' has clear pink flowers with dark red centres. 'Red Heart' has white flowers with dark magenta centres and veins. 'Woodbridge' has large, rich pink flowers, each to 10 cm (4 in) across, with dark pink centres and veins.

KEY FEATURES
• Deciduous shrub
• Colourful flowers

PLANT
In full sun in fertile, well-drained, neutral to alkaline soil

PROPAGATE
Greenwood cuttings in late spring; semi-ripe cuttings in summer

HARDINESS
Hardy; zones 6–9

PESTS AND DISEASES
Trouble free

Hosta

There are an enormous number of hosta cultivars, offering leaves in every imaginable shade of green, blue and yellow, often variegated, sometimes glaucous, and ranging in shape from long to almost round.

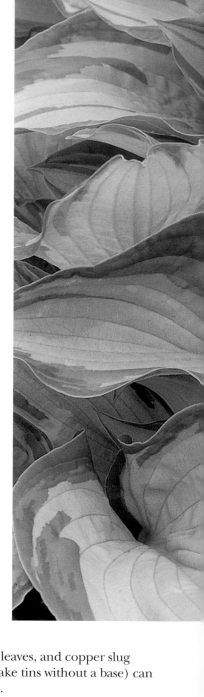

The leaves of hostas form dense mounds, which makes them useful for groundcover. Hostas can also be grown as companion plants for ferns, astilbes and roses, in mixed borders and in containers for summer interest.

Although hostas are grown primarily as foliage plants, they produce tall spikes of funnel-shaped flowers in mid- to late summer. Gardeners who are more interested in the foliage sometimes remove the flower spike.

Because they do best in shady sites in moist soil, hostas are the preferred food plant of slugs and snails, and many gardeners find the continual war just too much trouble, especially as winters become milder and slugs and snails are not killed by cold. Hostas with thick leaves grown in poor, gritty soil show some resistance to molluscs. Nematodes are useful against soil-dwelling slugs, but searching among the leaves for slugs and snails each evening is the best method of control. Encouraging frogs, toads and hedgehogs into the garden will help keep down numbers but not totally eliminate the problem. Clear plastic 'halos', which encircle plants and which are eventually hidden by the foliage, will prevent snails and

TOP 10 HOSTAS

Hosta fortunei var. albopicta
Narrow, heart-shaped, cream-yellow leaves with dark margins, 55 cm x 1 m (22 x 36 in)

'Frances Williams'
Sieboldiana type; large, heart-shaped, blue-green, puckered leaves, 60 cm x 1 m (2 x 3 ft)

'Ginko Craig'
Lance-shaped, dark green leaves edged with white, 25 x 45 cm (10 x 18 in)

'Hadspen Blue'
Tardiana type; heart-shaped, veined, blue-green leaves, 25 x 60 cm (10 x 24 in)

'Royal Standard'
Glossy, heart-shaped, pale green ribbed leaves, 60 cm x 1.2 m (2 x 4 ft)

Hosta sieboldiana var. elegans
Puckered, round- to heart-shaped, blue-green leaves, 1 x 1.2 m (3 x 4 ft)

'Sum and Substance'
Glossy, heart-shaped, green-yellow leaves, 75 cm x 1.2 m (30 in x 4 ft)

Hosta undulata var. undulata
Oval, slightly pointed green leaves with wavy margins and central white or cream-yellow variegation, 90 x 45 cm (36 x 18 in)

'Wide Brim'
Heart-shaped, puckered, dark blue-green leaves, 45 x 90 cm (18 x 36 in)

'Zounds'
Heart-shaped, puckered, yellow-green leaves, 55 cm x 1 m (22 in x 3 ft)

some slugs from reaching the leaves, and copper slug rings (which resemble small cake tins without a base) can also prove to be of some value.

Hostas grown in containers are often damaged by vine weevil larvae. In these circumstances, nematodes are useful, and you can prevent the adult weevils from getting into the compost to lay eggs by applying a barrier glue right around the top of each container.

If you are still determined to grow hostas, you will find a bewildering range. The main species are *Hosta fortunei, H. nigrescens, H. sieboldiana, H. sieboldii* (naturally variegated), *H. undulata, H. ventricosa* and the dwarf *H. venusta,* and these are the parent plants of thousands of hybrids.

◀ *Hosta undulata*

▲ *Hosta* 'Sum and Substance'

◄ *Hosta fortunei* var. *albopicta*

▼ *Hosta* 'Frances Williams'

KEY FEATURES
- Perennial
- Attractive foliage
- Good in containers
- Good groundcover

PLANT
In shade in fertile, moisture-
retentive but well-drained soil

PROPAGATE
Seed in spring; divide in early
spring or late summer

HARDINESS
Hardy; zones 3–9

PESTS AND DISEASES
Slugs and snails

Humulus

HOP

Hydrangea

▲ *Humulus lupulus* 'Aureus'

▲ *Hydrangea aspera* Villosa Group

The common hop, *Humulus lupulus*, is a twining perennial, with lobed, light green leaves. Female plants bear the decorative green flowers (hops) in autumn. These are hidden by aromatic bracts. On male plants small yellow flowers are borne in clusters 10 cm (4 in) long.

Although it is decorative, the species is rarely grown in gardens. Instead the golden-leaved *H. lupulus* 'Aureus' form is preferred, although it needs a position in full sun for the leaves to display their best colour. The twining stems can be trained over arches, fences, through trees and along hedges. They are fast-growing plants, getting to 6 m (20 ft) high in a season, and are useful as a summer screen when grown over pergolas or even over netting.

H. japonicus 'Variegatus' is not reliably hardy, often grown as a half-hardy annual. It, too, is a twining perennial. The dark green leaves are streaked and mottled white.

KEY FEATURES
• Perennial climber
• Unusual flowers
• Good for training over supports
• Good cover for birds

PLANT
In sun or partial shade in moisture-retentive but well-drained soil

PROPAGATE
Seed in spring; softwood cuttings in spring; greenwood cuttings in summer

HARDINESS
Hardy; zones 6–9

PESTS AND DISEASES
Largely trouble free

These plants are familiar from the many forms of *Hydrangea macrophylla* that are widely available and used as specimen plants, in mixed borders, in woodland gardens and in containers. They are easy to grow, needing little attention beyond the removal of old flowerheads in spring.

H. aspera is an upright deciduous shrub, 3 m (10 ft) high and across, that bears flattened flowerheads in late summer and autumn. Plants in the Villosa Group, 1.2 m (4 ft) high and across, have pink-purple or bluish-purple flowers. These plants do best in slightly acid soil.

The vigorous *H. paniculata* is an upright shrub, to 7 m (22 ft) high, although it responds well to pruning. It is grown for its large, conical, cream-white flowerheads. 'Kyushu' has glossy leaves and white flowers. 'Grandiflora' has especially large flowers.

The climbing *H. anomala* subsp. *petiolaris*, is a self-clinging plant, eventually covering an area 4 m (12 ft) high and across and bearing cream-white lacecap flowers in summer. It needs fertile, moisture-retentive soil.

KEY FEATURES
• Deciduous shrub or climber
• Large flowerheads
• Easy to grow

PLANT
In sun or partial shade in moisture-retentive but well-drained soil

PROPAGATE
Softwood cuttings in summer; hardwood cuttings in winter

HARDINESS
Hardy; zones 4–9

PESTS AND DISEASES
Honey fungus, leaf spot

Hypericum
ST JOHN'S WORT

Hyssopus
HYSSOP

▲ *Hypericum* x *cyathiflorum* 'Gold Cup'

▲ *Hyssopus officinalis*

This genus includes a wide range of plant types, including trees and perennials, but the most useful are the shrubs, grown for their bright yellow summer flowers.

The evergreen or semi-evergreen *Hypericum* 'Hidcote', 1.2 x 1.5 m (4 x 5 ft), makes a dense shrub and has large, golden-yellow flowers from midsummer to early autumn.

H. x *cyathiflorum* 'Gold Cup', 1.5 x 1.8 m (5 x 6 ft), is a deciduous shrub. It has mid-green leaves and, in summer, clusters of cup-shaped golden-yellow flowers.

A good groundcover plant, the deciduous *H. olympicum*, 25 x 30 cm (10 x 12 in), has clusters of golden-yellow flowers from midsummer on.

In a sheltered garden, the hybrid and only borderline hardy 'Rowallane', 1.8 x 1 m (6 x 3 ft), makes an elegant semi-evergreen shrub. The large, deep golden-yellow flowers, which can be 8 cm (3 in) across are borne from late summer into autumn.

KEY FEATURES
- Deciduous, evergreen or semi-evergreen shrub
- Attracts pollinating insects
- Good cover for ground-feeding birds

PLANT
In sun in moisture-retentive but well-drained soil

PROPAGATE
Softwood cuttings in late spring; greenwood or semi-ripe cuttings in summer

HARDINESS
Hardy to frost tender; zones 6–9

PESTS AND DISEASES
Rust but usually trouble free

These aromatic plants are often found in the herb garden, where they are grown both for their herbal properties and as neat, low hedging. They can also be grown in borders, gravel gardens and containers.

The most widely grown hyssop is the aromatic species *Hyssopus officinalis*, 60 x 90 cm (2 x 3 ft), which is a semi-evergreen subshrub or perennial. It has dense, erect spikes of tubular, deep purplish-blue flowers in late summer. *H. officinalis* f. *albus* has pure white flowers; 'Roseus' has flowers in shades of pink.

H. officinalis subsp. *aristatus* (dwarf hyssop, rock hyssop), 30 cm (12 in) high and across, has bright green leaves and dark blue flowers in midsummer. This plant is small enough for a rock garden.

KEY FEATURES
- Perennial or evergreen or semi-evergreen subshrub
- Colourful and fragrant summer flowers
- Attracts bees and butterflies

PLANT
In full sun in well-drained, neutral to alkaline soil

PROPAGATE
Seed in autumn; softwood cuttings in summer

HARDINESS
Hardy; zones 4–9

PESTS AND DISEASES
Trouble free

Iberis
CANDYTUFT

Ilex
HOLLY

▲ *Iberis umbellata*

▲ *Ilex x altaclarensis*

These little plants are ideal for rock gardens or sunny walls. The perennials are not long lived and will need to be replaced every two or three years.

Iberis sempervirens (syn. *I. commutata*), 30 x 40 cm (12 x 16 in), is a spreading, evergreen subshrub. It has dark green leaves and in late spring to early summer racemes of fragrant, small, white flowers.

Also an evergreen subshrub, *I. saxatilis*, 15 x 30 cm (6 x 12 in), bears flattened heads of small white flowers, which become purplish as they mature, from late spring to summer. The leaves are dark green.

Among the annual forms are *I. armara*, 45 x 15 cm (18 x 6 in), which has scented white or purplish-white flowers in large racemes in summer. From spring to summer *I. umbellata*, 30 x 23 cm (12 x 9 in) bears masses of small scented flowers, which may be pink, lavender, red or white. Plants in the Fairy Series have white, pink, lilac-purple or red-pink flowers.

KEY FEATURES
- Annual or perennial or evergreen subshrub
- Fragrant flowers
- Easy to grow

PLANT
In full sun in moisture-retentive but well-drained, neutral to alkaline soil

PROPAGATE
Seed in spring or autumn; softwood cuttings in spring

HARDINESS
Hardy to frost hardy; zones 4–9

PESTS AND DISEASES
Clubroot

Hollies are essential in the garden, providing height, hedging, specimen plants and even topiary. There are many cultivars with a range of leaf colour and shape; variegated forms produce their best colour in full sun. Female plants bear colourful winter berries. Hollies are slow-growing plants that respond well to pruning.

Ilex aquifolium (common holly) is the parent of some excellent garden plants. 'J. C. van Tol', 6 x 4 m (20 x 12 ft), has dark green leaves, but is self-fertile and produces bright red berries. 'Golden van Tol', 4 x 3 m (12 x 10 ft) a female form, has glossy dark leaves, irregularly edged with vivid yellow. 'Ferox Argentea', 8 x 4 m (25 x 12 ft) is a spreading form with cream-variegated, very spiny leaves.

Many cultivars have been developed from *I. x altaclerensis*, including the excellent 'Golden King', 6 m (20 ft) high and across, female with gold-edged leaves.

The slow-growing male *I. x meservae* 'Blue Prince', to 1.8 x 1.5 m (6 x 5 ft) after five years, has very dark green, very glossy leaves and dark purplish stems.

KEY FEATURES
- Evergreen shrub or tree
- Attractive foliage and berries
- Good hedging plant

PLANT
In sun or partial shade in moisture-retentive but well-drained soil

PROPAGATE
Semi-ripe cuttings in late summer or early autumn

HARDINESS
Hardy to frost tender; zones 7–9

PESTS AND DISEASES
Trouble free

Indigofera

Ipomoea
MORNING GLORY

▲ *Indigofera decora*

▲ *Ipomoea tricolor* 'Crimson Rambler'

Although there are more than 700 species in this genus, only a few are widely grown. They can be included in mixed borders or grown against a sunny wall, and they bear flowers over a long period in summer. Plant in a sheltered position, but even plants that are cut back to ground level by winter frosts often reshoot in spring.

The deciduous *Indigofera decora*, 60 x 90 cm (2 x 3 ft), is a spreading shrub, with glossy dark leaves and in mid- to late summer long racemes of pink, pea-like flowers.

I. heterantha (syn. *I. gerardiana*), 2.4 m (8 ft) high and across, bears long clusters of bright purple-pink flowers from early summer into autumn. This is a particularly attractive and elegant shrub with grey-green foliage.

I. potaninii is a slow-growing shrub, eventually growing to 1.8 m (6 ft) high and across. It has small, pink, pea-like flowers from early summer to early autumn.

KEY FEATURES
• Deciduous or evergreen shrub
• Pretty flowers
• Good wall shrub

PLANT
In full sun in moisture-retentive but well-drained soil

PROPAGATE
Greenwood cuttings in late spring; semi-ripe cuttings in midsummer

HARDINESS
Hardy to frost hardy; zones 5–10

PESTS AND DISEASES
Trouble free

These plants are grown for their large, trumpet-shaped flowers. They can be used to twine over arches or pergolas or grown into trees and shrubs. For early flowers on annuals, seed can be sown in a propagator in late winter and moved outdoors only after the last spring frosts. Perennials can be overwintered in a greenhouse.

Ipomoea lobata (Spanish flag), 1.8 m (6 ft) high and across, is a tender perennial climber, grown for its beak-like flowers, which are scarlet, ageing to orange, yellow and, finally, white. The twining *I. tricolor* is a fast-growing annual or short-lived perennial, growing to 4 m (12 ft) high. In summer it bears large, blue, white-throated flowers, each to 8 cm (3 in) across. 'Crimson Rambler' has dark red, white-throated flowers; 'Flying Saucers' has flowers striped with white and purplish-blue; 'Purpurea' has deep purple, white-throated flowers.

I. indica (blue dawn flower) is a vigorous annual climber, growing to 6 m (20 ft) or more in a season, with heart-shaped, mid-green leaves and, from late spring to autumn, deep purple flowers, each 8 cm (3 in) across.

KEY FEATURES
• Annual or perennial
• Large, colourful flowers
• Easy to grow

PLANT
In full sun in fertile, well-drained soil

PROPAGATE
Softwood cuttings in spring or summer

HARDINESS
Frost tender; zone 10

PESTS AND DISEASES
Mildew

Iris

This is a large and complex group of plants, including winter-, spring- and summer-flowering bulbs, as well as rhizomatous and fleshy rooted perennials. Some irises prefer well-drained soil, others flourish as marginal plants in ponds or in bog gardens.

Iris flowers are distinctive, with their three lower, spreading petals, usually known as the falls, and three more upright petals, the standards.

The widely grown bearded irises develop from rhizomes and have sword-shaped leaves, arranged in fans, and colourful flowers. There are conspicuous hairs on the falls, from which they get the name 'bearded'. These strong, sturdy irises need well-drained, neutral to slightly acid soil and a sunny position, and they range in size from the miniature forms, at about 10 cm (4 in) tall, to the tall forms, which grow to 70 cm (28 cm) or more tall. In mid-spring the dwarf *Iris pumila*, 15 cm (6 in) tall, has purple, yellow or brown-tinged yellow flowers. *I. germanica* (purple flag), 1 m (3 ft) tall, has blue-purple flowers in late spring.

There are numerous cultivars of bearded irises, many developed from *I. germanica*, but all with sturdy stems and colourful flowers. Many are named to indicate their colour – 'Pink Horizon', 'Glacier Gold', 'Study in Black' 'Orange Harvest', 'Tangerine Charm', 'Ruby Contrast' – and new forms appear every year.

In well-drained or even dry ground plant the evergreen, beardless *I. foetidissima* (stinking iris), 1 m (3 ft) tall, which has purplish, yellow-tinged flowers in early summer; the bright orange seeds that follow are useful food for birds. *I. lazica*, a rhizomatous beardless form, has evergreen leaves and pale violet-blue flowers in early spring.

▼ *Iris* 'Pink Horizon'

The variable and spreading *I. pseudacorus* (yellow flag), 1–1.5 m (3–5 ft) high, is found in the wild in water meadows and is ideal in a large bog garden. It has erect, grey-green leaves and pale yellow flowers in summer. Suitable for bog gardens or marginal planting in water about 10 cm (4 in) deep are *I. pseudacorus* 'Alba', 75 cm (30 in), which has cream-white flowers with yellow and grey markings on the falls, and *I. pseudacorus* var. *bastardii* (sometimes sold as 'Sulphur Queen'), 1.1 m (3 ft 6 in), which has beautiful primrose-yellow flowers.

In early summer the beardless Siberian iris *I. chrysographes* 'Goldvein', 45 x 30 cm (18 x 12 in), has handsome grey-green foliage and velvety, deep purple flowers with gold veins on the falls. 'Black Knight' has very dark purple flowers.

Bulbous irises include the Reticulata, Juno and Xiphium types. Reticulata irises, the smallest of all at about 15 cm (6 in) high, flower in late winter to early spring. They need a sunny position and well-drained, neutral to alkaline soil and can be grown in containers or rock gardens. The group includes 'Cantab' (mid-blue flowers), 'George' (rich purple flowers) and 'Joyce' (sky blue flowers).

The Juno group includes *I. bucharica*, 40 x 10 cm (16 x 4 in), which has glossy green leaves and, unusually for irises, bears scented, yellow and white flowers in the leaf axils in late spring to early summer; this is a good iris for a container.

The large Xiphium group contains the Dutch irises, which are popular as cut flowers. Flowering in late spring to early summer, these are excellent plants for a sunny border, growing to 45–60 cm (18–24 in) high. Colours range from white through yellow, blue and purple, and the flowers are usually to 15 cm (6 in) across. Consider planting 'Bronze Beauty' (deep bronze and gold flowers), 'Oriental Beauty' (lilac and yellow flowers), 'Sapphire Beauty' (blue and orange flowers) and 'Wedgwood' (clear blue flowers).

TOP 10 IRISES

'Annabel Jane'
Tall bearded; lilac-blue flowers, late spring to early summer, 1.2 m (4 ft)

Iris danfordiae
Reticulata; yellow flowers, late winter to early spring, 15 cm (6 in)

Iris ensata (syn. I. kaempferi) (Japanese water iris)
Beardless; purple-red flowers, midsummer, 1 m (3 ft)

Iris foetidissima var. citrina
Beardless; pale yellow flowers, early summer, bright red berries, 1 m (3 ft)

'Gypsy Beauty'
Dutch iris; deep blue and bronze flowers, summer, 45 cm (18 in)

Iris lutescens 'Nancy Lindsay'
Dwarf bearded; scented yellow flowers, early to mid-spring, 30 cm (12 in)

'Pauline'
Reticulata; dark purple flowers, early spring, 12 cm (5 in)

Iris pseudacorus 'Flore Pleno'
Beardless; deep lemon-yellow flowers, early to midsummer, 1 m (3 ft)

Iris sibirica 'Tropic Night'
Beardless; rich blue flowers, early summer, 60 cm (2 ft)

Iris xiphium (Spanish iris)
Xiphium; violet-blue flowers, late spring to summer, 60 cm (2 ft)

▲ *Iris pseudacorus*

◄ *Iris 'Cantab'*

▼ *Iris ensata*

KEY FEATURES
- Rhizomatous or bulbous perennial
- Beautiful flowers
- Suitable for a range of habitats
- Good cut flowers

PLANT
Different species have different requirements

PROPAGATE
Seed in autumn or spring; divide rhizomes; separate bulb offsets

HARDINESS
Hardy to frost tender; zones 4–9

PESTS AND DISEASES
Slugs and snails, grey mould, leaf spot

Jasminum
JASMINE

Juniperus
JUNIPER

▲ *Jasminum officinale*

▲ *Juniperus rigida* subsp. *conferta* 'Blue Pacific'

Of the 200 species in the genus, only two are regularly grown in gardens. Other climbers and shrubs are tender and need to be grown under glass or as houseplants.

The vigorous *Jasminum officinale* (common jasmine) is a twining climber, bearing beautifully fragrant, white flowers from summer to early autumn. It is an obliging plant, responding well to being pruned hard back. *J. officinale* f. *affine* has pink-tinged flowers. The attractive cultivars 'Argenteovariegatum' and 'Aureovariegatum' have cream-edged and yellow-splashed leaves, respectively.

J. nudiflorum (winter jasmine) is not strictly a climber, but its lax and trailing stems can be trained against a wall or trellis. It is grown for its pretty yellow flowers, which are borne on the bare stems from late autumn to early spring, opening wide on warm days. This plant needs little pruning, but remove wayward shoots after flowering.

KEY FEATURES
- Deciduous shrub or climber
- Fragrant summer flowers
- Winter flowers
- Easy to grow

PLANT
In sun or partial shade in fertile, well-drained soil

PROPAGATE
Semi-ripe cuttings in summer; layer in autumn

HARDINESS
Hardy to frost tender; zones 6–10

PESTS AND DISEASES
Aphids but largely trouble free

These easy-to-please plants will grow in almost any soil as long as it is not waterlogged and they rarely need pruning. They can be grown as specimen plants or even used as groundcover. Many of the plants grown in gardens today are cultivars of *Juniperus communis* (common juniper). The fastigiate 'Hibernica' will grow to 5 m (15 ft) high, but it rarely exceeds 30 cm (12 in) in width; the dense foliage is blue-green. The slow-growing *J. communis* 'Compressa', 80 x 45 cm (32 x 18 in), is an ideal feature plant in a heather garden or in a mixed border.

J. rigida (temple juniper), 8 x 6 m (25 x 20 ft) has bright green, rather sharply pointed leaves. *J. horizontalis* (creeping juniper), 30 cm (12 in) high, spreads indefinitely and can be used as groundcover.

J. chinensis (Chinese juniper), 20 x 6 m (70 x 20 ft), has attractive peeling bark, but it is too large for most gardens. The slow-growing 'Aurea' (Young's golden juniper), 11 x 5 m (35 x 15 ft), makes a dense golden-yellow column with aromatic foliage.

KEY FEATURES
- Evergreen conifer
- Year-round foliage and structure
- Range of sizes and colours

PLANT
In full sun or light shade in well-drained soil

PROPAGATE
Ripe seed; ripewood cuttings in early autumn

HARDINESS
Hardy to frost hardy; zones 5–9

PESTS AND DISEASES
Aphids, honey fungus

Kalmia

Kalopanax
CASTOR ARALIA, TREE ARALIA

▲ *Kalmia latifolia*

▲ *Kalopanax septemlobus*

These shrubs are ideal in woodland or shrub borders, but they must have acid soil. They are often grown as a feature plant in a heather bed. Plants can be pruned if they get too large, but they may not flower for several years after being cut back.

Kalmia latifolia (calico bush, mountain laurel), 3 m (10 ft) high and across, is a dense shrub with glossy, dark green leaves. From late spring to midsummer it bears pink to pink-purple flowers. 'Clementine Churchill' has rich pink flowers. 'Elf', 1 m (3 ft) high and across, has white flowers that open from pink buds. The large 'Ostbo Red' has pale pink flowers that open from bright red buds.

K. angustifolia (sheep laurel), 1.2 m (4 ft) high and across, is a suckering species, with red flowers in early summer. The smaller 'Rubra' has deep, red-pink flowers.

K. polifolia (eastern bog laurel), 60 x 90 cm (2 x 3 ft), has dark green leaves and purple-pink flowers in mid- to late spring. This is a rather straggling plant but is easy to grow.

KEY FEATURES
- Evergreen shrub
- Spring to summer flowers

PLANT
In partial shade in fertile, moisture-retentive but well-drained acid soil

PROPAGATE
Greenwood cuttings in late spring; semi-ripe cuttings in summer

HARDINESS
Hardy; zones 5–9

PESTS AND DISEASES
Trouble free

There is only one species in this genus. It is native to China, Japan, Korea and parts of Russia, where it grows in forests. *Kalopanax septemlobus* (syn. *K. pictus*, *K. ricinifolius*), 10 m (30 ft) high and across, is usually grown as a specimen tree in gardens, although it can be variable. Its dark green leaves are deeply lobed and grow to 35 cm (14 in) across. In summer it produces large panicles, to 30 cm (12 in) long, of white flowers, and these are followed by small, round, blue-black fruits. In winter the bare trunk and stems are shown to be heavily spined.

KEY FEATURES
- Deciduous tree
- Attractive leaves
- Summer flowers

PLANT
In full sun or partial shade in moisture-retentive but well-drained soil

PROPAGATE
Seed in autumn; greenwood cuttings in early summer

HARDINESS
Hardy; zones 5–9

PESTS AND DISEASES
Trouble free

Kerria

Kniphofia

RED-HOT POKER, TORCH LILY

▲ *Kerria japonica* 'Golden Guinea'

▲ *Kniphofia rooperi*

The only species in the genus, *Kerria japonica* is a familiar shrub, found in hedges, borders and woodland gardens. It can be grown as a wall shrub. The shrub will get to 1.8 m (6 ft) high and across if left unpruned, but it can be cut back as necessary. After flowering, old and woody stems can be removed from the base.

Kerrias are grown for their bright green leaves and especially for their single or double, golden-yellow flowers, to 5 cm (2 in) across, which are borne in spring.

Several cultivars have been developed. The single flowers of 'Golden Guinea' are to 6 cm (2^1/$_2$ in) across, and the vigorous 'Pleniflora' has masses of double flowers to 3 cm (1^1/$_4$ in) across. 'Picta' (syn. 'Variegata') is grown for its grey-green foliage, which is finely edged with white; it is not a profuse flowerer.

KEY FEATURES
• Deciduous shrub
• Spring flowers
• Wall shrub

PLANT
In sun or partial shade in fertile, well-drained soil

PROPAGATE
Greenwood cuttings in summer; divide in autumn

HARDINESS
Hardy; zones 5–9

PESTS AND DISEASES
Trouble free

Kniphofias have unmistakable flower spikes from late spring to early autumn. The reds, oranges and yellows do not always mix well with other plants, but some of the new cultivars have subtler colours, and smaller cultivars can be grown in mixed borders. Even hardy forms will benefit from a deep winter mulch in their first year.

Kniphofia rooperi, 1.2 m x 60 cm (4 x 2 ft) is a hardy evergreen species, with dark green leaves and orange-red flowers from early to late autumn.

Among the hardy hybrids are 'Atlanta', 1.2 m x 75 cm (4 ft x 30 in), with orange-red flowers fading to pale yellow in late spring to early summer; 'Candlelight', 50 x 30 cm (20 x 12 in), with yellow flowers in summer; 'Goldelse', 75 x 30 cm (30 x 12 in), with yellow flowers in early summer; 'Percy's Pride', 1.2 m x 60 cm (4 x 2 ft), with greenish-yellow flowers in late summer; 'Prince Igor', 1.8 x 1 m (6 x 3 ft), with deep orange flowers from late summer; 'Toffee Nose', 1 m x 45 cm (36 x 18 in), with brown-tipped cream flowers from midsummer.

KEY FEATURES
• Deciduous or evergreen perennial
• Erect spikes of flowers
• Attracts bees

PLANT
In sun or partial shade in fertile, moisture-retentive but well-drained soil

PROPAGATE
Seed in spring; divide late spring

HARDINESS
Hardy to frost tender; zones 6–9

PESTS AND DISEASES
Thrips, root rot

Kolkwitzia
BEAUTY BUSH

Laburnum
GOLDEN RAIN

▲ *Kolkwitzia amabilis* 'Pink Cloud'

▲ *Laburnum* x *watereri* 'Vossii'

The only species in the genus, *Kolkwitzia amabilis* can be grown in a shrub border or as a specimen plant. It makes a dense, twiggy bush, 3 x 4 m (10 x 12 ft), with dark green leaves to 8 cm (3 in) long. In spring and early summer it bears masses of bell-shaped pale pink flowers, each with a yellow throat, on long, arching branches. *K.a.* 'Pink Cloud', also 3 x 4 m (10 x 12 ft), has deeper pink flowers than the species.

Prune kolkwitzias immediately after flowering. The flowers are borne on shoots produced in the previous year.

KEY FEATURES
• Deciduous shrub
• Summer flowers

PLANT
In full sun in fertile, well-drained soil

PROPAGATE
Greenwood cuttings in late spring

HARDINESS
Hardy; zones 5–9

PESTS AND DISEASES
Trouble free

The only species in the genus, *Kolkwitzia amabilis* can be grown in a shrub border or as a specimen plant. It makes a dense, twiggy bush, 3 x 4 m (10 x 12 ft), with dark green leaves to 8 cm (3 in) long. In spring and early summer it bears masses of bell-shaped pale pink flowers, each with a yellow throat, on long, arching branches. *K.a.* 'Pink Cloud', also 3 x 4 m (10 x 12 ft), has deeper pink flowers than the species.

Prune kolkwitzias immediately after flowering. The flowers are borne on shoots produced in the previous year.

KEY FEATURES
• Deciduous shrub
• Summer flowers

PLANT
In full sun in fertile, well-drained soil

PROPAGATE
Greenwood cuttings in late spring

HARDINESS
Hardy; zones 5–9

PESTS AND DISEASES
Trouble free

Lamium

Larix

▲ *Lamium maculatum*

▲ *Larix kaempferi*

These useful and pretty spreading plants not only grow well in shade but they are also good groundcover.

Most lamiums grown are forms of *Lamium maculatum*, 20 cm x 1 m (8 x 36 in). This low-growing perennial has matt, mid-green leaves, irregularly marked with silver, and, in summer, spikes of red-purple, white or pink flowers. 'Album' has matt, mid-green leaves, marked with silver-white and white flowers from mid-spring to midsummer. The leaves of 'Aureum' are gold with white centres. 'Beacon Silver' has green-edged silver leaves and pale pink flowers. 'Pink Pewter' has grey-green leaves and pink flowers. 'White Nancy' has silver foliage edged with green, and white flowers.

L. galeobdolon (yellow archangel), 60 cm (24 in) high, will spread indefinitely and can be invasive. It has dark green leaves, to 6 cm (2½ in) long, sometimes marked with white, and tubular yellow flowers.

KEY FEATURES
• Annual or perennial
• Good groundcover
• Attractive foliage

PLANT
In shade in moisture-retentive but well-drained soil

PROPAGATE
Divide in autumn

HARDINESS
Hardy; zones 4–8

PESTS AND DISEASES
Slugs and snails

These are fairly fast-growing trees, with slender branches that droop gracefully as the plants mature. The soft, flat, needle-like leaves are bright green in spring, turning rich yellow or orange in autumn, and remain on the tree until early winter. The cones develop in spring and stay on the tree all year.

Larix decidua (European larch), 30 x 6 m (100 x 20 ft), has pale green leaves that turn yellow in winter. Mature trees have large, spreading crowns. The dwarf form 'Corley', 1 m (3 ft) high and across, can be grown in a rock garden.

The vigorous *L. kaempferi* (Japanese larch), 30 x 6 m (100 x 20 ft), has blue-green leaves and purplish winter shoots. The slow-growing 'Blue Dwarf', 1 x 1.5 m (3 x 5 ft), has bright bluish foliage. 'Wolterdingen' is a dense, dwarf bush with blue-grey foliage. 'Pendula', 25 x 7 m (80 x 22 ft), is a tall plant, with long, weeping branches.

KEY FEATURES
• Deciduous conifer
• Good autumn colour
• Specimen tree

PLANT
In full sun or partial shade in well-drained soil

PROPAGATE
Seed in spring; semi-ripe cuttings in late summer or autumn

HARDINESS
Hardy; zones 5–7

PESTS AND DISEASES
Trouble free

Lathyrus

Lavandula
LAVENDER

▲ *Lathyrus odoratus* 'White Supreme'

▲ *Lavandula stoechas* 'Willow Vale'

This genus is best known for the annual *Lathyrus odoratus* (sweet pea), which can be easily grown from seed, sown ideally in autumn to give the longest possible growing time. Planted out in spring, they provide colour and fragrance from early summer to early autumn. Even if you have only a balcony or terrace, you can still enjoy the fragrance: look out for compact forms, such as Snoopea Group, developed for hanging baskets and containers, which bear a flower in each leaf node all along the stems. Cut flowers regularly to keep new blooms coming.

There are dozens of cultivars, some better scented than others. Plants in the Galaxy Group are white, pink, red and lavender-blue. 'King Size Navy' is one of the best dark blue forms. 'Noel Sutton' has very fragrant blue flowers. The vigorous 'White Supreme' has scented flowers.

The perennial *L. latifolius*, 1.8 m (6 ft) high, is a climbing plant with blue-green leaves and deep pink-purple flowers from summer to early autumn.

KEY FEATURES
• Annual or perennial
• Fragrant flowers
• Good cut flowers

PLANT
In full sun in fertile, well-drained soil

PROPAGATE
Seed in spring; divide in early spring

HARDINESS
Hardy to frost hardy; zones 1–11

PESTS AND DISEASES
Aphids, slugs and snails, mildew, wilt

Always certain of its place in a herb garden, lavenders can also be grown for edging and hedging, in gravel gardens and in containers. *Lavandula angustifolia*, 1 x 1.2 m (3 x 4 ft), is a compact, hardy shrub and the parent of many lovely garden plants. 'Hidcote', 60 x 75 cm (24 x 30 in), has dark blue flowers; its neat habit makes it good for edging. 'Melissa Lilac', to 60 x 75 cm (24 x 30 in), has lilac-purple heads and is ideal for hedging. 'Blue Ice', 60 cm (24 in) high and wide, has pale blue flowers, and 'Wendy Carlile', 40 cm (16 in) high and wide, has pearly pink flowers.

The borderline hardy *L. stoechas* has distinctive flowers with an erect tuft of bracts at the top of each flowerhead. 'Pretty Polly', 45 x 45 cm (18 x 18 in), has dark violet flowerheads topped by white bracts. The compact and prostrate 'Roxlea Park', 40–50 cm (16–20 in) high and wide, has purple heads topped with pale pink-purple bracts. In a white garden, grow 'Snowman', which is a fragrant form, 40–45 cm (16–18 in) high and wide.

Leave plants untrimmed over winter to attract seed-eating birds. Insect-eating birds will be attracted by the insects surrounding lavender in the summer.

KEY FEATURES
• Evergreen shrub
• Fragrant flowers

PLANT
In full sun in well-drained soil

PROPAGATE
Seed in spring; semi-ripe cuttings in summer

HARDINESS
Hardy to half-hardy; zones 6–9

PESTS AND DISEASES
Honey fungus and mould

Lavatera

TREE MALLOW

Leucojum

SNOWFLAKE

▲ *Lavatera trimestris* 'Mont Blanc'

▲ *Leucojum aestivum*

Although there is a wide range of plant types in the genus, ranging from annuals to shrubs, they all produce large, funnel-shaped flowers in summer. They can be grown in beds and borders, against sunny walls or in containers.

The perennial forms, which are often not long lived, are derived from *Lavatera thuringiaca* (tree lavatera), and one of the best known is 'Barnsley', 1.8 m (6 ft) high and across, a semi-evergreen subshrub, which bears large red-eyed, white flowers in summer. 'Burgundy Wine' has dark pink flowers, 'Ice Cool' has pure white flowers, and 'Kew Rose' has bright pink flowers with darker veins.

The annual forms are derived from *L. trimestris*, and they are an easy-to-grow group, useful for filling gaps in borders and for providing cut flowers. The compact 'Mont Blanc', 50 cm (20 in) high and across, has dark green leaves and white flowers. 'Silver Cup', 75 x 45 cm (30 x 18 in), is a weather-resistant form with bright pink flowers.

KEY FEATURES
- Annual, perennial or shrub
- Colourful flowers
- Easy to grow
- Good cut flowers

PLANT
In full sun in well-drained soil

PROPAGATE
Seed in spring; softwood or greenwood cuttings in spring

HARDINESS
Hardy to frost hardy; zone 8

PESTS AND DISEASES
Rust, fungal diseases

The flowers of snowflakes superficially resemble those of snowdrops and they are delicately scented. The hardy *Leucojum aestivum* (summer snowflake), 60 cm (24 in) high, flowers in spring with up to eight, white, bell-shaped blooms. The taller and more robust *L. aestivum* 'Gravetye Giant', 1 m (3 ft) high, has two to eight white flowers, each petal tipped with green, in mid- to late spring.

The midwinter to early-spring flowers of *L. vernum* (spring snowflake), 30 cm (12 in) high, are similar to those of *L. aestivum*. They are borne singly and have the distinctive green tip at the end of each white petal. This is a good bulb for naturalizing in grass, as long as the ground does not dry out in summer. The flowers of *L. vernum* var. *carpathicum* are tipped with yellow. The shorter *L. vernum* var. *vagneri*, to 20 cm (8 in) high, is a vigorous plant that grows well around deciduous trees and shrubs.

L. roseum, 10 cm (4 in) high, bears one or two pale pink flowers in late summer or early autumn. This is not reliably hardy and is often grown in containers, when it can be protected in a greenhouse in winter.

KEY FEATURES
- Bulb
- Spring flowers
- Good for naturalizing

PLANT
In sun in moisture-retentive soil

PROPAGATE
Seed in autumn; remove offsets after flowering

HARDINESS
Hardy to frost hardy; zones 4–9

PESTS AND DISEASES
Narcissus bulb fly, slugs

Ligularia

Ligustrum
PRIVET

▲ *Ligularia przewalskii*

▲ *Ligustrum lucidum* 'Tricolor'

Ligularias are imposing plants, suitable for growing near a natural pond, in a bog garden or in a mixed border where the soil never dries out. They are useful for providing height and for flowering in late summer, when other plants are beginning to fade.

The clump-forming *Ligularia dentata* (golden groundsel), 1.5 x 1 m (5 x 3 ft), has bright orange, daisy-like flowers in a tall spike from mid- to late summer. 'Desdemona' has orange flowers and brown-green leaves, and 'Othello' has orange flowers and purplish-green leaves; both grow to 1 m (3 ft) high.

L. przewalskii, 1.8 x 1 m (6 x 3 ft), has large, deeply cut, green leaves. In mid- to late summer it bears clusters of yellow flowers on dark purple-green stems.

One of the best of the garden hybrids is *L.* 'Gregynog Gold', 1.8 x 1 m (6 x 3 ft). The large leaves, to 35 cm (14 in) long, are deeply veined and heart shaped. In late summer to early autumn it produces large, conical spires of orange-yellow flowers.

KEY FEATURES
• Perennial
• Tall flower spikes

PLANT
In full sun in moisture-retentive soil

PROPAGATE
Seed in autumn or spring; divide in spring

HARDINESS
Hardy; zones 4–8

PESTS AND DISEASES
Slugs and snails

This genus contains several shrubs that can be included in shrub borders, used as hedging or grown as standards.

L. ovalifolium, 4 m (12 ft) high and across, is evergreen or semi-evergreen, and in midsummer it produces white flowers, which are followed by black fruits. The more interesting 'Argentum' has leaves edged in cream-white; 'Aureum' (golden privet) is variegated with golden-yellow.

The evergreen *L. lucidum* (Chinese privet), 10 m (30 ft) high and across, will develop into a small tree, although it can be pruned to keep it small. It has glossy, dark green leaves and white flowers in late summer. The leaves of 'Tricolor' are grey-green edged with pink-white. The striking 'Excelsum Superbum' is usually grown as a shrub. The leaves are variegated and edged with yellow-green.

L. sinense, 4 m (12 ft) high and across, is a deciduous shrub, with pale green leaves. In midsummer it bears masses of white flowers, followed by blue-black fruit.

KEY FEATURES
• Deciduous, semi-evergreen or evergreen shrub or tree
• Good hedging
• White flowers

PLANT
In sun or partial shade in well-drained soil

PROPAGATE
Seed in spring or autumn; semi-ripe cuttings in summer; hardwood cuttings in winter

HARDINESS
Hardy to frost hardy; zones 6–10

PESTS AND DISEASES
Aphids, leaf miners, honey fungus, leaf spot

Lilium

LILY

This genus contains about 100 species, from which an enormous number of hybrids and cultivars have been developed, with new forms appearing every year. Lilies are much-loved garden plants, reminiscent of cottage gardens and Mediterranean holidays.

Like dahlias and daffodils, lilies are such a huge group of plants that they are classified in nine divisions, some of which are further categorized according to flower shape. Asiatic hybrids, for example, are divided into subgroups according to whether the flowers are upward facing, outward facing or pendent.

Most lilies do best in neutral to acid soil, but some, such as *Lilium candidum* and *L. henryi*, like alkaline soil, and the Asiatic hybrids, *L. pyrenaicum*, *L. regale* and *L. martagon* will tolerate alkaline conditions.

The Asiatic hybrids are sturdy, stem-rooting lilies. This is a large group, which includes 'Apollo', 60 cm (2 ft), with unscented white flowers; 'Connecticut King', 1 m (3 ft), with star-shaped, yellow flowers; 'Fata Morgana', 70 cm (2 ft 4 in), with double, yellow flowers.

The martagon hybrids are mainly stem-rooting lilies with turkscap (recurved petals) flowers. They tolerate a range of conditions, including dry shade. 'Marhan', 1.5 m (5 ft), has orange turkscap flowers; 'Mrs R. O. Backhouse', 1.3 m (4 ft 6 in), has orange-yellow turkscap flowers.

Candidum hybrids have turkscap flowers and are not usually stem rooting. They will tolerate alkaline soil. The hybrid *L.* x *testaceum* (Nankeen lily), 1.5 m (5 ft) has up to 12 light apricot-pink flowers, lightly spotted with red.

▲ *Lilium* Bellingham Hybrid

American hybrids are rhizomatous lilies with often scented, usually turkscap flowers. They are not stem rooting. The group includes the excellent Bellingham hybrids, which have flowers that range in colour from yellow to orange and orange-red, all spotted with red-brown. They need acid, preferably moist soil and are good for naturalizing in light shade.

Longiflorum hybrids have been developed from *L. formosanum* and *L. longiflorum*. They have fragrant, trumpet- or funnel-shaped flowers and are often used as cut flowers. They will tolerate a range of soils, including alkaline conditions, but they are not hardy. 'Casa Rosa', 1 m (3 ft), has white, pink-flushed flowers; and 'White American', 1 m (3 ft), has green-tipped white flowers.

The Trumpet and Aurelian hybrids are mostly hardy, fragrant, stem-rooting lilies, which will tolerate alkaline conditions. The group includes the Golden Splendor Group, 1.8 m (6 ft), with scented, yellow and dark red flowers; and 'White Henryi', 1.5 m (5 ft), with large, fragrant, orange-flushed, white flowers.

Oriental hybrids are mostly scented and flower in late summer. Most need acid soil. 'Hotlips', 1 m (3 ft), has fragrant white flowers, streaked and spotted with red; 'Mona Lisa', 1 m (3 ft), has red-spotted white flowers; the popular and reliable 'Star Gazer', 1 m (3 ft), has rose-red flowers, edged in white; and 'White Mountain', 80 cm (32 in), has white flowers with a yellow band down each petal.

Hybrids not included in other divisions are known simply as 'Other hybrids'. The group includes *L.* x *dalhansonii*, 1.5 m (5 ft), with small, maroon, turkscap flowers, and 'Moneymaker', 1 m (3 ft), with clear pink flowers in midsummer.

The final division, species lilies and their true forms, includes some of the best-known and most beautiful of all plants. *L. auratum* (golden-rayed lily), 1.5 m (5 ft), has fragrant white and gold flowers; plant in acid soil in full sun. *L. candidum* (Madonna lily), 1.8 m (6 ft), has scented,

◀ *Lilium martagon*

▲ *Lilium longiflorum*

▲ *Lilium* 'Connecticut King'

KEY FEATURES
- Bulb
- Beautiful, colourful flowers
- Easy to grow
- Good cut flowers
- Good in containers

PLANT
In sun in well-drained soil

PROPAGATE
Ripe seed; remove scales, offsets or bulblets from dormant bulbs; remove bulbils from stems in late summer

HARDINESS
Hardy to frost hardy; zones 4–8

PESTS AND DISEASES
Aphids, lily beetle, grey mould

TOP 10 LILIES
'African Queen'
Trumpet hybrid; fragrant, orange-apricot flowers, brownish-purple on the outside, 1.8 m (6 ft)
***Lilium candidum* (Madonna lily)**
Species; fragrant, pure white, trumpet flowers, 1.8 m (6 ft)
'Casa Rosa'
Longiflorum hybrid; pink-flushed, white flowers, 1 m (3 ft)
'Mont Blanc'
Asiatic hybrid; pale pink, upward-facing flowers, 70 cm (28 in)
Lilium* x *dalhansonii
Hybrid lily, maroon turkscap flowers, 1.5 m (5 ft)
***Lilium lancifolium* (tiger lily)**
Species; orange-red turkscap flowers, 1.5 m (5 ft)
'Mrs R. O. Backhouse'
Martagon hybrid; orange-yellow turkscap flowers with maroon spots, 1.3 m (4 ft 6 in)
'Shuskan'
American hybrid; orange-yellow flowers with red-brown spots, 1.2 m (4 ft)
'Star Gazer'
Oriental hybrid; white-edged, deep rose-red flowers, 1 m (3 ft)
***Lilium* x *testaceum* (Nankeen lily)**
Candidum hybrid; apricot-pink turkscap flowers with red spots, 1.5 m (5 ft)

trumpet-shaped, white flowers, each to 8 cm (3 in) long. *L. longiflorum* (Easter lily), 1 m (3 ft), is tolerant of alkaline conditions; it has very fragrant, trumpet-shaped white flowers, each to 20 cm (8 in) long. *L. regale* (regal lily), 1.8 m (6 ft), has trumpet-shaped, fragrant, white flowers, streaked with purple on the reverse; not only is this one of the most beautiful of all lilies, it is among the easiest to grow, tolerating most conditions (except very alkaline soil) but needing staking to support its lovely flowers.

If you suffer from pollen allergy, look out for lilies with 'Kiss' in their name. They have been developed specially without stamens.

Lobelia

Lonicera
HONEYSUCKLE

▲ *Lobelia cardinalis*

▲ *Lonicera x heckrottii*

Lobelias are often thought of in the context of summer bedding, with trailing heads of blue, white, pink and red flowers cascading from containers. These annuals come from *Lobelia erinus*, and there are dozens of hybrids. Cascade Mixed is a free-flowering, trailing mixture, with masses of miniature blooms in shades of blue, mauve, lilac, crimson and white. This is an ideal choice for a hanging basket. 'Mrs Clibran' is a compact form, to 15 cm (6 in) high, with blue, white-eyed flowers. 'Cambridge Blue', to 10 cm (4 in) high, has sky blue flowers.

Many people don't realize that the genus also contains one of the finest plants for the bog garden. *L. cardinalis* (cardinal flower), 90 x 30 cm (3 x 1 ft), is a clump-forming perennial. It has bright green leaves, often glossy and tinged with bronze, and in summer to early autumn erect racemes, 35 cm (14 in) long, of bright red flowers with red-purple bracts.

L. tupa, 1.8 x 1 m (6 x 3 ft), is a useful perennial for a mixed border. It has grey-green leaves and tall racemes of bright reddish-orange flowers. An unusual and eye-catching plant.

KEY FEATURES
- Annual, perennial or shrub
- Colourful summer flowers

PLANT
In full sun or partial shade in fertile, moisture-retentive soil

PROPAGATE
Seed in spring; divide in spring

HARDINESS
Hardy to frost tender; zones 5–8

PESTS AND DISEASES
Slugs and snails

This genus contains some of the finest flowering climbers, used to clothe walls and fences, and also some fine flowering shrubs. The best-known is the deciduous *Lonicera periclymenum* (woodbine), which has fragrant, cream-white, often red-tinged flowers mid- to late summer. Bright red berries follow. 'Graham Thomas' bears cream-white flowers all summer long.

L. x heckrottii deserves to be more widely grown. It is deciduous or semi-evergreen with blue-green leaves. In summer it bears fragrant orange-yellow flowers, pink outside, which are followed by red berries.

L. fragrantissima, 1.8 x 3 m (6 x 10 ft), is a deciduous or semi-evergreen shrub. It is grown for its fragrant, cream-white flowers, which are borne in winter and early spring. It does best in a sheltered position or as a wall shrub.

KEY FEATURES
- Deciduous or evergreen climber or shrub
- Fragrant winter or summer flowers
- Autumn berries

PLANT
In full sun or partial shade in well-drained soil

PROPAGATE
Ripe seed; semi-ripe cuttings (evergreen) in summer; greenwood or hardwood cuttings (deciduous) in summer or autumn

HARDINESS
Hardy; zones 5–9

PESTS AND DISEASES
Trouble free

Lunaria

HONESTY, SATIN FLOWER

Lupinus

LUPIN

▲ *Lunaria annua* 'Munstead Purple'

▲ *Lupinus* Russell Hybrids

Honesty is often grown for its oval, translucent seedheads, which can be left in the garden to provide new plants or used in dried-flower arrangements. It is an essential cottage-garden plant, but is also grown in mixed borders and woodland gardens.

Lunaria annua, 90 x 30 cm (36 x 12 in), is an annual or biennial, although once planted and allowed to self-seed plants will appear every year. It has mid-green, toothed leaves and, from late spring to summer, clusters of small white or light purple flowers. For white flowers only plant *L. annua* var. *albiflora*. The leaves of the white-flowered *L. annua* var. *albiflora* 'Alba Variegata' are edged and variegated with white. 'Munstead Purple' has dark red-purple flowers. 'Variegata' has red-purple flowers and leaves that are finely edged in white.

L. rediviva, 90 x 30 cm (36 x 12 in) is a hardy perennial, with dark green leaves and fragrant, pale lilac flowers in spring to early summer. The flowers are followed by the attractive seedheads.

KEY FEATURES
• Annual, biennial or perennial
• Attractive seedheads
• Source of winter food for birds

PLANT
In full sun or partial shade in fertile, well-drained soil

PROPAGATE
Seed in spring; divide in spring

HARDINESS
Hardy; zone 8

PESTS AND DISEASES
Clubroot but usually trouble free

The perennial lupins, with spires of pea-like flowers, are essential plants in a cottage garden, but they can also be grown in mixed borders or wildflower gardens. They are not long lived and are best treated as annuals or biennials.

Most garden plants are hybrids derived from *Lupinus polyphyllus*, of which there is an enormous number. Cut plants back after flowering and before they can set seed and some may send up a second, if sparser, flower spike. The lupins offered as Russell Hybrids grow to about 1 m (3 ft) tall and have bicoloured flowers in blue and white, cream-white and white, and pink and white.

Among the best of the named hybrids, which get to 1.2 m (4 ft) tall unless indicated, are 'Alan Titchmarsh', yellow flowers; 'Blushing Bride', 1 m (3 ft), pink-flushed white flowers; 'Esmerelder', 1 m (3 ft), lilac flowers; 'My Castle', brick red flowers; 'Olive Tolley', rose-pink flowers; 'Noble Maiden', white flowers; 'Rosalind Woodfield', apricot-pink flowers; and 'The Governor', 1 m (3 ft), white and dark lavender-blue flowers.

KEY FEATURES
• Annual or perennial
• Tall flower spikes
• Attracts bees

PLANT
In full sun or partial shade in well-drained, neutral to acid soil

PROPAGATE
Seed in spring; basal cuttings in mid-spring

HARDINESS
Hardy to half-hardy; zones 4–8

PESTS AND DISEASES
Aphids, slugs and snails, mildew

Lychnis
CAMPION, CATCHFLY

Lysichiton
SKUNK CABBAGE

▲ *Lychnis coronaria*

▲ *Lysichiton americanus*

These brightly coloured plants are suitable for sunny borders and wildlife gardens where they will extend the flowering season to late summer. Most will self-seed freely.

Lychnis chalcedonica (Jerusalem cross, Maltese cross), 1.2 m x 30 cm (4 x 1 ft), has scarlet flowers in midsummer. 'Flore Pleno' has striking double flowers. *L. chalcedonica* var. *albiflora* has white, pink-flushed flowers, but it does not grow as strongly as its red cousins.

L. coronaria (dusty miller, rose campion), 80 x 45 cm (32 x 18 in), has grey, rather felty leaves which are an excellent contrast to the magenta flowers, each to 3 cm (1^1/$_4$ in) across, which are borne in midsummer. *L. coronaria* 'Alba', to 75 cm (30 in) tall, has white flowers borne on grey stems above greyish leaves.

L. flos-cuculi (ragged robin), 75 x 80 cm (30 x 32 in), has grey-green leaves and, from late spring to early summer, star-shaped, pale pink, dark pink or white flowers.

KEY FEATURES
• Biennial or perennial
• Easy to grow
• Colourful flowers
• Good cut flowers

PLANT
In full sun or partial shade in well-drained soil

PROPAGATE
Seed in spring; divide in early spring

HARDINESS
Hardy; zones 4–8

PESTS AND DISEASES
Slugs and snails

The hardy perennials in this genus are often grown as aquatic plants in the shallow margins of a natural pond. They also do well in bog gardens. Although the spathes look exotic, they are hardy plants and will colonize ground that suits them.

The imposing *Lysichiton americanus* (yellow skunk cabbage), 1 x 1.2 m (3 x 4 ft), has rosettes of glossy, mid-green leaves, which grow to 1 m (3 ft) or more long. In early spring it produces bright yellow spathes, like those on an arum, surrounding the greenish-yellow spadix.

L. camtschatcensis, 75 cm (30 in) high and across, has glossy dark green leaves and, in spring, white spathes, to 40 cm (16 in) long, around the green spadix. This is less vigorous than *L. americanus* and is better suited to small ponds and bog gardens.

KEY FEATURES
• Perennial
• Good in bog gardens
• Eye-catching spathes

PLANT
In full sun or partial shade in fertile, moisture-retentive soil or in water to a depth of 2.5 cm (1 in)

PROPAGATE
Ripe seed; remove offsets in spring

HARDINESS
Hardy; zones 7–9

PESTS AND DISEASES
Trouble free

Lysimachia
LOOSESTRIFE

Macleaya
PLUME POPPY

▲ *Lysimachia clethroides*

▲ *Macleaya microcarpa*

These useful perennials can be included in mixed borders and woodland gardens. Some are suitable for bog gardens, and the low-growing plants are excellent groundcover. They are tolerant, easy-to-grow plants and can be invasive.

Lysimachia clethroides, 90 x 60 cm (3 x 2 ft), has long, slender stems that end in clusters of white flowers in mid- and late summer. The mid-green leaves are paler beneath.

L. nummularia 'Aurea' (golden creeping jenny), 5 cm (2 in) high, will spread indefinitely. It has yellow leaves, which darken in shade and as they age, and, throughout summer, bright yellow flowers. This is not only useful groundcover at the edges of a natural pond, but it can be used in a well-watered hanging basket or trailing over the sides of a large container.

L. punctata (dotted loosestrife), 90 x 60 cm (3 x 2 ft), can be invasive. It has green leaves, 8 cm (3 in) long, and in summer upright stems of yellow, cup-shaped flowers.

KEY FEATURES
• Perennial
• Tall flower spikes
• Good groundcover

PLANT
In sun or partial shade in fertile, moisture-retentive but well-drained soil

PROPAGATE
Seed in spring; divide in spring or autumn

HARDINESS
Hardy to frost hardy; zones 4–8

PESTS AND DISEASES
Slugs and snails

These perennials are grown for their graceful flowerheads, which take the form of airy plumes of tiny flowers. Although they grow quite tall, they have attractive foliage, which is best admired when plants are at the front of the border. They are also large enough to be specimen plants, although they do not provide year-round interest.

Macleaya cordata (plume poppy, tree celandine), 2.4 x 1 m (8 x 3 ft), has large, greyish-blue leaves and in summer large, feathery plumes of cream-white flowers.

M. x kewensis, 2.4 x 1 m (8 x 3 ft), has large, grey-green leaves. In early summer it bears large panicles of cream-coloured flowers. 'Flamingo' has pink-brown flowers.

M. microcarpa is similar to *M. cordata*, with plumes of cream-coloured flowers, but it can be invasive. More appealing is *M. microcarpa* 'Kelway's Coral Plume', 2.1 x 1 m (7 x 3 ft). The large, lobed leaves are grey-green and whitish underneath. Panicles of rich pink flowers are borne in early to midsummer on pink stems.

KEY FEATURES
• Perennial
• Airy flowerheads

PLANT
In full sun in fertile, well-drained soil

PROPAGATE
Seed in spring; divide in spring or autumn

HARDINESS
Hardy; zones 4–9

PESTS AND DISEASES
Slugs and snails

Magnolia

Mahonia

▲ *Magnolia* x *soulangeana*

▲ *Mahonia* x *media* 'Lionel Fortescue'

This genus contains both evergreen and deciduous trees and shrubs, all bearing beautiful, often fragrant flowers.

The slow-growing, deciduous *M. stellata* (star magnolia) is ideal for a small garden, eventually getting to 3 m (10 ft) tall and to 4 m (12 ft) across; it has a mass of white flowers in early spring. In early spring the deciduous *M.* x *soulangeana*, 6 m (20 ft) high and across, bears large flowers, which may be white to deep rose pink; grow it as a specimen so that its graceful shape can be appreciated.

One of the best cultivars of the deciduous hybrid *M.* x *loebneri* is 'Leonard Messel', 8 m (25 ft) high and across, which has pale pink flowers in early spring.

The evergreen *M. grandiflora* (bull bay) is a large, handsome tree, potentially to 18 m (60 ft) tall and 15 m (50 ft) across; the lovely white flowers are borne from late summer into autumn.

KEY FEATURES
- Evergreen or deciduous tree or shrub
- Wonderful showy flowers
- Often fragrant

PLANT
In sun or partial shade in neutral to acid soil

PROPAGATE
Seed in autumn; layer in early spring; greenwood cuttings in early summer; semi-ripe cuttings in late summer

HARDINESS
Hardy to frost tender; zones 4–9

PESTS AND DISEASES
Scale insects, coral spot, honey fungus

These useful and tolerant evergreen shrubs deserve a place in every garden for their year-round interest. The glossy dark green leaves are spiny, and the winter or spring flowers are followed by small, blue-black berries. They are useful for filling inhospitable corners, and because they can be cut back with no ill-effects are useful in mixed and shrub borders.

The justifiably popular *M.* x *media* 'Charity', to 3 m (10 ft) high and across, has clusters of sweetly fragrant, yellow flowers from late autumn to winter. 'Lionel Fortescue' has upright plumes of bright yellow flowers.

M. aquifolium (Oregon grape, mountain grape holly), eventually to about 1.5 m (5 ft) high and across, has scented yellow flowers in spring, and in winter the leaves often turn red-orange. The young leaves of the compact cultivar 'Smaragd', 60 x 90 cm (2 x 3 ft), have a wonderful bronze tinge; this is a perfect choice for a small garden.

KEY FEATURES
- Evergreen shrub
- Striking foliage
- Fragrant winter flowers

PLANT
In sun or shade in well-drained soil

PROPAGATE
Seed in spring; semi-ripe cuttings in summer or autumn; layer in spring

HARDINESS
Hardy; zones 6–9

PESTS AND DISEASES
Rust but usually trouble free

Malus

Malva
MALLOW

▲ *Malus pumila* 'Dartmouth'

▲ *Malva alcea* var. *fastigiata*

As well as apple trees, this genus includes many decorative trees, including crab apples, which are grown for blossom as well as fruit and leaf colour and are ideal in small gardens, providing interest for so much of the year.

Malus floribunda (Japanese crab apple), 10 m (30 ft) high and across, has dark green leaves. Pale pink flowers, borne in mid- to late spring, are followed by yellow fruits.

One of the most popular crab apples is *M.* 'John Downie', 10 x 6 m (30 x 20 ft), which makes an upright, rather conical tree. It has bright green leaves, white flowers in late spring and orange-red fruits in autumn. The compact 'Evereste', 7 x 6 m (22 x 20 ft), has dark green leaves, white spring flowers and red-orange fruits.

M. pumila 'Dartmouth', 8 x 7 m (25 x 22 ft), has dark green leaves, white spring flowers and red-purple fruits. The excellent *M. zumi* 'Golden Hornet', 10 x 8 m (30 x 25 ft), has white flowers and abundant bright yellow fruits.

KEY FEATURES
• Deciduous tree or shrub
• Blossom in spring
• Fruits in autumn
• Attracts wide range of birds

PLANT
In sun in fertile, well-drained soil

PROPAGATE
Seed in autumn; graft in midwinter

HARDINESS
Hardy; zones 5–8

PESTS AND DISEASES
Aphids, honey fungus, mildew, rust, scab

These are good plants for a cottage garden or wildflower garden but look equally at home in a mixed border. Perennials may be short lived but often self-seed. Taller plants will need staking, especially in exposed areas.

The perennial *Malva alcea* (hollyhock mallow), 1.2 m x 60 cm (4 x 2 ft), has light green, scalloped leaves and from early summer to early autumn clusters of pink flowers. *M. alcea* var. *fastigiata* (cut-leaved mallow), 1.5 m x 50 cm (5 ft x 20 in) has bright pink flowers.

M. moschata (musk mallow), 90 x 60 cm (3 x 2 ft), a woody-based perennial has musk-scented foliage. Large pale pink or white flowers are borne through summer.

The annual or biennial *M. nicaeensis*, 50 x 23 cm (20 x 9 in), produces large lilac-pink flowers in summer.

KEY FEATURES
• Annual, biennial or perennial
• Large flowers
• Easy to grow

PLANT
In full sun in well-drained soil

PROPAGATE
Seed in spring

HARDINESS
Hardy; zones 5–9

PESTS AND DISEASES
Rust

Meconopsis

Melianthus

▲ *Meconopsis cambrica*

▲ *Melianthus major*

This genus is perhaps best known for its glorious blue poppies, which thrive as perennials in cool climates. In warmer areas and in dry ground the plants may die after flowering. The Himalayan poppies have cup-shaped flowers with prominent yellow stamens. They are beautiful but not easy to grow, and if your garden is dry and hot these are not the plants for you. *Meconopsis betonicifolia*, 1.2 m x 45 cm (4 ft x 18 in), produces large, bright blue flowers in early summer. *M. grandis*, 1.2 m x 60 cm (4 x 2 ft), is a clump-forming perennial, producing blue-purple flowers in summer. *M. horridula*, 90 x 45 cm (36 x 18 in), has blue-red flowers; this will die after flowering no matter what conditions it grows in.

The perennial and more reliable *M. cambrica* (Welsh poppy), 45 x 25 cm (18 x 10 in), also prefers cool conditions and soil that is on the acid side of neutral, when it will produce appealing yellow or orange flowers on upright stems in spring. It self-seeds and can be invasive.

KEY FEATURES
• Annual, biennial or perennial
• Spring or summer flowers
• Eye-catching blue blooms

PLANT
In partial shade in fertile, moisture-retentive but well-drained, neutral to acid soil

PROPAGATE
Seed in spring; divide after flowering

HARDINESS
Hardy; zones 4–8

PESTS AND DISEASES
Slugs and snails, downy mildew

These plants are grown for their attractive blue-green, serrated leaves, and in very cold areas they are best regarded as conservatory plants. In temperate areas they will usually survive outdoors, though they should be regarded as herbaceous perennials – that is, they will be cut back by winter frosts, but if you provide a good winter mulch, they should reshoot in spring. These plants flower best in poor soil, but if you want the handsome leaves make sure the soil is fertile and moisture retentive.

Melianthus major (honey bush), 2.4 x 1.8 m (8 x 6 ft), has large, spreading leaves, to 50 cm (20 in) long, made up of sharply toothed, grey-green leaflets. In a hot summer it will produce a spike of dark brown-red flowers. It looks lovely next to a pond or amid a group of cannas. *M. minor*, 1.8 x 1 m (6 x 3 ft), is similar but smaller.

KEY FEATURES
• Evergreen shrub
• Beautiful foliage
• Unusual flowers

PLANT
In full sun in moisture-retentive but well-drained soil

PROPAGATE
Seed in spring; softwood cuttings in spring

HARDINESS
Half-hardy; zones 9–10

PESTS AND DISEASES
Trouble free

Mimulus

MONKEY FLOWER, MUSK

Miscanthus

▲ *Mimulus cupreus* 'Whitecroft Scarlet'

▲ *Miscanthus sinensis* 'Silberfeder'

This large genus contains plants that are most at home in reliably moist soil, and some do best in bog gardens or near the margins of a natural pond. They can also be grown in borders that have deep, fertile soil that does not dry out in summer, and they are good companion plants for hostas. The perennials are often short lived but they will self-seed.

The hardy annual *Mimulus cupreus*, 30 x 20 (12 x 8 in), bears masses of small, golden-yellow flowers in spikes in summer. 'Whitecroft Scarlet', 10 x 15 cm (4 x 6 in), has deep scarlet flowers from early to late summer.

Plant *M. cardinalis*, 1 m (3 ft) high and across, in a bog garden. It is an erect perennial, producing vertical sprays of red, two-lipped flowers in late summer. Cut back after flowering to encourage new growth. *M. luteus* (yellow musk), 45 cm (18 in) high and across, is a spreading perennial, with yellow flowers in midsummer. It will grow in a bog garden but tends to self-seed rather freely and may look better in a wild garden or near a natural pond.

KEY FEATURES
• Annual or perennial
• Colourful flowers
• Attracts bees

PLANT
In full sun or light shade in fertile, moist, neutral to acid soil

PROPAGATE
Seed in spring; divide in spring

HARDINESS
Hardy to frost tender; zones 6–9

PESTS AND DISEASES
Slugs and snails, mildew

These deciduous and evergreen grasses make dense clumps, and inflorescences can be left on the plants to provide winter interest. Many of the most widely available forms have been developed from *Miscanthus sinensis*, 4 x 1.2 m (12 x 4 ft), a clump-forming, deciduous grass that has blue-grey leaves and, in autumn, large panicles of pale grey, purple-tinged spikelets. 'Goliath', 2.1 m (7 ft) tall, has green leaves and pink-tinged inflorescences in late summer. 'Gracillimus' (maiden grass), 1.3 m (4 ft 6 in) tall, has narrow leaves that curl at the ends and have white midribs and, in autumn, plumes of buff-yellow spikelets; the leaves become bronze in autumn. 'Kleine Fontäne' ('Little Fountain'), to 1 m (3 ft) tall, has upright leaves and pink inflorescences in late summer. The fluffy, pinkish flowerheads of 'Malepartus', 1.8 m (6 ft) tall, are popular with flower arrangers. 'Silberfeder' ('Silver Feather'), 2.4 m (8 ft) tall, has feathery, slightly pink-tinged plumes of silver spikelets from midsummer. 'Zebrinus', 1.2–1.5 m (4–5 ft) tall, has narrow green leaves, marked with bold horizontal bands of yellow.

KEY FEATURES
• Deciduous grass
• Variegated foliage
• Attractive inflorescences

PLANT
In full sun in moisture-retentive but well-drained soil

PROPAGATE
Seed in spring; divide in spring

HARDINESS
Hardy to frost hardy; zones 5–9

PESTS AND DISEASES
Trouble free

Monarda
BERGAMOT

Muscari
GRAPE HYACINTH

▲ *Monarda* 'Cambridge Scarlet'

▲ *Muscari latifolium*

The showy, long-lasting flowerheads of monardas are carried on erect stems from mid- to late summer. They are excellent in mixed borders and in wildlife gardens.

Many of the garden hybrids have been developed from the clump-forming perennial *Monarda didyma* (Oswego tea, sweet bergamot), 90 x 45 cm (36 x 18 in), which is often grown in herb gardens. It has red-pink flowers surrounded by reddish bracts and mid-green leaves. The cultivars grow to 90 x 45 cm (36 x 18 in) unless otherwise indicated. 'Beauty of Cobham' has pale pink flowers with purple-pink bracts. 'Cambridge Scarlet' has red flowers and plum red bracts. 'Croftway Pink' has rose-pink flowers and pinkish bracts. 'Loddon Crown' has dark red-purple flowers with purple-brown bracts. 'Mahogany' has purplish-red flowers with brown-red bracts. 'Mohawk', 1.2 m (4 ft) tall, has light mauve flowers with paler bracts. 'Snow Queen' has pale pink-white flowers. 'Squaw' has scarlet flowers. 'Vintage Wine' has red-purple flowers and green-brown bracts.

KEY FEATURES
- Perennial
- Colourful flowers
- Attracts bees

PLANT
In full sun in fertile, well-drained soil

PROPAGATE
Seed in spring; divide in spring

HARDINESS
Hardy; zones 4–9

PESTS AND DISEASES
Slugs and snails

The dense racemes of dark blue flowers of *Muscari armeniacum*, 20 x 5 cm (8 x 2 in), appear in mid-spring and last for many weeks above the narrow mid-green leaves. This is an excellent hardy bulb for naturalizing under deciduous shrubs. The main disadvantage is that the foliage can get straggly and overgrown, developing at the expense of the flowers. Lift and divide congested clumps, or simply dig them up and plant one of the other species or new cultivars, such as *M*. 'Blue Spike', 15 x 5 cm (6 x 2 in), which has double, pale blue flowers in spring.

The borderline hardy *M. latifolium*, 20 x 5 cm (8 x 2 in), has dark violet-blue flowers topped by a crown of paler flowers. Grow in containers and protect in winter.

Also borderline hardy is *M. comosum* (tassel grape hyacinth), 60 x 5 cm (24 x 2 in), which has cream-brown flowers topped by a tassel of sterile, violet-blue flowers. 'Plumosum' has entirely purple-blue, sterile flowers.

M. botryoides 'Album', 20 x 5 cm (8 x 2 in), has dense racemes of fragrant white flowers. It is hardy.

KEY FEATURES
- Bulb
- Spring flowers
- Easy to grow

PLANT
In full sun in fertile, moisture-retentive but well-drained soil

PROPAGATE
Seed in autumn; offsets in summer

HARDINESS
Hardy to frost hardy; zones 2–9

PESTS AND DISEASES
Viruses but usually trouble free

Myosotis

FORGET-ME-NOT

Nandina

HEAVENLY BAMBOO

▲ *Myosotis sylvatica* (pink flowered)

▲ *Nandina domestica*

It is hard to image a spring garden without tulips and forget-me-nots or without a carpet of blue under deciduous shrubs. Although forget-me-nots self-seed, sow fresh seed every couple of years because the intensity of the blue tends to diminish as the years pass. If plants get mildew, pull them up and burn them.

Myosotis sylvatica, 30 x 15 cm (12 x 6 in), the familiar blue-flowered (sometimes pink or white), yellow-eyed plant with grey-green leaves, is the parent of many hybrids. 'Blue Ball', 20 cm (8 in) high and across, has azure flowers. 'Compinidi', 20 cm (8 in) high and across, has dark blue flowers. 'Rosylva', 30 x 15 cm (12 x 6 in), has pink flowers. 'Victoria Rose', 10 cm (4 in) high and across, has bright pink flowers.

Unlike other members of the genus, *M. scorpiodes* (water forget-me-not), 30 cm (12 in) high and across, will grow in water to a depth of 15 cm (6 in). It is a spreading perennial, producing bright blue flowers, with a central eye of white, pink or yellow, in early to midsummer.

KEY FEATURES
- Annual, biennial or perennial
- Blue flowers
- Easy to grow

PLANT
In full sun in moisture-retentive but well-drained soil

PROPAGATE
Seed in spring; divide in spring

HARDINESS
Hardy; zones 4–10

PESTS AND DISEASES
Slugs and snails, mildew

Nandina domestica, 1.8 x 1.5 m (6 x 5 ft), the only species in the genus, is an evergreen or semi-evergreen, upright shrub. Although it is related to *Berberis*, it looks nothing like those useful shrubs. It has bright green leaves, which are flushed with purple and red in spring and autumn. In midsummer it bears sprays of small, star-shaped flowers and, after hot summers, in autumn it produces round, bright red berries, which persist into winter.

A number of cultivars have been developed, and the smaller ones are good groundcover. The dwarf 'Fire Power', 1.2 m x 60 cm (4 x 2 ft), has yellow-green leaves that turn red-purple in autumn. 'Harbor Dwarf' grows to 1 x 1.2 m (3 x 4 ft). 'Richmond', 2.4 x 1.5 m (8 x 5 ft), has scarlet berries in autumn.

KEY FEATURES
- Evergreen or semi-evergreen shrub
- Summer flowers
- Autumn foliage colour
- Autumn berries
- Easy to grow
- Good groundcover

PLANT
In full sun

PROPAGATE
Ripe seed; semi-ripe cuttings in summer

HARDINESS
Frost hardy; zones 7–10

PESTS AND DISEASES
Viruses but largely trouble free

Narcissus

DAFFODIL

Daffodils are probably the most familiar and most popular of all spring flowers. They are easy to grow and tolerate a range of different conditions – being naturalized in grass, growing on a rock garden, in clumps in beds and borders, or as cheery subjects for containers.

▲ *Narcissus* 'February Gold'

From the 50 or so species, thousands of cultivars have been developed, offering an almost bewildering selection of flower shape and size. Not only is it possible to find daffodils in white and every conceivable shade of yellow, but new forms have been hybridized with pink flowers.

For many people Trumpet daffodils, which have one flower to each stem and a trumpet which is the same length, or longer than, the petals, are the spring flower par excellence. The group includes 'Golden Harvest', 35 cm (14 in), good for naturalizing; the excellent 'King Alfred', 35 cm (14 in), golden-yellow flowers in mid-spring; and 'W.P. Milner', 23 cm (9 in), white and cream trumpet, milky white petals in early spring.

Large-cupped daffodils have one flower to a stem and have a trumpet that is longer than one-third of, but not as long as, the petals. The group includes 'Carlton', 45 cm (18 in), soft yellow flowers in mid-spring; 'Ice Follies', 35 cm (14 in), cream-white flowers in mid-spring; and 'Salome', 35 cm (14 in), pink trumpet and cream petals late spring.

Small-cupped daffodils have one flower to a stem, and the cup is less than one-third of the length of the petals. This group includes 'Merlin', 45 cm (18 in), white petals and pale yellow cup from mid- to late spring, and also 'Segovia', 25 cm (10 in), white petals and pale yellow cup from mid- to late spring.

Double daffodils have more than one ring of petals. 'Bridal Crown', 40 cm (16 in), has fragrant white flowers with orange-yellow centres in early spring. 'Sir Winston Churchill', 40 cm (16 in), has white flowers in late spring;

it is good for borders or grass. 'Tahiti', 45 cm (18 in), has golden petals and a red-orange trumpet in mid-spring.

Triandrus daffodils have been developed from *N. triandrus*, which is native to Spain, Portugal and northwest France. They flower in mid-spring, with two to six slightly drooping flowers on each stem. The dainty 'Hawera', 18 cm (7 in), has lemon flowers from mid- to late spring; this is a good choice for a container. 'Thalia', 35 cm (14 in), has white flowers with reflexed petals in mid-spring.

Cyclamineus daffodils produce a single flower with swept-back petals on each stem. In early to mid-spring the long-lasting flowers of 'Jack Snipe', 20 cm (8 in), have lemon-yellow trumpets and white petals. 'Jenny', 23 cm (9 in), has very pale yellow trumpets with strongly reflexed white petals in early spring.

Jonquilla daffodils have from one to five, usually scented flowers on each stem. 'Quail', 40 cm (16 in), has all-yellow flowers from mid- to late spring. 'Sun Disc', 15 cm (6 in), has neat all-yellow flowers in mid-spring; it is ideal for a small container or rock garden.

TOP 10 NARCISSI

'Altruist'
Small-cupped daffodil; pale apricot petals, orange-red trumpet, mid-spring, 45 cm (18 in)

***Narcissus bulbocodium* (hoop-petticoat daffodil)**
Species daffodil; all-yellow flowers, mid-spring, 10 cm (4 in)

'Cantabile'
Poeticus daffodil; red-rimmed, green and yellow cup, white petals, late spring, 25 cm (10 in)

'February Gold'
Cyclamineus daffodil; golden-yellow flowers with reflexed petals, early spring, 30 cm (12 in)

'Grand Soleil d'Or'
Tazetta daffodil; scented flowers with orange-red trumpet, golden petals, early spring, 45 cm (18 in)

'Ice Wings'
Triandrus daffodil; all-white flowers, mid-spring, 30 cm (12 in)

'Misty Glen'
Large-cupped daffodil; pure white petals, green-white trumpet, mid-spring, 42 cm (17 in)

'Mount Hood'
Trumpet daffodil; pure white petals, ivory trumpet, mid-spring, 42 cm (17 in)

'Pipit'
Jonquilla daffodil; scented, long-lasting flowers with pale yellow trumpet, lemon-yellow petals, mid- to late spring, 30 cm (12 in)

'Rip van Winkle' (syn. *N. minor* var. *pumilus* 'Plenus')
Double daffodil, all-yellow flowers, early spring, 20 cm (8 in)

Tazetta daffodils, which are usually scented, may be small-flowered forms with up to 20 flowers on each stem or large-flowered forms with three or four flowers on each stem. 'Silver Chimes', 30 cm (12 in), has fragrant creamy petals and cream-yellow trumpets in mid- to late spring. 'Minnow', 18 cm (7 in), has cream-yellow petals and yellow trumpets in mid-spring. For scented flowers at Christmas, grow prepared bulbs of *N. papyraceus* (Paper White), 35 cm (14 in), forcing them into growth early.

Poeticus daffodils have shallow, red-edged cups and white petals. 'Actaea', 45 cm (18 in), has fragrant flowers in late spring, white petals and a red-edged yellow cup.

Bulbocodium daffodils have the typical hoop-petticoat trumpet. *N. bulbocodium* 'Golden Bells', 10 cm (4 in), has dainty all-yellow flowers in mid-spring.

Split-corona daffodils are usually borne one to a stem. The cups are divided for more than half their length. 'Cassata', 40 cm (16 in) flowers in mid-spring with white petals and a lemon-yellow, almost flattened cup.

A group known as 'Miscellaneous' contains those that do not fit into any other category. The multi-headed 'Jumblie', 20 cm (8 in), bears golden-yellow flowers in early spring. The popular and reliable 'Tête-à-tête', 15 cm (6 in), has all-yellow flowers in early spring.

Species narcissi include the fragrant *N. poeticus* (poet's daffodil), 50 cm (20 in), which attracts beneficial insects before other plants come into bloom. The attractive *N. cyclamineus*, 20 cm (8 in), has golden-yellow flowers with a long trumpet and strongly swept-back petals.

▲ *Narcissus* 'Tahiti'

KEY FEATURES
- Bulb
- Spring flowers
- Good for naturalizing
- Good in containers
- Good cut flowers

PLANT
In sun or partial shade in moisture-retentive but well-drained soil

PROPAGATE
Ripe seed; offsets in summer or early autumn

HARDINESS
Hardy to half-hardy; zones 3–9

PESTS AND DISEASES
Narcissus bulb fly, eelworms, fungal infections

▼ *Narcissus papyraceus* (Paper White)

Nepeta
CATMINT

Nephrolepis
SWORD FERN

▲ *Nepeta nervosa*

▲ *Nephrolepis exaltata*

These plants are recognizable from their toothed, aromatic leaves. They are ideal in cottage and wildlife gardens but can also be used for edging.

Nepeta x *faasenii*, 45 cm (18 in) high and across, is the widely grown catmint. The soft grey-green leaves make a dense mound, with lavender flowers borne in succession in summer. Deadhead regularly to encourage new growth.

N. nervosa, 60 x 30 cm (2 x 1 ft), has the typical veined, aromatic, grey-green leaves. Purple-blue flowers are borne in cylindrical whorls from midsummer to early autumn.

The spreading *N. racemosa*, 30 x 45 cm (12 x 18 in), has lavender-blue summer flowers. It is the parent of 'Snowflake', which has white flowers, and 'Little Titch', 15 cm (6 in) high and across, with lavender-blue flowers.

N. 'Six Hills Giant', 90 x 60 cm (3 x 2 ft) is one of the best hybrids. It has soft, veined, aromatic, grey-green leaves and masses of erect spikes of lavender-blue flowers.

KEY FEATURES
• Perennial
• Fragrant foliage
• Attracts bees

PLANT
In full sun or partial shade in well-drained, alkaline soil

PROPAGATE
Seed in autumn; divide in spring or autumn

HARDINESS
Hardy to half-hardy; zones 4–9

PESTS AND DISEASES
Mildew

Although these ferns are tender, they can be grown in containers and moved outside in summer. In frost-free areas they can be grown in shady sites in reliably moist soil. When they are grown in a container they must have free-draining compost and filtered light. They are often grown in hanging baskets, when the arching fronds can be seen to great effect. Plants grown indoors benefit from regular misting with soft water to maintain humidity around them.

The fast-growing *Nephrolepis exaltata* is often grown as a houseplant. It makes neat clumps, 1 m (3 ft) high and wide, of narrow arching fronds. It is the parent plant of many cultivars, of which the best known and most widely grown is 'Bostoniensis' (Boston fern), which has broad, lance-shaped fronds. The vigorous 'Hillii', 1 x 1.8 m (3 x 6 ft), has attractively lobed and crisped fronds.

N. cordifolia, 80 cm x 1.5 m (32 in x 5 ft), has gracefully arching fronds formed of near-oblong pinnae. This is a wonderful fern to stand on a patio in summer, although it does need the protection of a conservatory in winter.

KEY FEATURES
• Evergreen or
  semi-evergreen fern
• Good in containers

PLANT
In sun or partial shade in moisture-retentive but well-drained soil

PROPAGATE
Divide in spring or autumn

HARDINESS
Half-hardy to frost tender; zone 10

PESTS AND DISEASES
Trouble free

Nerine

Nicotiana
TOBACCO PLANT

▲ *Nerine sarniensis*

▲ *Nicotiana* 'Lime Green'

The showy *Nerine bowdenii* will survive happily outdoors against the shelter of a sunny wall. *N. sarniensis*, *N. undulata* and late-flowering cultivars of *N. bowdenii* should be grown in containers so that the flowers can be protected from cold weather. These bulbs grow best when congested.

The silvery pink, rather spidery flowers of *N. bowdenii*, 45 x 8 cm (18 x 3 in), appear in mid-autumn and are followed by the strap-shaped leaves. The plants have a summer dormancy when they need warm, dry conditions. Plant with the nose of the bulb just above soil level. The cultivars include 'Alba' with white flowers. In early to mid-autumn 'Codora' has rich red flowers. 'Pink Triumph', a late-flowering form, has pink flowers with wavy petals. 'Mark Fenwick', 60 x 8 cm (24 x 3 in), has large pink flowers.

The many hybrids include *N.* 'Stephanie', with cream-white, pink-flushed flowers in early to mid-autumn, and *N.* 'Zeal Giant', which has long-stemmed, broad pink flowers.

N. sarniensis (Guernsey lily), 60 x 15 cm (24 x 6 in), has deep orange-pink flowers in early autumn. *N. undulata*, 45 x 8 cm (18 x 3 in), has umbels of funnel-shaped, mid-pink flowers with crinkled petals.

KEY FEATURES
• Bulb
• Autumn flowers
• Suitable for containers

PLANT
In full sun in well-drained soil

PROPAGATE
Ripe seed; divide after flowering

HARDINESS
Hardy to half-hardy; zones 8–10

PESTS AND DISEASES
Slugs and snails

The tubular, five-petalled flowers are borne in late summer to autumn, and many nicotianas open in the evening or only when they are grown in shade. They are best in mixed borders, and plants derived from *Nicotiana alata* can be used as summer bedding.

N. alata, 1.5 m x 30 cm (5 x 1 ft) is a perennial but is often grown as an annual. It has tubular, greenish-white flowers, which are fragrant at night.

N. langsdorfii, 1.5 m x 35 cm (5 ft x 14 in), is a sticky annual. Branching stems arise from a rosette of leaves and bear drooping, pale lime-green flowers.

The widely grown *Nicotiana* 'Lime Green', 60 x 25 cm (24 x 10 in), bears lime-green flowers, each to 12 cm (5 in) long, throughout the summer.

Many annuals have been developed from the hybrid *N.* x *sanderae*. Plants in the Domino Series have red, white, pink or green flowers. The Merlin Series includes compact, bushy plants that are perfect for containers or the front of a border; the flowers are purple, crimson, lime-green and white.

KEY FEATURES
• Annual, biennial or perennial
• Fragrant flowers
• Attracts night-flying moths

PLANT
In sun or partial shade in moisture-retentive but well-drained soil

PROPAGATE
Seed in spring

HARDINESS
Hardy to half-hardy; zone 7

PESTS AND DISEASES
Grey mould, mosaic virus

Nothofagus
SOUTHERN BEECH

Nyssa

▲ *Nothofagus menziesii*

▲ *Nyssa sylvatica*

These ornamental trees are fast growing and have very attractive habits of growth, making them ideal specimen trees. They will not grow in chalky soil and they will not do well in exposed positions.

The deciduous *Nothofagus antarctica* (Antarctic beech), 15 x 10 m (50 x 30 ft), has a broadly conical shape. The dark green, heart-shaped leaves, which are glossy and crinkled at the edges, turn yellow in autumn.

The half-hardy *N. menziesii* (silver beech), 15 x 8 m (50 x 25 ft), is a graceful evergreen tree. It has round, toothed leaves.

N. obliqua (Roblé beech), 20 x 15 m (70 x 50 ft), is a fast-growing deciduous tree. The dark green leaves are blue-green underneath and have strongly toothed edges. They turn yellow, orange or red in autumn.

KEY FEATURES
• Deciduous or evergreen tree
• Good autumn colour

PLANT
In full sun in moisture-retentive but well-drained, acid soil

PROPAGATE
Seed in autumn

HARDINESS
Hardy to half-hardy; zones 7–9

PESTS AND DISEASES
Trouble free

If you have a small garden with acid soil these neat deciduous trees would be an excellent and unusual specimen plant. In a larger garden they could be grown in a woodland setting.

Nyssa sinensis (Chinese tupelo), 10 m (30 ft) high and across, has narrow dark green leaves, each to 20 cm (8 in) long. The young leaves are suffused with red, and in autumn all the foliage turns brilliant shades of red, yellow and orange. Insignificant flowers appear in early summer and are followed by small bluish fruits.

The larger but slow-growing *N. tupelo* (black gum, sour gum, tupelo), 20 x 10 m (70 x 30 ft), also has dark green leaves that turn red, orange and yellow in autumn.

N. 'Jermyns Flame' and 'Sheffield Park' are hybrids with relatively large leaves, giving even better autumn colour.

KEY FEATURES
• Deciduous tree
• Autumn colour

PLANT
In sun or partial shade in moisture-retentive but well-drained, acid soil

PROPAGATE
Seed in autumn; greenwood cuttings in summer; semi-ripe cuttings in midsummer

HARDINESS
Hardy; zones 3–7

PESTS AND DISEASES
Trouble free

Oenothera

EVENING PRIMROSE

Onopordum

SCOTCH THISTLE

▲ *Oenothera macrocarpa*

▲ *Onopordum acanthium*

The perennial or biennial *Oenothera biennis* (evening primrose), 1.5 m x 60 cm (5 x 2 ft), will self-seed itself around the garden and can be invasive. The fragrant yellow flowers, each to 8 cm (3 in) wide, are borne from early summer to mid-autumn and open in the evening.

O. macrocarpa (Ozark sundrops), 15 x 50 cm (6 x 20 in), bears a long succession of bright yellow flowers, which open from red buds, all summer long. Grow at the front of a sunny border.

The flowers of *O. fruticans* (sundrops), 90 x 30 cm (36 x 12 in), which is often grown as a biennial, are borne from late spring to late summer and open in the day. The cup-shaped, bright yellow flowers are borne in racemes.

In a wildlife garden, plant evening primrose to attract warblers, which feed on the insects attracted to the flowers. The tiny seeds in the fruit capsules are eaten by finches and siskins.

KEY FEATURES
• Annual, biennial or perennial
• Colourful flowers

PLANT
In sun or partial shade in fertile, moisture-retentive soil

PROPAGATE
Divide in late spring

HARDINESS
Hardy to frost hardy; zones 4–8

PESTS AND DISEASES
Slugs and snails

Grow these imposing, tap-rooted plants at the back of a border or in a wildlife garden, where they will readily self-seed. The flowers do not appear until the second year.

Onopordum acanthium, 3 x 1 m (10 x 3 ft), bears pink-purple, white or pink flowerheads, to 5 cm (2 in) across, encased in spiny bracts in summer. The spiny, grey, toothed leaves, to 35 cm (14 in) long, form dense rosettes.

O. nervosum, 2.4 x 1 m (8 x 3 ft), has purple-red to purple-pink flowerheads, to 5 cm (2 in) across in summer. The silver-grey leaves, to 50 cm (20 in) long, are toothed and spiny and form basal rosettes. This is not as reliably hardy as *O. acanthium* and needs a position in full sun.

KEY FEATURES
• Biennial
• Silvery foliage

PLANT
In full sun in fertile, well-drained, neutral to alkaline soil

PROPAGATE
Seed in spring or autumn

HARDINESS
Hardy; zones 6–9

PESTS AND DISEASES
Slugs and snails

Ophiopogon

Ornithogalum
STAR-OF-BETHLEHEM

▲ *Ophiopogon planiscapus* 'Nigrescens'

▲ *Ornithogalum pyrenaicum*

These grass-like plants bear small white or purple bell-shaped flowers, but they are grown mainly for their handsome and architectural foliage.

Ophiopogon planiscapus, 20 x 30 cm (8 x 12 in), has strap-shaped, curving, dark green leaves and pale purple-white flowers in summer. The flowers are followed by little dark blue berries. This species is rather dull and is represented in gardens by the cultivar 'Nigrescens', which has black-purple leaves and purplish, bell-shaped flowers.

O. japonicum, 30 cm (12 in) high and across, has dark green leaves and white or lilac-white flowers followed by round blue-black berries. It, too, is rather uninteresting, but 'Silver Dragon', 30 x 15 cm (12 x 6 in), has white-variegated leaves and makes a good front-of-border plant.

O. jaburan (white lilyturf), 60 x 30 cm (2 x 1 ft), has dark green leaves and white or pale lilac flowers, followed by violet-blue fruits. It, too, is best represented by cultivars. 'Vittatus' has pale green leaves which are striped with cream or yellow, and the leaves of 'White Dragon' are boldly striped in white.

KEY FEATURES
• Evergreen perennial
• Attractive foliage

PLANT
In full sun in moisture-retentive but well-drained, acid soil

PROPAGATE
Ripe seed; divide in spring

HARDINESS
Hardy to half-hardy; zones 6–9

PESTS AND DISEASES
Slugs and snails

This genus contains about 80 species, but only a few of these are widely grown and not all are hardy enough to be left in the ground all year round.

Ornithogalum nutans, 20–60 x 5 cm (8–24 x 2 in), is hardy. In late spring it bears racemes of up to 20 funnel-shaped, white flowers with green stripes. Also hardy is *O. pyrenaicum* (Bath asparagus), 1 m x 10 cm (3 ft x 4 in), which has grey-green leaves and, in early summer, racemes of up to 40 star-shaped, white flowers, also striped green.

The summer-flowering *O. thyrsoides* (chincherinchee), 40 x 10 cm (16 x 4 in), is tender. It bears erect, dense racemes of cup-shaped, white flowers, greenish at the base, which open in succession.

The half-hardy *O. arabicum*, 45 x 15 cm (18 x 6 in), can be grown outdoors if you are prepared to lift the bulbs in autumn; alternatively, grow it in a container that can be moved into a frost-free greenhouse in winter. In early summer it produces erect stems with about ten fragrant, white flowers, each with a distinctive black centre.

KEY FEATURES
• Bulb
• White flowers
• Suitable for containers

PLANT
In sun in well-drained soil

PROPAGATE
Seed in spring; offsets in autumn

HARDINESS
Hardy to frost tender; zones 6–10

PESTS AND DISEASES
Trouble free

Osmanthus

Oxalis

▲ *Osmanthus delavayi*

▲ *Oxalis oregana*

These small shrubs can be used for hedging and edging and also for topiary. They can also be grown in shrub borders and trained as wall shrubs. They do not usually need any pruning, but straggling, dead or damaged shoots can be removed in mid- to late spring.

The neat rounded *Osmanthus delavayi*, 1.8 x 2.4 m (6 x 8 ft) or more, has glossy, dark green leaves that are toothed (like holly leaves). In mid-spring it bears fragrant white flowers, and these are followed by round, blue-black fruit.

O. x *burkwoodii*, 3 x 3 m (10 x 10 ft), is a dense shrub with oval, slightly toothed, glossy dark green leaves. In mid- to late spring it bears clusters of small fragrant white flowers.

O. decorus, 3 x 5 m (10 x 15 ft), is a rather spreading shrub with glossy, toothed, dark green leaves. Like other plants in the genus it bears fragrant white flowers in spring; they are followed by blue-black fruits.

KEY FEATURES
- Evergreen shrub
- Attractive foliage
- Fragrant flowers

PLANT
In sun or partial shade in fertile, well-drained soil

PROPAGATE
Ripe seed; semi-ripe cuttings in summer; layer in autumn

HARDINESS
Hardy; zones 6–9

PESTS AND DISEASES
Trouble free

This large genus contains about 500 species of bulbs, tubers, rhizomes and fibrous-rooted annuals and perennials.

The clump-forming hardy perennial *Oxalis adenophylla*, 10 x 15 cm (4 x 6 in), develops from fibre-covered bulbs. It has attractive grey-blue leaves, which consist of up to 12 radiating leaflets, and, in late spring, purplish-pink flowers, each to 2.5 cm (1 in) across and with darker veining and throats. Plant in full sun in well-drained soil.

The spreading and hardy *O. oregana*, to 20 cm (8 in) high, is a rhizomatous perennial with clover-like leaves, each with a grey mark. From late spring to midsummer it bears cup-shaped, white, pale pink or lilac flowers, each to 2 cm ($^3/_4$ in) across. This is good groundcover in a shady area where the soil is fertile and moist.

O. tetraphylla (good-luck plant, lucky clover), 15 x 10 cm (6 x 4 in), is only borderline hardy. In summer it bears loose clusters of reddish-purple flowers, each 2.5 cm (1 in) across, above the clover-like, deeply lobed leaflets.

KEY FEATURES
- Annual or perennial
- Pretty flowers
- Attractive foliage
- Good groundcover
- Good in shade

PLANT
Different species have different requirements

PROPAGATE
Seed in late winter or early spring; divide in spring

HARDINESS
Hardy to frost tender; zones 7–10

PESTS AND DISEASES
Slugs and snails, rust

Paeonia
PEONY

Papaver
POPPY

▲ *Paeonia delavayi*

▲ *Papaver orientale* 'Black and White'

This genus contains both the lovely herbaceous peonies and some shrubs. Newly planted peonies probably won't flower in the first year, and you might even have to wait until the third summer after planting before you see any flowers. Peonies don't respond well to being moved.

The tree peony *Paeonia delavayi*, 1.8 x 1.2 m (6 x 4 ft), has dark red, bowl-shaped flowers in late spring. *P. suffruticosa*, 2.1 m (7 ft) high and across, is a fine plant for a shrub border and is the parent of many good cultivars, including 'Mrs William Kelway', with double white flowers.

Most herbaceous peonies are derived from *P. lactiflora*. They grow to about 1 m (3 ft) high and across and have mid- to dark green leaves. 'Bowl of Beauty' has large flowers, white in the centre and with a broad, deep pink-red edge to the petals. 'Dinner Plate', which has very large double pink flowers, is fragrant. 'Primevere' has beautiful cream flowers with a yellow centre. 'Sarah Bernhardt' has double, silver-pink flowers in late spring. 'Yellow Crown' is, as the name suggests, a yellow-flowered form, with fragrant, double flowers.

KEY FEATURES
- Perennial or shrub
- Beautiful flowers
- Good cut flowers

PLANT
In sun or partial shade in fertile, moisture-retentive soil

PROPAGATE
Seed in spring; divide herbaceous plants in early spring

HARDINESS
Hardy; zones 5–8

PESTS AND DISEASES
Eelworms, honey fungus

Poppies are found in cottage gardens, wildlife gardens, mixed borders and rock gardens. They can be fast-growing annuals or robust herbaceous perennials.

Papaver orientale (oriental poppy), 90 x 30 cm (3 x 1 ft), is the parent of most of the perennial poppies, which flower in late spring to midsummer. The species has red flowers with a dark splodge at the base of each petal. The cultivars grow to 75–90 cm (30–36 in) tall. 'Allegro' has bright red petals with a black mark at the centre. 'Beauty of Livermore' has scarlet flowers with a black mark. 'Black and White' has white flowers with a crimson-black mark. 'Cedric Morris' has grey-pink flowers. 'Marcus Perry' has red-orange flowers with a black mark. 'Perry's White' has pure white flowers with a dark centre. 'Picotee' has pink-flushed white flowers with frilly petals.

The flowers of the annual *Papaver rhoeas* (corn poppy, field poppy), 90 x 30 cm (3 x 1 ft), are red. They attract pollinating insects, and the seeds are eaten by birds. There are several cultivars, including 'Mother of Pearl', with soft grey-pink flowers. The Shirley Series has single, semi-double and double flowers in yellow, pink, orange or red.

KEY FEATURES
- Annual or perennial
- Colourful flowers
- Easy to grow

PLANT
In sun in fertile, well-drained soil

PROPAGATE
Seed in spring; divide in spring

HARDINESS
Hardy; zones 3–7

PESTS AND DISEASES
Aphids, mildew

Parthenocissus
VIRGINIA CREEPER

Passiflora
PASSIONFLOWER

▲ *Parthenocissus quinquefolia*

▲ *Passiflora caerulea*

These deciduous foliage plants are grown largely for their wonderful autumn colours. They cling by means of suckering pads and are useful for covering walls and fences, and they offer valuable cover for a wide range of wildlife. They can also be allowed to grow up into sturdy deciduous trees. Shoots that grow too long for their allotted space can be removed in summer.

Parthenocissus henryana (Chinese Virginia creeper), 10 m (30 ft) high and across, has palmate, dark green leaves, to 12 cm (5 in) long, with distinctive white veins. They turn red in autumn.

The vigorous *P. quinquefolia* (Virginia creeper), 15 m (50 ft) high and across, has dark green leaves, to 10 cm (4 in) in length, which turn vivid red in autumn.

P. tricuspidata (Boston ivy), 20 m (70 ft) high and across, has large bright green leaves, to 20 cm (8 in) long. They turn brilliant reds and purples in autumn.

KEY FEATURES
- Clinging deciduous climber
- Wonderful autumn colour
- Attracts birds

PLANT
In sun or shade in fertile, well-drained soil

PROPAGATE
Seed in autumn; softwood cuttings in early summer; greenwood cuttings in midsummer; hardwood cuttings in winter

HARDINESS
Hardy; zones 4–9

PESTS AND DISEASES
Trouble free

The beautiful, intricate flowers of these tendril climbers are instantly recognizable. The tender forms can be grown in conservatories or greenhouses, but *Passiflora caerulea* (blue passionflower) will grow outside in a sheltered garden. Plants cut down by frost often reshoot from ground level. They need the support of a trellis or arch or they can be trained into a tree.

P. caerulea, 10 m (30 ft) high and across but less in cool areas, has glossy, divided, dark green leaves. From summer and into autumn it produces white flowers, each to 10 cm (4 in) across, the filaments banded with blue, white and purple. Oval, orange-yellow fruits, 6 cm ($2^1/_2$ in) long, follow the flowers after warm, sunny summers. They are edible but flavourless. 'Constance Elliott' has especially lovely fragrant, pale cream flowers with pale blue filaments and red stigmas.

The tender *P. quadrangularis* (giant granadilla), 10 m (30 ft) high and across but less in a container, has very fragrant, pale to dark red flowers with an extraordinary mass of wavy filaments.

KEY FEATURES
- Evergreen climber
- Exotic-looking flowers

PLANT
In full sun in moisture-retentive but well-drained soil

PROPAGATE
Seed in spring; semi-ripe cuttings in summer; layer in autumn

HARDINESS
Hardy to frost tender; zones 7–9

PESTS AND DISEASES
Cucumber mosaic virus

Pelargonium

Pelargoniums are used as summer planting, when the succession of colourful, five-petalled flowers provides summer-long displays in hanging baskets, windowboxes, containers and summer borders.

This is a large genus of some 230 species, but most of the pelargoniums grown today are cultivars developed from only about 20 of the species. They are tender plants and have to be overwintered in bright, frost-free conditions in barely moist compost.

The huge selection of cultivars is usually divided into six main groups: angel, ivy-leaved, regal, scented-leaf, unique and zonal. Zonal pelargoniums are further categorized by flower or leaf type.

Angel pelargoniums, which are derived from regal pelargoniums, are small plants, to about 30 cm (12 in) high and across. 'Catford Belle' has mauve-purple flowers with frilled petals. 'Starlight Magic' has maroon and pink-white flowers with darker veins.

Ivy-leaved pelargoniums have thick leaves borne on trailing stems to 60 cm (24 in) long, making them ideal for hanging baskets. 'Eclipse' has salmon-pink flowers. 'Rio Grande' has black-red flowers and glossy green leaves.

Regal pelargoniums have large, richly coloured flowers. The group includes 'Fleur d'Amour', 35 cm (14 in) high and across, with pink and white, frilly-edged flowers; 'Sunrise', 40 cm (16 in) high and across, with salmon-orange flowers with white throats and magenta marks.

Scented-leaf pelargoniums have highly aromatic leaves but the flowers are small and uninteresting. 'Lady Scarborough', 50 cm (20 in) high and across, has small pink flowers with dark veins; 'Little Gem', 45 cm (18 in), has leaves scented of rose-lemon and mauve flowers.

Unique pelargoniums have rounded or lobed, soft aromatic leaves and usually mauve or purple flowers. 'Pink Aurore', 50 cm (20 in) high and across, has petals

KEY FEATURES
- Evergreen perennial
- Succession of colourful flowers

PLANT
In sun in fertile, well-drained neutral to alkaline soil

PROPAGATE
Seed in early spring; cuttings in spring, late summer or early autumn

HARDINESS
Tender; zone 10

PESTS AND DISEASES
Aphids, vine weevils, grey mould, rust

TOP 10 PELARGONIUMS
'Attar of Roses'
Scented-leaf; mauve flowers, 50 x 30 cm (20 x 12 in)
'Black Magic'
Regal; rich black-red flowers, 35 cm (14 in) high and across
'Chocolate Peppermint'
Scented-leaf; pale mauve-pink flowers, 1 m x 75 cm (36 x 30 cm)
'Golden Lilac Gem'
Ivy-leaved; golden-green leaves, double lilac flowers, 60 cm (24 in) high and across
'Lord Bute'
Regal; dark crimson-purple flowers, 45 x 30 cm (18 x 12 in)
'Moon Maiden'
Angel; pale pink flowers with dark red marks, 45 x 50 cm (18 x 20 in)
'Mrs Pollock'
Fancy-leaved zonal; single pink-orange flowers, 30 x 15 cm (12 x 6 in)
'Polka'
Unique; orange-red flowers marked with purple, 50 x 25 cm (20 x 10 in)
'Red Black Vesuvius'
Zonal; rich scarlet flowers; 12 cm (5 in) high and wide
'Rois des Balcons Lilas'
Cascade; pale lilac flowers, 60 x 25 cm (24 x 10 in)

▲ *Pelargonium* 'Lord Bute'

▲ *Pelargonium* 'Rois des Balcons Lilas'

◄ *Pelargonium* 'Polka'

with a burgundy mark. 'Rollisson's Unique', 45 cm (18 in) high and across, has magenta-purple flowers which are marked with darker purple.

The leaves of zonal pelargoniums are banded (zoned) with a darker colour. The group includes 'Appleblossom Rosebud', 35 cm (14 in) high and across, double, pale pink flowers; 'Joan Fontaine', 30 cm (12 in) high and across, pale salmon-pink flowers; and 'Plum Rambler', 40 cm (16 in) high and across, double, plum-red flowers.

One of the most unusual pelargoniums is *P.* 'Schottii' (syn. *P.* x *schottii*), 30 cm (12 in) high and across, which has attractive, velvety grey leaves and long-stemmed, wine red blooms with faint red stripes. This tender plant is best grown in a conservatory.

▲ *Pelargonium* 'Hindoo'

Pennisetum

MILLET

Penstemon

▲ *Pennisetum setaceum*

▲ *Penstemon 'Evelyn'*

These grasses are good border plants, but they need to be grown where the dense flowerheads can be appreciated.

Pennisetum setaceum (fountain grass), 90 x 45 cm (36 x 18 in), is a half-hardy perennial, which is often grown as an annual. It has upright, mid-green leaves and, from midsummer to early autumn, purplish-pink flowerheads on upright stems.

The green leaves of the evergreen perennial *P. alopecuroides* (fountain grass), 1.5 x 1.2 m (5 x 4 ft), form dense tufts, above which the yellow-green to purplish, bottlebrush-like flower spikes are borne in late summer.

The half-hardy *P. orientale*, 60 cm (2 ft) high and across, has narrow, dark green leaves and, in late summer, tall spikelets of pink-grey flowers.

The recent introduction *P. glaucum* 'Purple Majesty', 1.2–1.5 m (4–5 ft) high, has deep purple leaves and purple-brown flower spikes. Grow in full sun for best colour. It is not reliably hardy and is best treated as an annual.

KEY FEATURES
• Annual or perennial grass
• Attractive inflorescences
• Good for cutting

PLANT
In full sun in fertile, well-drained soil

PROPAGATE
Seed in spring; divide in spring

HARDINESS
Hardy to half-hardy; zones 7–9

PESTS AND DISEASES
Trouble free

Traditional cottage-garden plants, penstemons provide reliable colour for months through summer and autumn. Some are small enough for a rock garden, but most are grown in borders. Border penstemons need more fertile soil than alpine types, and they benefit from a sheltered position and a winter mulch. Penstemons are continually being hybridized, and almost every supplier will offer a selection of colours and heights. 'Apple Blossom', 45–60 cm (18–24 in) high and across, has pink flowers with a white throat, 'Evelyn', 45 cm (18 in) high and across, has pale pink flowers. 'Raven', 70 x 45 cm (28 x 18 in), has dark purple flowers with a white throat, 'Sour Grapes', 60 x 45 cm (24 x 18 in), has (despite the name) delightfully shaded pinkish-purplish-whitish flowers. 'White Bedder' (syn. 'Snow Storm'), 60 x 45 cm (24 x 18 in), has pure white flowers, turning pink as they age.

P. heterophyllus (foothill penstemon), 50 cm (20 in) high and across, is an evergreen plant, bearing large, pink-blue flowers in summer. 'Heavenly Blue', to 70 x 45 cm (28 x 18 in), has bright blue flowers. *P. heterophyllus* subsp. *purdyi* is a compact form with sky blue flowers.

KEY FEATURES
• Perennial
• Beautiful flowers in a wide range of colours

PLANT
In sun in well-drained soil

PROPAGATE
Seed in spring; softwood cuttings in summer

HARDINESS
Hardy to half-hardy; zones 7–9

PESTS AND DISEASES
Slugs and snails, mildew

Philadelphus

MOCK ORANGE

Phlomis

▲ *Philadelphus* 'Manteau d'Hermine'

▲ *Phlomis fruticosa*

These shrubs are grown for the lovely, scented early-summer flowers, but for the rest of the year all but the plants with variegated leaves can be rather uninteresting, so they are best planted at the back of a mixed border. When pruning is necessary do it immediately after flowering because the next season's flowers will be borne on shoots produced in the current year.

Philadelphus coronarius is the parent of two of the most widely grown cultivars. 'Aureus', 2.4 x 1.5 m (8 x 5 ft) has yellow-green leaves; site it out of direct sun, which will scorch the foliage. The leaves of 'Variegatus', 2.4 x 1.8 m (8 x 6 ft), are edged in cream.

The compact *P.* 'Manteau d'Hermine', 60 x 75 cm (24 x 30 cm), produces double, very fragrant cream-white flowers in early to midsummer.

P. 'Innocence', which grows to 1.5 x 1.2 m (5 x 4 ft), bears masses of lovely pure white, single flowers in midsummer. The attractive leaves are splashed with cream.

KEY FEATURES
• Deciduous shrub
• Summer flowers

PLANT
In sun or partial shade in fertile, well-drained soil

PROPAGATE
Softwood cuttings in summer; hardwood cuttings in autumn

HARDINESS
Hardy to half-hardy; zones 5–9

PESTS AND DISEASES
Aphids, mildew

These plants do well in hot sunny corners, and the hairy, grey-green leaves are designed to withstand drought and do well in gravel gardens. They are likely to suffer in winter in heavy soil that becomes waterlogged. The shrubs do not normally need pruning, although straggly stems can be cut back in spring.

The evergreen shrub *Phlomis fruticosa* (Jerusalem sage), 1 x 1.5 m (3 x 5 ft), has slightly wrinkled, grey-green leaves and, in summer, whorls of yellow flowers.

The shrub *P. italica*, 60 cm (24 in) high and across, is also evergreen. In midsummer it produces lilac-pink flowers in small whorls above the dull green leaves.

The perennial *P. russeliana*, 90 x 75 cm (36 x 30 in), flowers from late spring to early autumn, bearing strong, upright stems that are ringed with hooded, pale yellow flowers. These are followed by attractive seedheads.

KEY FEATURES
• Perennial or evergreen shrub
• Attractive foliage
• Colourful flowers

PLANT
In full sun in fertile, well-drained soil

PROPAGATE
Seed in spring; divide in spring; softwood cuttings in summer

HARDINESS
Hardy to frost hardy; zones 5–8

PESTS AND DISEASES
Trouble free

Phormium

FLAX LILY

Photinia

▲ *Phormium* 'Maori Sunrise'

▲ *Photinia glabra* 'Rubens'

Phormiums have stiff, upright leaves, and there are many cultivars with variegated or striking coloured foliage. In summer clusters of small flowers are borne on tall, erect stems. The leaves are sharply pointed, so take care when gardening around them. Many handsome cultivars have been developed, but the plants with plain green leaves tend to be hardier than the variegated and coloured forms.

Many of the most popular plants have been derived from *Phormium tenax* (New Zealand flax), which is a clump-forming perennial. The dwarf *P.* 'Bronze Baby', 80 cm (32 in) high and across, has bronze-purple, arching leaves. If you have more space, plants in the Purpureum Group grow to 2.4 x 1.8 m (8 x 6 ft); they have bronze-purple leaves.

P. cookianum (mountain flax), 1.8 x 3 m (6 x 10 ft), has plain green leaves, but it is the parent plant of 'Maori Sunrise', which has yellow and pink striped leaves with bronze edges.

KEY FEATURES
• Evergreen perennial
• Striking foliage
• Good focal point
• Good in containers

PLANT
In full sun in moisture-retentive but well-drained soil

PROPAGATE
Seed in spring; divide in spring

HARDINESS
Frost hardy to half-hardy; zones 8–10

PESTS AND DISEASES
Mealybugs

Both evergreen and deciduous photinias are grown for their colourful foliage. The young leaves of evergreen plants are usually brilliant shades of red, while the foliage of deciduous plants often turns red in autumn.

The evergreen hybrid *Photinia* x *fraseri*, 5 m (15 ft) high and across, has leathery dark green leaves, which are red or bronze when they emerge. Clusters of small white flowers are born in mid- to late spring. 'Red Robin' 1.5 m (5 ft) high and across, has bright red stems and leaves in spring and glossy green older leaves.

The young leaves of the evergreen *P. glabra*, 3 m (10 ft) high and across, are bright red, and the white flowers are often followed by small red fruits. 'Rubens' has especially bright and glossy leaves in spring.

The deciduous *P. villosa*, 5 m (15 ft) high and across, has dark green leaves, which turn red and orange before they fall. The late-spring flowers are followed by red fruits.

KEY FEATURES
• Deciduous or evergreen shrub
• Colourful foliage

PLANT
In full sun or partial shade in moisture-retentive but well-drained soil

PROPAGATE
Seed in autumn; semi-ripe cuttings in summer

HARDINESS
Hardy to frost hardy; zones 7–9

PESTS AND DISEASES
Fireblight, mildew

Phyllostachys

Picea
SPRUCE

▲ *Phyllostachys nigra*

▲ *Picea orientalis* 'Aurea'

These useful bamboos can be used as a barrier or screen, at the back of a border or in a large container. They are imposing plants and need space to be appreciated. When plants get congested remove old canes (culms) in the centre of clumps and cut out dead culms after flowering. In warm areas they can be invasive. Clumps that grow beyond their allotted space can be cut back to size with a sharp spade. Alternatively, insert a barrier to a depth of about 30 cm (12 in) into the soil when you plant.

The canes of *Phyllostachys nigra* (black bamboo), 5 x 3 m (15 x 10 ft), become black as they age. The mid- to dark green leaves, to 10 cm (4 in) long, are carried on numerous shoots that grow from the branches that emerge from the cane nodes. *P. nigra* 'Bornyana' has brown markings on the canes, and the green canes of *P. nigra* var. *henonis* age to yellow-green; both bamboos grow to about 5 x 1.8 m (15 x 6 ft),

P. aurea (fishpole bamboo, golden bamboo), 4 x 1.8 m (12 x 6 ft) or more, has graceful, golden-yellow canes and mid- to light green leaves.

KEY FEATURES
• Evergreen bamboo
• Good in containers
• Good for hedging

PLANT
In sun in fertile, moisture-retentive but well-drained soil

PROPAGATE
Divide in spring

HARDINESS
Hardy; zones 7–10

PESTS AND DISEASES
Slugs and snails in spring but usually trouble free

This genus contains many useful garden plants, which can be grown as specimens, as hedges or even in a rock garden. *Picea abies* is often used as a Christmas tree.

The handsome *P. orientalis* (Caucasian spruce, oriental spruce) grows to 30 x 8 m (100 x 25 ft) and is probably too large for most gardens. 'Aurea', which has attractive cream-yellow young foliage that turns pale green, is deceptively slow growing, but it will eventually grow to the same size as the species.

P. glauca (white spruce), 50 x 6 m (160 x 20 ft), makes a fine specimen, but more appropriate for most gardens is the widely available *P. glauca* var. *albertiana* 'Conica', 6 x 2.4 m (20 x 8 ft), which makes a dense cone, useful as a focal point or for year-round foliage.

P. pungens (Colorado spruce), 15 x 5 m (50 x 15 ft), is the parent of many useful garden plants, including the silver-blue 'Globosa', 1 m (3 ft) high and across, and the slow-growing 'Montgomery', 1.5 x 1 m (5 x 3 ft), which also has silver-blue foliage.

KEY FEATURES
• Evergreen conifer
• Good specimen plant

PLANT
In full sun in moisture-retentive but well-drained, neutral to acid soil

PROPAGATE
Seed in spring; ripewood cuttings in summer

HARDINESS
Hardy to frost hardy; zones 3–8

PESTS AND DISEASES
Adelgids, honey fungus

Pieris

Pinus
PINE

▲ *Pieris formosa* var. *forrestii*

▲ *Pinus radiata* Aurea Group

These small shrubs make ideal container plants, especially as they can be given ericaceous compost, no matter what the soil in the open garden. In a garden with acid soil they can be grown in a shrub border or woodland garden. Little pruning is needed, but straggly stems can be cut back in late winter. Old, dead stems should be removed in late summer.

The young leaves of *Pieris formosa*, 5 x 4 m (15 x 12 ft), are red-bronze, turning glossy dark green as they mature. Clusters of white flowers are borne in mid- to late spring. Among the smaller forms that are suitable for containers are *P. formosa* var. *forrestii* 'Jermyns', 2.4 m (8 ft) high and across, which has white flowers opening from pink buds, and *P. formosa* var. *forrestii* 'Wakehurst', 1.8 m (6 ft) high and across, which has bright red young leaves.

The hybrid *P.* 'Forest Flame', 4 x 1.8 m (12 x 6 ft), has vivid red young leaves, which turn cream-white then green.

KEY FEATURES
- Evergreen shrub
- Spring flowers
- Colourful foliage
- Good in containers

PLANT
In sun or light shade in fertile, moisture-retentive but well-drained, acid soil

PROPAGATE
Seed in spring; greenwood cuttings in early summer; semi-ripe cuttings in late summer

HARDINESS
Hardy to frost hardy; zones 7–9

PESTS AND DISEASES
Root rot but usually trouble free

The species in this genus are too large for most gardens, but there are many excellent small and even dwarf forms that can be used as feature plants, in heather beds, in shrub borders and even in rock gardens. Although they are fairly easy going about the soil they grow in (as long as it is not shallow chalk), they do not tolerate pollution.

The useful *Pinus mugo* (dwarf mountain pine), 3.5 x 5 m (11 x 15 ft), is the parent of many small conifers, some small enough for a rock garden. The prostrate 'Corley's Mat', 1 x 1.8 m (3 x 6 ft), makes a spreading carpet. The slow-growing 'Mops', which gets to only 1 m (3 ft) high and across, is almost spherical.

P. radiata (Monterey pine), 40 x 12 m (130 x 40 ft), is best known as a forest plant, but plants in the Aurea Group, which have golden-yellow foliage, grow to about 35 x 4 m (115 x 12 ft).

KEY FEATURES
- Evergreen conifer
- Seeds for birds
- Good cover for nesting birds

PLANT
In full sun in well-drained soil

PROPAGATE
Seed in spring; graft in late winter

HARDINESS
Hardy; zones 3–7

PESTS AND DISEASES
Adelgids, honey fungus

Potentilla

Primula

▲ *Potentilla 'Gibson's Scarlet'*

▲ *Primula rosea*

There are more than 500 species in this genus, all bearing five-petalled flowers over a long period from spring to summer. Overgrown shrubs usually respond well to being cut right back. Many of the shrubby potentillas are derived from *Potentilla fruticosa*. They have saucer-shaped flowers and divided leaves and can be trained as wall shrubs or included in shrub or mixed borders. 'Abbotswood', 75 cm x 1.2 m (30 in x 4 ft), has blue-green leaves and white flowers. 'Elizabeth', 1 x 1.5 m (3 x 5 ft), has grey-green leaves and yellow flowers. The dwarf 'Goldfinger' has blue-green leaves and golden flowers. 'Manchu', 30 x 75 cm (12 x 30 cm), has grey foliage and white flowers.

Many other hybrid shrubs have been developed. *P.* 'Gibson's Scarlet', 45 x 60 cm (18 x 24 in), has single, very bright red flowers from early to late summer. 'Blazeaway', 1 m (3 ft) high and across, has dark green leaves and orange red-flowers.

Among the best of the perennial potentillas is the clump-forming *P. atrosanguinea*, 90 x 60 cm (3 x 2 ft), which has yellow, orange or red flowers on erect stems in summer to autumn.

KEY FEATURES
• Perennial or deciduous shrub
• Flowers over a long period

PLANT
In full sun in fertile,
well-drained soil

PROPAGATE
Seed in spring; divide in spring;
greenwood cuttings in summer

HARDINESS
Hardy; zones 3–8

PESTS AND DISEASES
Trouble free

This large and complicated genus ranges from the polyanthus group, the small, colourful flowers that are often used in spring bedding arrangements, to *Primula florindae* (giant cowslip), which can get to 1.2 m (4 ft) tall.

P. rosea, 20 cm (8 in) high and across, bears clusters of yellow-eyed, deep pink flowers in late spring.

P. japonica (Japanese primrose), 45 cm (18 in) high and across, is a candelabra-type primrose, with clusters of red-purple, pink or white flowers on erect stems. 'Miller's Crimson' has crimson flowers, and 'Postford White' has white, red-eyed flowers.

P. vialli, 60 x 30 cm (24 x 12 in), forms rosettes of mid-green leaves above which stiff stems bear heads of tightly packed pink flowers, the unopened red buds appearing in a little point above them. Like *P. rosea*, this species needs moist, acid to neutral soil and a position in shade.

The lovely yellow flowers of *P. vulgaris* (primrose) attract bees and butterflies early in the year, and they bring insect-eating birds in their wake. Leave flowers to go to seed – chaffinches will appreciate the extra food.

KEY FEATURES
• Perennial
• Lovely spring flowers
• Good for pots and rock gardens

PLANT
Different species have different
requirements

PROPAGATE
Seed in spring; divide in
early spring

HARDINESS
Hardy to frost tender; zones 5–7

PESTS AND DISEASES
Slugs and snails, grey mould

Prunus
ORNAMENTAL CHERRY

Pulmonaria
LUNGWORT

▲ *Prunus* x *subhirtella* 'Autumnalis'

▲ *Pulmonaria saccharata*

This large genus contains some of the loveliest winter- and spring-flowering trees. There are also trees with colourful foliage as well as many with elegant, spreading habits of growth. Several forms, including *Prunus serrula* (Tibetan cherry), have handsome bark. These are excellent plants for small gardens, offering interest in every season, being easy to grow and requiring little pruning, unless wayward stems have to be shortened in midsummer.

The hybrid *P.* x *subhirtella* (higan cherry, rosebud cherry), 8 m (25 ft) high and across, has dark green leaves and, from autumn to spring, white or pink flowers. 'Autumnalis' bears pink-tinged white flowers throughout winter. The leaves turn yellow in autumn.

P. triloba (flowering almond), 3 m (10 ft) high and across, has dark green leaves and, in early to mid-spring, pink flowers, which are followed by red fruits.

P. cerasifera (cherry plum, myrobalan), 10 m (30 ft) high and across, is the parent of 'Nigra', which has dark purple leaves, reddish when they emerge in spring, and pink flowers.

KEY FEATURES
- Deciduous or evergreen tree
- Winter and spring blossom

PLANT
In sun in well-drained soil

PROPAGATE
Seed in autumn; greenwood cuttings in summer

HARDINESS
Hardy; zones 7–9

PESTS AND DISEASES
Aphids, caterpillars, honey fungus, peach leaf curl

Pulmonarias are grown for their spring flowers and their long-lasting leaves. They do best in shade, although they will blossom in sun as long as the soil never dries out. They can be grown in mixed borders and woodland gardens.

The evergreen leaves of *Pulmonaria saccharata* (Bethlehem sage), 30 x 60 cm (12 x 24 in), are heavily spotted with silver-white. From late winter to late spring red-violet, violet or white flowers are borne in clusters. There are several attractive cultivars, including plants in the Argentea Group, which have leaves so heavily spotted that they appear almost completely silver-white; the flowers are reddish, turning purple as they age.

P. officinalis (Jerusalem cowslip, spotted dog), 25 x 45 cm (10 x 18 in), has mid-green leaves that are spotted with white. The flowers are pink, ageing to blue. 'Cambridge Blue' has pale blue flowers; 'Sissinghurst White' has white flowers and the leaves are heavily spotted.

KEY FEATURES
- Deciduous or evergreen perennial
- Spring flowers
- Attractive leaves

PLANT
In sun or partial shade in moisture-retentive but well-drained soil

PROPAGATE
Seed in spring; divide in autumn

HARDINESS
Hardy; zones 4–8

PESTS AND DISEASES
Slugs and snails, mildew

Pulsatilla
PASQUE FLOWER

Pyracantha
FIRETHORN

▲ *Pulsatilla vulgaris*

▲ *Pyracantha* 'Orange Charmer'

These clump-forming perennials are grown for their beautiful spring flowers, which are so large that they seem out of proportion to the small plants. They must have very well-drained soil and will do well in a scree or rock garden.

Pulsatilla vulgaris, 20 cm (8 in) high and across, has ferny, hairy, dark green leaves. In spring solitary, deep blue or purple bell-shaped flowers are borne on short stalks. The flowers have prominent yellow stamens and are followed by feathery seedheads. There are several cultivars, including the white-flowered 'Alba' and 'Röde Klokke' ('Red Clock'), which has dark red flowers, but few are as lovely as the species.

P. vernalis, 10 x 20 cm (4 x 8 in), has deep green, finely divided leaves and bears bell-shaped, white flowers, flushed lilac-blue on the outside, in early to mid-spring. This is an evergreen perennial and is often grown in an alpine house. When grown in the garden it must be protected from winter wet.

KEY FEATURES
- Perennial
- Large spring flowers
- Attractive seedheads

PLANT
In full sun in fertile, well-drained soil

PROPAGATE
Ripe seed; root cuttings in winter

HARDINESS
Hardy; zones 3–5

PESTS AND DISEASES
Trouble free

These spiny, evergreen shrubs are ideal for hedging, forming a dense barrier against intruders. Most of the popular cultivars grow to 3–4 m (10–12 ft) high and across, but they can be kept smaller by pruning between spring and midsummer. Plants grown as hedges should also be pruned at this time. They are also ideal for training as wall shrubs. They have fairly small, dark green leaves and, in summer, clusters of little white flowers. The flowers are followed by masses of colourful and long-lasting autumn berries. 'Mohave' and 'Santa Cruz' have red berries; 'Orange Charmer' and 'Orange Glow' have dark orange berries; 'Soleil d'Or' has masses of golden-yellow berries; 'Knap Hill Lemon' has light yellow berries.

Pyracantha coccinea, 3 m (10 ft) high and across, has dark green leaves. Clusters of cream-white flowers are borne in early summer, and these are followed by bright red berries. The compact 'Red Column', 1.5 x 1 m (5 x 3 ft), has reddish shoots and vivid berries; it has some resistance to fireblight.

KEY FEATURES
- Evergreen shrub
- Summer flowers
- Autumn berries
- Good hedging

PLANT
In sun or partial shade in well-drained soil

PROPAGATE
Semi-ripe cuttings in summer

HARDINESS
Hardy; zones 7–8

PESTS AND DISEASES
Aphids, leaf miners, scale insects, fireblight, scab

Ranunculus

Ribes
FLOWERING CURRANT

▲ *Ranunculus acris 'Flore Pleno'*

▲ *Ribes sanguineum*

This genus is often represented in gardens by *Ranunculus repens* (creeping buttercup), a common lawn weed. There are, however, some more desirable species. *R. acris* (meadow buttercup), 60 x 45 cm (24 x 18 in), is rarely grown, but the cultivar 'Flore Pleno' (fair maids of France) has double flowers on upright, wiry stems. The single flowers of 'Farrer's Yellow' are pale yellow. The cultivars are not invasive and make attractive clumps.

The half-hardy *R. asiaticus* (Persian buttercup), 25 x 20 cm (10 x 8 in), has brilliantly coloured, peony-like, single or double flowers in white, red, pink, orange and yellow with dark purple centres. Outdoors the flowers appear in summer, under glass in late spring.

The annual or perennial *R. aquatilis* (water crowfoot) is a submerged plant for a natural garden pond, which will survive in water to 1 m (3 ft) deep, although it does best in water 15–60 cm (6–24 in) deep. It bears its leaves and white and yellow flowers above water. In shallower water at the margins of a natural pond, to a depth of no more than 15 cm (6 in), *R. lingua* (greater spearwort), 1.5 x 1.8 m (5 x 6 ft), bears heart-shaped leaves and golden flowers.

KEY FEATURES
• Annual, biennial or perennial
• Good cut flowers

PLANT
Different species have different requirements

PROPAGATE
Ripe seed; divide in spring or autumn

HARDINESS
Hardy to half-hardy; zones 8–10

PESTS AND DISEASES
Trouble free

You may prefer to grow culinary currants and gooseberries instead of the ornamental species in the genus, but it is worth making space for both kinds. Flowering currants are useful as ornamental plants in their own right or as hedging. Flowers are produced on the previous year's growth, so pruning should be carried out after flowering. If necessary at the same time cut about one-third of the old shoots back to ground level to encourage new growth.

The popular *Ribes sanguineum* (flowering currant), 1.8 m (6 ft) high and across, bears red-pink flowers in mid-spring, and these are followed by blue-black fruit. The more compact 'Brocklebankii', 1.2 m (4 ft) high and across, has bright yellow leaves and pink flowers.

R. speciosum (fuchsia-flowered currant), 1.8 m (6 ft) high and across, is a spiny shrub. Small, narrow, red flowers with long stamens are borne in spring and are followed by round, rather bristly, red berries. It needs a sheltered corner and a position in full sun.

KEY FEATURES
• Deciduous shrub
• Spring flowers
• Easy to grow

PLANT
In full sun in fertile, well-drained soil

PROPAGATE
Hardwood cuttings in winter; layer in autumn

HARDINESS
Hardy to frost hardy; zone 7

PESTS AND DISEASES
Aphids, honey fungus, mildew

Rodgersia

Romneya
CALIFORNIA POPPY, TREE POPPY

▲ *Rodgersia pinnata*

▲ *Romneya coulteri*

Rodgersias are often grown around the edges of natural ponds or in wildlife gardens. They can also be grown in a bog garden, although they will not tolerate permanently waterlogged soil.

Plant the imposing *Rodgersia podophylla*, 1.5 x 1.8 m (5 x 6 ft), where its beautiful, bronze-tinged young foliage can be appreciated. The leaves, each to 40 cm (16 in) long, consist of five sections, and they form a dense clump, above which branched stems bear clusters of tiny cream flowers in mid- to late summer.

R. pinnata, 1.2 m x 75 cm (4 ft x 30 in), has deeply veined, dark green leaves, each to 90 cm (36 in) long, borne on red-green stems and flushed with red. Clusters of small pink, red or cream-white flowers are borne on sturdy stems in summer. The leaves of 'Superba' are strongly flushed with red, and the flowers are deep pink.

R. sambucifolia, 1 m (3 ft) high and across, has dark green leaves and dense clusters of star-shaped, white flowers in early to midsummer.

KEY FEATURES
• Perennial
• Attractive leaves
• Large flower spikes

PLANT
In sun or partial shade in fertile, moisture-retentive soil

PROPAGATE
Seed in spring; divide in spring

HARDINESS
Hardy; zones 3–9

PESTS AND DISEASES
Slugs and snails

Romneyas are grown for their lovely, fragrant summer flowers. They are actually subshrubs but are usually grown as perennials, with all topgrowth cut down to ground level in autumn and the crown covered with a thick winter mulch. They are not always easy to establish and do best against a sunny wall, protected from blustery winds, but when they are growing strongly they can produce suckers and even become invasive.

Romneya coulteri, 1–2.4 x 1 m (3–8 x 3 ft), has lobed, grey-green leaves, to 12 cm (5 in) long. The flowers, to 12 cm (5 in) across, which last from midsummer to early autumn, have papery white petals around brilliant yellow stamens, and they are followed by seedpods. The cultivar 'White Cloud' is even more vigorous than the species; its leaves are greyer and its flowers are larger.

KEY FEATURES
• Perennial or subshrub
• Fragrant flowers

PLANT
In full sun in well-drained soil; shelter from strong winds

PROPAGATE
Seed in spring; root cuttings in winter

HARDINESS
Frost hardy; zones 6–9

PESTS AND DISEASES
Caterpillars

Rosa

ROSE

There can be few gardens in which there is not a single rose. As well as the traditional forms, there is now such a vast range of what are known as patio and groundcover roses that even the smallest plot can have a rose in a container or at the front of a sunny border.

Roses need pruning. Even miniature roses must be pruned from time to time if they are to continue to grow and flower well. Although the idea of regular pruning deters some gardeners from planting a rose, once a routine has been established it takes little time, and the benefits in terms of plant health and number of flowers produced more than makes up for the time it takes. Different types of rose have different requirements, and it is worth consulting a specialist book to find out when and how you should prune your plant.

The way in which roses are classified can be confusing, but they are usually categorized as follows: species roses (wild roses and a few hybrids); old garden roses (damask, centifolia, moss roses and so on); hybrid teas (now known as large-flowered bush roses); polyantha roses; floribundas (cluster-flowered bush roses); modern shrub roses; rugosa roses; patio roses (dwarf cluster-flowered roses); miniature roses, which are usually shorter than 30 cm (12 in); groundcover roses, which have a lax habit and may be regarded rather like miniature climbers; climbing roses; and rambling roses.

▲ *Rosa* 'Treasure Trove'

▼ *Rosa* 'William Lobb'

An arch or wall covered with a rose like the fragrant and vigorous 'Albertine' might be appropriate in a large garden, but in a small garden a more biddable climber, such as 'Dublin Bay' or 'Aloha' (which will grow in a container) might be more suitable. If fragrance is the criterion governing your choice, you might prefer the pink flowers of 'Ispahan' or the less strongly scented yellow flowers of 'Graham Thomas', which are borne over a longer period from summer and autumn.

In a wildlife garden the fruits of *R. canina* (dog rose) will attract birds, and the aphids that might infest the leaves and shoots will be sought by tits and house sparrows.

KEY FEATURES
• Deciduous or semi-evergreen shrub or climber
• Fragrant flowers

PLANT
In sun in fertile, well-drained soil

PROPAGATE
Hardwood cuttings in summer

HARDINESS
Hardy to frost hardy; zones 4–9

PESTS AND DISEASES
Aphids, leaf-cutting bees, sawfly larvae, blackspot, canker, honey fungus, mildew, rust, soil sickness

▲ *Rosa* 'Alec's Red'　　　　　　　　▶ *Rosa* 'Abraham Darby'

TOP 10 ROSES
'Abraham Darby'
Shrub rose; lovely double, apricot-yellow flowers, 1.5 m (5 ft) high and across

'Alec's Red'
Hybrid tea; fragrant, fully double red flowers, 1 x 1.8 m (3 x 6 ft)

'Baby Masquerade'
Miniature; semi-double, yellow-pink flowers, 40 cm (16 in) high and across

'Cécile Brünner'
Polyanthus China rose; double, pale pink flowers, 75 x 60 cm (30 x 24 in)

'Chinatown'
Floribunda; scented, double pink-flushed, yellow flowers, 1.2 x 1 m (4 x 3 ft)

'Fritz Nobis'
Shrub rose; fully double, blush pink to pale salmon flowers, orange hips, 1.5 x 1.2 m (5 x 4 ft)

'Treasure Trove'
Rambler; semi-double, cream-apricot flowers, 10 x 6 m (30 x 20 ft)

'William Lobb'
Centifolia; moss rose, fragrant, fully double, bright pink-red flowers, 1.2 x 1 m (4 x 3 ft)

***Rosa xanthina* 'Canary Bird'**
Shrub rose; masses of single pale yellow flowers, 2.4 x 1.8 m (8 x 6 ft)

'Zéphirine Drouhin'
Bourbon climber; thornless, fragrant, semi-double deep pink flowers, 3 x 1.8 m (10 x 6 ft)

Rubus
BRAMBLE

Rudbeckia
CONEFLOWER

▲ *Rubus phoenicolasius*

▲ *Rudbeckia fulgida* var. *speciosa*

This genus includes raspberries and loganberries, but there are many ornamental plants as well, which are grown for their foliage, flowers and, sometimes, attractive winter shoots. Some are good groundcover; others are useful in shady borders or woodland gardens.

The stems of *Rubus phoenicolasius* (Japanese wineberry), 1.5 m (5 ft) high and across, are densely covered with reddish bristles. In midsummer spikes of pale pink flowers are borne and these are followed by edible red berries.

The deciduous *R.* 'Benenden', 3 m (10 ft) high and across, produces masses of large white flowers in late spring to early summer. The leaves are dark green, and the attractively peeling bark is thornless.

R. thibetanus, 2.4 m (8 ft) high and across, is also deciduous. It has small purple-red flowers in summer, and in winter the stems are covered with an attractive white bloom. *R. cockburnianus* also has striking white winter stems, which can be improved by hard pruning in spring.

KEY FEATURES
• Deciduous or evergreen shrub
• Autumn berries
• Attracts birds

PLANT
In sun or partial shade in fertile, well-drained soil

PROPAGATE
Divide in autumn; greenwood cuttings in summer; hardwood cuttings in early winter

HARDINESS
Hardy to frost hardy; zones 5–9

PESTS AND DISEASES
Grey mould but usually trouble free

The daisy-like flowers with prominent central bosses are borne on erect, sturdy stems and will make a spreading clump in a mixed border, flowering in late summer and into early autumn.

The perennial *Rudbeckia fulgida* (black-eyed Susan), 75 x 30 cm (30 x 12 in), bears striking yellow flowers with black-brown centres. It is a good border plant in its own right and is also the parent of some fine plants, all with golden-yellow summer flowers. *R. fulgida* var. *speciosa* (syn. *R. newmannii*) will grow to 1 m (3 ft) tall, but *R. fulgida* var. *sullivantii* 'Goldsturm' is more compact, at about 60 cm (24 in) tall.

Among the cultivars of *R. laciniata* is 'Goldquelle' ('Golden Fountain'), 90 x 60 (3 x 2 ft), which has double flowers with greenish centres. From midsummer to early autumn 'Herbstonne' ('Autumn Sun'), 1.8 x 1 m (6 x 3 ft), bears golden-yellow, daisy flowers with green centres. Each flower is to 12 cm (5 in) across and the petals are reflexed.

KEY FEATURES
• Annual, biennial or perennial
• Colourful summer flowers
• Easy to grow

PLANT
In sun or partial shade in moisture-retentive but well-drained soil

PROPAGATE
Seed in spring; divide in spring or autumn

HARDINESS
Hardy to half-hardy; zones 3–9

PESTS AND DISEASES
Slugs and snails

Ruscus

Salix
WILLOW

▲ *Ruscus aculeatus*

▲ *Salix hastata* 'Wehrhahnii'

These are the ideal plants for areas of dry shade, which can be difficult to fill. The 'leaves' are actually leaf-like shoots (cladodes). Tiny star-shaped flowers are followed on female plants by attractive berries. Encourage berries by planting both a male and a female plant or a hermaphrodite type. They do not need pruning.

The small, erect shrub *Ruscus aculeatus* (butcher's broom), 75 x 90 cm (30 x 36 in), is unusual in this genus in not needing both male and female plants in the garden to produce berries, although they are seen only on female plants and will be more prolific if a male plant is also present. The glossy, dark green 'leaves' end in sharp spines, and the round, bright red berries appear in autumn and last into winter.

R. hypoglossum, 45 x 90 cm (18 x 36 in), can be used for groundcover in a shady corner. It has glossy, mid-green cladodes, with tiny, star-shaped, pale green flowers borne on the upper surface of each cladode. Round, bright red berries follow the flowers and last into winter.

This genus is best known for weeping willows, which are far too large for most gardens, but there are also some small shrubs and trees with pretty spring catkins.

The slow-growing, multi-stemmed shrub *Salix hastata* 'Wehrhahnii', 1 m (3 ft) high and across, has woolly silver-white catkins in early spring, before the bright green leaves emerge. The dark, red-purple stems are an attractive winter feature.

The weeping miniature *S. caprea* 'Kilmarnock' (Kilmarnock willow), 1.5 x 1.8 m (5 x 6 ft), bears silver-white catkins in winter. This is a suitable feature plant for the centre of a lawn, and it has an elegant head of trailing shoots that reach almost to ground level.

Rather larger and more spreading is *S. gracilistyla*, 3 x 4 m (10 x 12 ft), which has furry stems and grey-green leaves, which become glossy as they mature. In spring it produces grey catkins, to 4 cm (1½ in) long. The form 'Melanostachys' has black catkins, which turn red and then golden-yellow and are borne on plum-purple stems.

KEY FEATURES
• Evergreen subshrub
• Autumn berries
• Good for dry shade

PLANT
In sun or shade in
well-drained soil

PROPAGATE
Ripe seed; divide in spring

HARDINESS
Hardy; zone 7

PESTS AND DISEASES
Trouble free

KEY FEATURES
• Deciduous tree or shrub
• Spring catkins

PLANT
In sun in moisture-retentive but
well-drained soil

PROPAGATE
Greenwood cuttings in summer;
hardwood cuttings in winter

HARDINESS
Hardy; zones 2–8

PESTS AND DISEASES
Aphids, caterpillars, anthracnose,
honey fungus

Salvia
SAGE

Sambucus
ELDER

▲ *Salvia involucrata* 'Bethellii'

▲ *Sambucus nigra* 'Guincho Purple'

This genus is best known for its culinary herbs, but it also contains many useful border plants, which can be used for summer bedding and in containers.

Salvia involucrata is a subshrubby, borderline hardy perennial, 1.5 x 1 m (5 x 3 ft), with hairy, dark green leaves and, from late summer to autumn, spikes of purple-red flowers. The flowers of 'Bethellii' are larger and a brighter purple-red.

S. splendens (scarlet sage), 40 x 35 cm (16 x 14 in), is a tender perennial, usually grown as an annual and used in summer bedding. The scarlet flowers are borne in dense spikes from early to midsummer. The dark green leaves have toothed edges.

S. verticillata, 90 x 45 cm (36 x 18 in), is a hardy perennial, forming a loose clump of mid-green leaves. In late summer and into autumn it bears arching stems that end in clusters of small, lilac-blue flowers, which are surrounded by reddish bracts that persist after the flowers have faded.

KEY FEATURES
- Annual or perennial
- Colourful flowers
- Easy to grow
- Attracts bees and butterflies

PLANT
In full sun in fertile,
well-drained soil

PROPAGATE
Seed in spring; divide in spring

HARDINESS
Hardy to frost tender;
zones 6–10

PESTS AND DISEASES
Slugs and snails

These trees and shrubs are grown for their foliage, flowers and autumn berries. If you do not mind losing flowers and foliage for a season, cut back overgrown plants to ground level in spring. Otherwise, cut out dead or damaged shoots at ground level and younger shoots by about half.

Sambucus nigra (black elder), 6 m (20 ft) high and across, can be invasive, but it is the parent of some excellent garden plants. The leaves of 'Guincho Purple' emerge dark green but turn black-purple as they mature and red before they fall. Pink-tinged white flowers are borne in clusters, followed by purple-black berries. 'Aurea' (golden elder) produces the best leaf colour when it is grown in sun; the flowers are followed by red fruit.

S. racemosa, 3 m (10 ft) high and across, is the parent of 'Plumosa Aurea', which has finely cut leaves, bronze in spring and ageing to golden-yellow. Plant in good light but out of direct sun, which will scorch the delicate leaves.

KEY FEATURES
- Deciduous shrub or tree
- Spring flowers
- Autumn berries
- Attracts birds
- Cover for roosting and
  nesting birds

PLANT
In sun or partial shade in fertile,
moisture-retentive soil

PROPAGATE
Greenwood cuttings in summer;
hardwood cuttings in winter

HARDINESS
Hardy; zone 5

PESTS AND DISEASES
Blackfly

Santolina

Sarcococca
CHRISTMAS BOX, SWEET BOX

▲ *Santolina rosmarinifolia* subsp. *rosmarinifolia*

▲ *Sarcococca hookeriana* var. *digyna*

Santolinas can be grown in mixed borders and rock gardens, and they can be clipped to create low hedges around a herb garden. To keep plants neat, cut stems back by about half every spring. After flowering, lightly shear over plants to remove the heads. Old, overgrown and straggly plants are best replaced.

Santolina chamaecyparissus (cotton lavender), 60 cm (24 in) high and across, has finely cut, grey-white leaves, which form a dense clump. Bright lemon-yellow, button flowers are borne on erect stems in midsummer. 'Lambrook Silver' has especially attractive, finely cut, silver-white foliage.

S. rosmarinifolia, 60 x 90 cm (2 x 3 ft), has bright green, aromatic, thread-like leaves, to 5 cm (2 in) long, and, from mid- to late summer, lemon-yellow flowers. *S. rosmarinifolia* subsp. *rosmarinifolia* 'Primrose Gem', 60 cm (24 in) high and across, has pale yellow, button-like flowers above the aromatic, feathery, evergreen foliage.

KEY FEATURES
- Evergreen shrub
- Easy to grow
- Attracts beneficial insects

PLANT
In sun in well-drained soil

PROPAGATE
Seed in spring; semi-ripe cuttings in late summer

HARDINESS
Hardy; zones 6–9

PESTS AND DISEASES
Trouble free

These useful shrubs are grown for their glossy green leaves, berry-like fruits and, above all, fragrant winter flowers. They can be grown in mixed and shrub borders, and because they prefer shady conditions they are ideal groundcover. They tolerate pollution.

Sarcococca confusa, 1.2 x 1 m (4 x 3 ft), has glossy, dark green leaves. In winter it bears very fragrant cream-white flowers, which are followed by glossy black fruits.

S. hookeriana, 1.5 x 1.8 m (5 x 6 ft), is a suckering shrub with glossy, dark green leaves and fragrant white winter flowers. The naturally occurring hybrid *S. hookeriana* var. *digyna*, 1.2 m (4 ft) high and across, has white flowers with pink stamens, and *S. hookeriana* var. *humilis* has spidery but fragrant white flowers in winter and, sometimes, black berries in autumn. The slim, dark green leaves are evergreen. This compact shrub, to 60 cm (24 in) high and across, is ideal for groundcover or low hedging.

KEY FEATURES
- Evergreen shrub
- Fragrant winter flowers

PLANT
In shade in fertile, moisture-retentive but well-drained soil

PROPAGATE
Seed in spring or autumn; semi-ripe cuttings in late autumn

HARDINESS
Hardy to frost hardy; zones 6–9

PESTS AND DISEASES
Trouble free

Saxifraga

Scabiosa
SCABIOUS, PINCUSHION FLOWER

▲ *Saxifraga* 'Gregor Mendel'

▲ *Scabiosa caucasica* 'Stäfa'

This large genus includes many of the plants that are grown in scree and rock gardens and in alpine houses. Most form dense cushions or mats of foliage above which the flowers are borne on slender stems.

One of the most popular saxifrages is the spreading *Saxifraga* x *urbium* (London pride), 30 cm (12 in) high, which prefers moisture-retentive but well-drained soil and shade. It forms rosettes of fleshy, mid-green leaves, each rosette about 8 cm (3 in) across. In early summer airy clusters of pale pink flowers are borne on erect, wiry stems.

The cushion-forming 'Gregor Mendel', which is derived from the hybrid *S.* x *apiculata*, needs well-drained, neutral to alkaline soil and a bright position not in direct sun. It is easy to grow, forming a mound 15 x 30 cm (6 x 12 in). In early spring it bears clusters of primrose-yellow flowers.

S. 'Kathleen Pinsent', 40 x 10 cm (16 x 4 in), is a short-lived plant, forming rosettes of silvery leaves above which clusters of pink flowers are borne in late spring.

KEY FEATURES
- Evergreen or deciduous perennial
- Suitable for rock gardens
- Good groundcover

PLANT
Different species have different requirements but plant all in well-drained soil

PROPAGATE
Seed in autumn; divide in spring; remove rosettes in spring

HARDINESS
Hardy; zones 5–7

PESTS AND DISEASES
Slugs and snails

These mainstays of the cottage and wild garden can also be grown in containers and windowboxes, and many of the taller forms are good for cutting.

The flowers of the annual or biennial *Scabiosa atropurpurea*, 90 x 23 cm (36 x 9 in), may vary in colour from white, pink, lavender-blue to the desirable dark red. Among the single-colour strains are 'Ace of Spades', with very dark purple, almost black flowers, and 'Blue Cockade', with lavender-blue flowers.

The clump-forming perennial *S. caucasica*, 60 cm (24 in) high and across, has grey-green leaves, which form a dense cluster above which the long-stemmed flowers are borne. Among the best cultivars are 'Clive Greaves' (lavender-blue), 'Bressingham White' and 'Miss Willmott' (white), 'Floral' Queen' (pale blue) and 'Stäfa' (dark blue).

Compact forms, suitable for containers, include the perennial *S. columbaria*, 30 cm (12 in) high and across, and its cultivars, such as the widely available 'Butterfly Blue' and 'Pink Mist'.

KEY FEATURES
- Annual or perennial
- Summer flowers
- Good for cutting
- Attracts bees and butterflies

PLANT
In full sun in well-drained, neutral to alkaline soil

PROPAGATE
Seed in spring; divide in spring

HARDINESS
Hardy; zones 4–6

PESTS AND DISEASES
Trouble free

Scilla

Sedum
STONECROP

▲ *Scilla siberica*

▲ *Sedum spurium* 'Schorbuser Blut'

These useful bulbs are closely related to chionodoxas and puschkinias; they have similar pretty flowers, borne in clusters on upright stems.

The reliable and hardy *S. siberica* (Siberian squill), 20 x 5 cm (8 x 2 in), has bright blue, nodding flowers in spring. The cultivar 'Spring Beauty' is deeper blue.

In early spring the hardy *S. bifolia*, 15 x 5 cm (6 x 2 in), produces spikes of star-shaped, blue to purple-blue flowers, which naturalize well under deciduous shrubs. Also hardy and also good for naturalizing is *S. bithynica* (Turkish squill), 15 x 8 cm (6 x 3 in). It bears spikes of pale-blue flowers in early to mid-spring.

The borderline hardy *Scilla peruviana*, 30 x 20 cm (12 x 8 in), is almost evergreen, with new basal leaves appearing in autumn almost as soon as the old ones are dying away. The flowers appear in early summer. Each raceme has between 50 and 100 star-shaped, purple-blue flowers. *S. peruviana* 'Alba' has lovely white flowers.

KEY FEATURES
• Bulb
• Colourful flowers
• Good for naturalizing
• Suitable for rock gardens

PLANT
In sun or partial shade in well-drained soil

PROPAGATE
Ripe seed; divide offsets in summer

HARDINESS
Hardy to half-hardy; zones 1–8

PESTS AND DISEASES
Viruses but usually trouble free

Many of the smaller sedums are grown in rock or scree gardens or in alpine houses, while larger forms can be grown at the front of mixed borders. Once established they need little attention.

One of the best is *Sedum spectabile* (ice plant), 45 cm (18 in) high and across, which produces rosettes of fleshy, grey-green, deciduous leaves. The clusters of pink-purple flowers are covered with bees and butterflies on warm, sunny days in late summer and autumn.

The mat-forming *S. spurium*, 10 x 60 cm (4 x 24 in), has reddish stems and toothed, dark green, evergreen leaves. In mid- to late summer it bears clusters of pink-purple flowers on erect stems. *S. spurium* 'Schorbuser Blut' ('Dragon's Blood') has deep pink flowers.

S. lydium, 5 x 20 cm (2 x 8 in), has bright green, evergreen leaves. Clusters of white flowers are borne from early to midsummer. This sedum will do better in cooler, shadier conditions than others in the genus.

KEY FEATURES
• Deciduous or evergreen perennial
• Attracts bees and butterflies

PLANT
In full sun in well-drained, neutral to alkaline soil

PROPAGATE
Seed in spring or autumn; divide in spring

HARDINESS
Hardy; zones 3–9

PESTS AND DISEASES
Slugs and snails

Senecio

Skimmia

▲ *Senecio cineraria* 'Silver Dust'

▲ *Skimmia japonica*

There are more than 1,000 species of annuals, biennials, perennials, climbers, shrubs and even small trees in this genus, which includes the weed groundsel. In addition, some popular plants formerly included in the genus have been renamed as *Brachyglottis* and *Pericallis*. Most widely grown are the subshrubs and perennials that have silver-grey or blue-grey foliage and are often used in summer bedding or at the front of mixed borders. Although they produce flowers in summer, many people prefer to remove the flowering stems in spring so that all the plants' energies go into the foliage.

The evergreen subshrub *Senecio cineraria*, 60 cm (24 in) high and across, has oval, deeply lobed, silver-grey leaves, to 15 cm (6 in) long. In summer it bears loose clusters of yellow flowers. If you allow the flowers to bloom, deadhead after flowering. It is not reliably hardy but can be easily raised from seed each year. 'Cirrus' also has oval leaves, but they are silver-green and deeply toothed. 'Silver Dust' has deeply divided, almost white leaves.

KEY FEATURES
• Perennials or subshrubs
• Handsome foliage
• Yellow flowers

PLANT
In sun in well-drained soil

PROPAGATE
Seed in spring; semi-ripe cuttings in late summer

HARDINESS
Hardy to frost tender; zones 4–9

PESTS AND DISEASES
Rust

These easy-to-grow shrubs are ideal in borders, and young plants of *Skimmia japonica* 'Rubella' are often included in containers for winter interest. The only problem that might arise is that on excessively alkaline soil magnesium deficiency sometimes causes the leaves to turn yellow.

The best-known species is *S. japonica*, which can form a large shrub 5 m (15 ft) high and across. It has dark green glossy leaves, and fragrant white flowers, often flushed with pink or red, are borne in clusters in spring. On female plants the flowers are followed by red berries, although both male and female plants must be present.

More often grown than the species are the many compact cultivars. Throughout winter the male 'Rubella', 1.5 m (5 ft) high and across, bears clusters of red buds, which open in spring to reveal the white flowers. The dark green leaves are finely edged in red. The female 'Wakehurst White' (syn. 'Fructu Albo'), 60 cm (24 in) high and across, has green flower buds and white berries. 'Fragrans', 1 m (3 ft) high and across, is a male form with narrow leaves and a mass of flowers.

KEY FEATURES
• Evergreen shrub
• Early-spring flowers
• Good in containers

PLANT
In shade in fertile, moisture-retentive but well-drained soil

PROPAGATE
Semi-ripe cuttings in late summer

HARDINESS
Hardy; zones 7–9

PESTS AND DISEASES
Trouble free

Solidago
GOLDEN ROD

Sorbus
WHITEBEAM, ROWAN

▲ *Solidago 'Goldkind'*

▲ *Sorbus hupehensis var. obtusa*

An invaluable plant in the wildlife garden, the flowers of golden rod attract pollinating insects, which in turn attract birds. Seedheads left in winter will provide food for finches, linnets and siskins. Although species are rarely grown, being altogether too thuggish for most gardens, there are several more manageable cultivars, flowering from late summer to early autumn and producing feathery heads of small yellow flowers.

'Crown of Rays', 60 x 45 cm (24 x 18 in), has golden-yellow flowers in broad heads to 25 cm (10 in) long. 'Goldenmosa', 75 x 45 cm (30 x 18 in), has mid-green leaves, the bright yellow flowers are borne on yellow stems. 'Loddon Gold', 90 x 45 cm (36 x 18 in), has broad clusters of golden-yellow flowers.

Among the dwarfer forms for the front of a border are 'Cloth of Gold', 45 x 25 cm (18 x 12 in), which has bright yellow flowers on sturdy stems. 'Goldkind' (syn. 'Golden Baby', 'Babygold'), 45 cm (18 in) high and across, has soft yellow flowers. 'Queenie' (syn. 'Golden Thumb'), 30 cm (12 in) high and across, has bright yellow flowers and green and yellow leaves.

KEY FEATURES
- Perennial
- Summer flowers
- Easy to grow
- Attracts beneficial insects

PLANT
In full sun in well-drained soil

PROPAGATE
Divide in spring or autumn

HARDINESS
Hardy; zones 5–8

PESTS AND DISEASES
Mildew

This genus contains some of the best ornamental trees for small gardens, where they can be grown as specimens or in a woodland glade. They tolerate pollution and also withstand wind, so are useful in exposed areas.

Sorbus hupehensis (Hubei rowan), 8 m (25 ft) high and across, has blue-green leaves, which turn red in autumn. White spring flowers are followed by white berries. The berries of *S. hupehensis* var. *obtusa* turn pink as they ripen.

S. aucuparia (mountain ash), 15 x 7 m (50 x 22 ft), is a rounded tree with dark green leaves that turn red and yellow in autumn. White flowers, borne in late spring, are followed by red-orange berries.

S. 'Joseph Rock', 10 x 7 m (30 x 21 ft), has bright green leaves, which turn orange, red and purple in autumn. In late spring it bears clusters of white flowers, and these are followed by orange-yellow berries. Unfortunately, this lovely tree is susceptible to fireblight.

KEY FEATURES
- Deciduous tree
- Spring to early-summer flowers
- Colourful berries
- Good autumn colour
- Attracts birds

PLANT
In sun or light shade in fertile, well-drained soil

PROPAGATE
Greenwood cuttings in summer

HARDINESS
Hardy; zones 4–7

PESTS AND DISEASES
Fireblight

Spiraea

Stachys
BETONY

▲ *Spiraea japonica*

▲ *Stachys macrantha*

These useful shrubs can be grown in mixed or shrub borders and smaller forms are suitable for rock gardens.

Spiraea japonica, 1.8 x 1.5 m (6 x 5 ft), is a clump-forming shrub with dark green leaves and clusters of white or pink flowers in mid- to late summer. More often grown are the many attractive cultivars that have been developed from the species. 'Anthony Waterer' has dark leaves and dark pink flowers. The popular 'Goldflame', 75 cm (30 in) high and across, has yellow-green leaves, which are sometimes marked with red, and dark pink flowers; any shoots bearing all-green leaves should be cut out to prevent the entire plant from reverting. 'Nana' (syn. 'Nyewoods'), 45 x 60 cm (18 x 24 in), has pale green leaves, turning red in autumn, and dark pink flowers.

S. 'Arguta' (bridal wreath), 2.4 m (8 ft) high and across, forms a dense shrub with graceful, arching stems. In spring, clusters of white flowers are borne on the tips of the stems. Cut back the twiggy growths after flowering each year to ensure a good display in the following year.

KEY FEATURES
• Deciduous shrub
• Summer flowers
• Easy to grow

PLANT
In full sun in well-drained soil

PROPAGATE
Greenwood cuttings in summer

HARDINESS
Hardy; zones 4–9

PESTS AND DISEASES
Trouble free

This genus contains about 300 species, including annuals and shrubs, but it is the perennials that are most widely grown, usually in mixed borders or as edging plants. The flowers attract butterflies and bees.

Stachys byzantina (lambs' ears, lambs' tails), 45 x 60 cm (18 x 24 in), has silvery, softly hairy leaves, which are borne in rosettes. From early summer to early autumn pink-purple flowers are borne in spikes. Several cultivars have been developed, most for their foliage. 'Big Ears', for example, has large, white-felted, mid-green leaves, each to 25 cm (10 in) long; the flowers are purple. 'Silver Carpet' is a non-flowering form, which is useful where a groundcovering mat is needed; its grey-white leaves are covered with silvery hairs. 'Cotton Ball' has silvery leaves and flowers that look like balls of cotton wool.

S. *macrantha*, 60 x 30 cm (24 x 12 in), has dark green, wrinkled, hairy leaves and dense spires of deep purple-pink, funnel-shaped flowers in early summer to autumn.

KEY FEATURES
• Perennial
• Attractive foliage

PLANT
In full sun in well-drained soil

PROPAGATE
Divide in spring

HARDINESS
Hardy; zones 4–8

PESTS AND DISEASES
Mildew

Stipa

FEATHER GRASS, NEEDLE GRASS, SPEAR GRASS

Symphytum

COMFREY

▲ *Stipa gigantea*

▲ *Symphytum* x *uplandicum* 'Variegatum'

These handsome grasses make good border plants or feature plants. The inflorescences are popular with flower arrangers, but do not cut them back in autumn: they are a valuable source of winter food for many birds, which will also find insects and snails overwintering among the dense clumps formed by the grass stalks.

A fully grown *Stipa gigantea* (giant feather grass, golden oats), 2.4 x 1.2 m (8 x 4 ft), is an imposing sight. The dense clumps are evergreen or semi-evergreen, and in summer the mid-green leaves are topped with panicles, up to 50 cm (20 in) long, of silvery spikelets, which turn golden as they age.

More appropriate for a smaller border is *S. arundinacea* (pheasant's tail grass), 1 x 1.2 m (3 x 4 ft), which has dark green, evergreen leaves, which are streaked with orange in summer and turn orange-brown in autumn. In mid-summer to early autumn it bears arching panicles of purplish-green spikelets.

The deciduous *S. tenuissima*, 60 x 30 cm (24 x 12 in), has delicate, bright green leaves. In summer it has feathery panicles of green-white, later brown-yellow spikelets.

KEY FEATURES
- Deciduous or evergreen grass
- Attractive inflorescences

PLANT
In full sun in well-drained soil

PROPAGATE
Divide in late spring

HARDINESS
Hardy; zones 7–9

PESTS AND DISEASES
Trouble free

These perennials are grown for their small, tubular flowers and sometimes their attractive foliage. The plants are easy to grow and can colonize ground that suits them, but they are easily controlled and can be divided and moved. They are useful groundcover and can be grown in mixed borders and woodland gardens. Use *Symphytum officinale* (common comfrey), 1.2 x 1 m (4 x 3 ft), to make a good, if smelly, liquid fertilizer or add the leaves to the compost heap, where they will act as an activator.

S. x *uplandicum*, 1.8 x 1.2 m (6 x 4 ft), has mid-green leaves and pink-blue buds in late spring, which open to blue-purple flowers. The more manageable *S.* x *uplandicum* 'Variegatum', 90 x 60 cm (3 x 2 ft), has attractive sage-green leaves, edged with white, and lilac-pink flowers on erect stems.

S. 'Hidcote Blue', 45 cm (18 in) high and across, has mid-green leaves and pale blue flowers, which open from pink-red buds in mid- to late spring. 'Hidcote Pink' has pale pink flowers, which fade to white as they age.

KEY FEATURES
- Perennial
- Attracts pollinating insects

PLANT
In sun or partial shade in fertile, moisture-retentive soil

PROPAGATE
Seed in spring; divide in spring

HARDINESS
Hardy; zones 4–8

PESTS AND DISEASES
Trouble free

Syringa
LILAC

Taxus
YEW

▲ *Syringa vulgaris* 'Primrose'

▲ *Taxus baccata* 'Standishii'

Lilacs are grown for their fragrant spring flowers, and a tree or shrub covered in the clusters of white, pink, yellow or purple flowers is a beautiful sight. Unfortunately, for the rest of the year they are rather dull. If you have space for a tree, plant it in a far corner of the garden. If you only have room for a shrub, choose a species rather than one of the showier cultivars.

That said, for most people lilac means one of the many cultivars of *Syringa vulgaris*, which has the potential to grow to 7 m (22 ft) high and across. The heart-shaped leaves are to 10 cm (4 in) long, and in late spring, sometimes to early summer, fragrant clusters of single or double lilac-coloured flowers are borne. Choose a flower colour to suit your garden: 'Mme Lemoine' has double white flowers; 'Primrose' has small clusters of yellow flowers; 'Président Grévy' has lilac-blue flowers.

S. reticulata, 10 x 6 m (30 x 20 ft), has fragrant cream flowers in spring to summer and the winter interest of red-brown bark. The compact 'Ivory Young' is a more freely flowering form.

Unlike most conifers, yews can be pruned hard back and will regrow from old wood. This makes them uniquely useful for hedging and topiary. The dense, dark foliage creates an excellent backdrop for more flamboyant plants, while single plants make splendid specimen trees and prostrate forms are useful groundcover. Female plants bear berries in summer to autumn.

The species *Taxus baccata*, 20 x 10 m (70 x 30 ft), is less often seen than the many excellent cultivars. The female 'Fastigiata' (Irish yew, Florence Court yew), 10 x 6 m (30 x 6 ft), is an upright plant, slowly spreading with age. The leaves of 'Fastigiata Aureomarginata', also female, are edged in golden-yellow. The female 'Standishii', 1.5 m x 60 cm (5 x 2 ft), is a good container plant, forming a slim, yellow-green column. 'Repandens', 60 cm x 5 m (2 x 15 ft), another female, can be used as groundcover. 'Dovastonii Aurea', 5 x 1.8 m (15 x 6 ft), has spreading branches and makes a good specimen shrub or small tree; both male and female forms are available.

KEY FEATURES
- Deciduous shrub or tree
- Fragrant flowers

PLANT
In sun in fertile, well-drained, neutral to alkaline soil

PROPAGATE
Greenwood cuttings in summer; layer in summer

HARDINESS
Hardy; zones 4–7

PESTS AND DISEASES
Honey fungus

KEY FEATURES
- Evergreen tree
- Excellent hedging plant
- Responds well to pruning
- Midsummer to autumn berries

PLANT
In sun or shade in well-drained soil

PROPAGATE
Ripe seed; semi-ripe cuttings in late summer

HARDINESS
Hardy; zones 6–7

PESTS AND DISEASES
Trouble free

Thalictrum

MEADOW RUE

Trachelospermum

▲ *Thalictrum diffusiflorum*

▲ *Trachelospermum jasminoides*

These useful perennials can be grown in mixed borders or wild and woodland gardens, and the smaller species are perfect for rock gardens. The taller plants are best grown among shrubs, which will provide some necessary support for the slender stems.

The clump-forming *Thalictrum delavayi*, 1.2 m x 60 cm (4 x 2 ft), has mid-green leaves on purplish-pink stems. In midsummer purple flowers with long white stamens are borne on erect stems. The all-white flowers of the cultivar 'Album' have a delightful fluffy appearance. 'Hewitt's Double' bears masses of small, double, lilac-coloured flowers on greyish stems and mounds of mid-green leaves.

T. diffusiflorum, 90 x 30 cm (36 x 12 in), has grey-green, deeply divided leaves and, in summer, semi-pendent, pale purple flowers with pinkish sepals.

T. flavum (yellow meadow rue), 90 x 45 cm (36 x 18 in), has blue-green, lobed leaves and, in summer, clouds of yellow flowers. 'Illuminator' has bright green leaves and will grow to 1.2 m (4 ft) tall.

KEY FEATURES
- Perennial
- Summer flowers
- Attractive foliage

PLANT
In partial shade in fertile, moisture-retentive soil

PROPAGATE
Seed in spring; divide in spring

HARDINESS
Hardy; zones 5–8

PESTS AND DISEASES
Mildew

Although they are not reliably hardy, these twining evergreen climbers have such attractive foliage and flowers that it is worth finding a sheltered position against a sunny wall. Plants need to be protected from cold, blustery winds, and in an exposed garden plastic bubble-wrap around the topgrowth and a thick mulch over the roots may be sufficient to see them through cold winters. In areas that suffer from prolonged and piercing frosts they can be grown in a large conservatory.

The dark green, glossy leaves of *Trachelospermum jasminoides* (star jasmine, confederate jasmine), to 9 m (28 ft) high, turn reddish in winter. From mid- to late summer, sweetly scented, white flowers 2.5 cm (1 in) across, are borne in clusters. 'Variegatum' has grey-green leaves, which are variegated with cream-white.

T. asiaticum is slightly hardier. It has glossy dark green, evergreen leaves and, in summer, fragrant cream-white flowers which age to yellow.

KEY FEATURES
- Evergreen climber
- Fragrant flowers

PLANT
In sun or partial shade in fertile, well-drained soil

PROPAGATE
Semi-ripe cuttings in summer; layer in autumn

HARDINESS
Frost hardy; zones 8–10

PESTS AND DISEASES
Trouble free

Trillium

TRINITY FLOWER, WAKE ROBIN, WOOD LILY

Trollius

GLOBEFLOWER

▲ *Trillium sessile*

▲ *Trollius chinensis*

These plants have distinctive whorls of three broad leaves, from which grows a flower consisting of three green sepals and three petals. They are ideal for woodland gardens or shady corners of borders that do not dry out. They may take a season to become established.

Trillium sessile (toad-shade), 30 x 20 cm (12 x 8 in) is a clump-forming perennial with large leaves, irregularly marbled with pale green, grey and white. In late spring dark red, stemless flowers emerge above the leaves.

In spring *T. luteum* (yellow wake robin), 40 x 30 cm (16 x 12 in), bears fragrant yellow or bronze flowers above the mid-green leaves, which are marbled with light green.

The vigorous *T. grandiflorum* (wake robin), 40 x 30 cm (16 x 12 in), has pure white flowers, borne in spring and summer above dark leaves. *T. grandiflorum* f. *roseum* has pale pink flowers, which open wide to show the wavy petals.

T. undulatum (painted trillium), 20 x 30 cm (8 x 12 in), needs acid soil. It has unusual funnel-shaped flowers, with three white or pink petals surrounded by three green, red-edged sepals. The petals have dark red marks at the base.

KEY FEATURES
- Rhizomatous perennial
- Grows in shade
- Lovely flowers

PLANT
In shade in fertile, moisture-retentive but well-drained soil

PROPAGATE
Divide rhizomes in autumn or early spring

HARDINESS
Hardy; zones 5–9

PESTS AND DISEASES
Slugs and snails

Among the most colourful of all spring-flowering bog garden plants, these clump-forming herbaceous perennials need reliably moist soil, but they will not grow in waterlogged soil or shallow water.

Trollius chinensis, 90 x 45 cm (36 x 18 in), flowers in midsummer, bearing orange-yellow flowers, to 5 cm (2 in) across, above the finely divided green leaves.

T. europaeus, 60–80 x 45 cm (24–32 x 18 in), is a rather variable plant with deeply divided, mid-green leaves. In late spring to early summer spherical lemon flowers, each to 5 cm (2 in) across, are borne on erect stems.

The compact *T. pumilus*, 30 x 20 cm (12 x 8 in), has crinkled, finely divided, glossy leaves. In late spring to early summer yellow flowers, dark maroon on the outside, are borne on erect stems.

Several cultivars have been developed, mostly forms of *T. x cultorum*, flowering from mid-spring to midsummer and about 60 x 40 cm (24 x 16 in): 'Alabaster' has pale yellow flowers; 'Lemon Queen' has large pale yellow flowers; and 'Orange Princess' has orange-yellow flowers.

KEY FEATURES
- Perennial
- Large yellow flowers
- Good for bog gardens
- Good for cut flowers

PLANT
In sun or partial shade in fertile, moisture-retentive soil

PROPAGATE
Ripe seed; divide in spring

HARDINESS
Hardy; zones 5–9

PESTS AND DISEASES
Mildew

Tsuga
HEMLOCK

Tulipa
TULIP

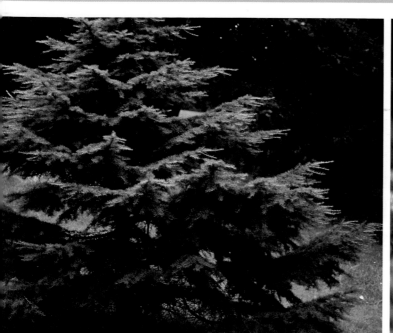

▲ *Tsuga mertensiana*

▲ *Tulipa* 'Queen of Bartigons'

These graceful trees have a broadly conical habit with drooping or arching branches, and they make fine specimen plants. Tsugas are among the few conifers that can be safely clipped and pruned, and for this reason they make good hedges, when they should be clipped from early to late summer.

Tsuga mertensiana (mountain hemlock), 15 x 6 m (50 x 20 ft), is a columnar, densely branched tree, with blue-green foliage and oblong cones. The slow-growing 'Glacua', 3 x 1.8 m (10 x 6 ft), has glaucous leaves.

The narrowly conical *T. heterophylla* (western hemlock), 40 x 10 m (130 x 30 ft) is an elegant tree, with attractively cracked, purplish bark. The needles are dark green but silvery beneath. The cones are pale green at first, ripening to dark brown. This makes a good specimen plant or a fine hedge.

T. canadensis (eastern hemlock), 25 x 10 m (80 x 30 ft), has dark green leaves, silvery beneath, and light brown cones. The slow-growing 'Pendula', 4 x 8 m (12 x 25 ft), develops into a mound of drooping branches.

KEY FEATURES
- Evergreen conifer
- Attractive habit of growth

PLANT
In sun or partial shade in moisture-retentive but well-drained, slightly acid soil

PROPAGATE
Seed in spring; semi-ripe cuttings in summer

HARDINESS
Hardy; zones 3–8

PESTS AND DISEASES
Largely trouble free

Tulips provide an enormous range of flower colour and shape and, like narcissi, they are classified by division.

Most of the modern hybrids are 40–50 cm (16–20 in) tall. 'Apeldoorn Elite' has yellow-edged red flowers; 'Golden Apeldoorn' has golden flowers, both mid-spring. Among the lily-flowered tulips, 'White Triumphator' has pure white flowers in late spring. Also flowering in late spring is 'Queen of Night', which bears single, silky, dark purple-brown flowers. The tall and elegant 'Queen of Bartigons' has salmon-pink flowers in late spring.

Among the smaller tulips are *T. praestans*, to 30 cm (12 in) high, which bears several orange-red flowers on each stem in early spring; 'Fusilier' has bright red flowers. *T. humilis*, to 25 cm (10 cm) tall, has grey-green leaves and star-shaped, deep pink flowers in early spring.

Plant bulbs in late autumn two or three times the height of the bulb deep. Many tulips benefit from being lifted after flowering, and the bulbs should be kept in a dry, dark place until they are planted out again in autumn. Some, including Darwin, Kaufmanniana, Greigii and Triumph hybrids, can be left in the ground to naturalize.

KEY FEATURES
- Bulb
- Vividly coloured spring flowers

PLANT
In sun in well-drained soil

PROPAGATE
Separate offsets in summer

HARDINESS
Hardy; zones 3–8

PESTS AND DISEASES
Eelworms, slugs and snails, rot, tulip fire, viruses

Ulmus

ELM

Vaccinium

▲ *Ulmus parvifolia 'Frosty'*

▲ *Vaccinium glaucoalbum*

Dutch elm disease is fatal, and although Asiatic species and some forms of *Ulmus* x *hollandica*, *U. parvifolia* and *U. pumila* appear to have some resistance, if you are thinking of planting a specimen tree for the long term, elm should not be your first choice. However, many of the smaller, disease-resistant plants should be welcomed to the garden.

U. parvifolia (Chinese elm), 18 x 12 m (60 x 40 ft), has small, glossy green leaves, which persist well into late autumn or even early winter. Small flowers open in early autumn and are followed by winged fruits. The shrub-like 'Frosty', 2.4 m (8 ft) high and across, has small, white-edged leaves.

In a small garden plant the elegant and slender *U.* x *hollandica* 'Dampieri Aurea' (syn. 'Wredi'), which has golden-yellow leaves and grows to 3.5 m (11 ft) but is only about 60 cm (2 ft) across.

The fast-growing and apparently disease-resistant *U.* 'Sapporo Autumn Gold', 18 x 12 m (60 x 40 ft), has glossy green leaves, which are tinged with red in spring and turn yellow-green in autumn.

KEY FEATURES
• Deciduous or semi-evergreen tree
• Good autumn colour

PLANT
In sun or partial shade in well-drained soil

PROPAGATE
Greenwood cuttings in summer

HARDINESS
Hardy; zones 3–8

PESTS AND DISEASES
Dutch elm disease, honey fungus

This genus contains bilberries and cranberries, but there are several attractive ornamental species that are easy to grow in well-drained, acid soil. They rarely need pruning, but straggly shoots can be cut back in spring if necessary.

The borderline hardy *Vaccinium glaucoalbum*, 1.2 x 1 m (4 x 3 ft), has evergreen, dark green leaves, with waxy, blue-white undersides. In late spring and early summer cylindrical, pale pink flowers are borne in clusters, and these are followed by edible blue-black berries.

V. corymbosum (highbush blueberry), 1.5 m (5 ft) high and across, is attractive and useful. The mid-green leaves turn orange and red before they fall in autumn. White or pink-tinged, white flowers are borne in late spring, and these are followed by large, edible, blue-black berries.

The dwarf evergreen, *V. delavayi*, 60 x 90 cm (2 x 3 ft), has dark green, rather leathery leaves. Pink-flushed, cream-white flowers in early summer are followed by edible red berries.

KEY FEATURES
• Deciduous or evergreen shrub
• Attractive foliage
• Autumn berries

PLANT
In sun or partial shade in well-drained, acid soil

PROPAGATE
Greenwood cuttings (deciduous) in early summer; semi-ripe cuttings (evergreen) in late summer

HARDINESS
Hardy to frost hardy; zones 5–9

PESTS AND DISEASES
Trouble free

Valeriana
VALERIAN

Verbascum
MULLEIN

▲ *Valeriana phu* 'Aurea'

▲ *Verbascum* 'Pink Domino'

Although this genus contains annuals and evergreen shrubs, it is for the perennials that it is best known. They are suitable for cottage gardens and mixed borders, or they can be allowed to naturalize in a wild garden.

The variable *Valeriana officinalis* (common valerian, garden heliotrope), 1.5 x 1.2 m (5 x 4 ft), has many herbal uses, not least its attraction for cats. It has aromatic, divided, bright green leaves, to 20 cm (8 in) long. In midsummer it bears clusters of tiny pink or white flowers.

V. phu 'Aurea', 1.5 m x 60 cm (5 x 2 ft), is grown for its aromatic foliage, which is bright golden-yellow in spring, maturing to bright green in summer. In early summer clusters of small white flowers appear.

Less often grown is the clump-forming perennial *V. alliariifolia*, 1 m (3 ft) high and across, which has divided, mid-green leaves and, in midsummer, clusters of white or pink flowers, which are followed by fluffy seedheads.

KEY FEATURES
• Perennial
• Aromatic foliage
• Summer flowers

PLANT
In sun or shade in moisture-retentive soil

PROPAGATE
Seed in spring; divide in spring

HARDINESS
Hardy; zones 4–8

PESTS AND DISEASES
Trouble free

Verbascums are useful herbaceous perennials, easy to grow and flowering over a long period from late spring to early autumn. They are versatile plants and will even grow in poor soil, although they prefer alkaline conditions. The flowers are borne in dense, erect spikes.

From mid- to late summer *Verbascum chaixii*, 90 x 45 cm (36 x 18 in), bears erect panicles of pale yellow flowers above the rosettes of grey-haired, mid-green leaves.

There are many cultivars available. *V.* 'Caribbean Crush', to 80 x 30 cm (32 x 12 in), has orange-peach flowers above rosettes of grey, felted foliage. 'Catherine', 45 x 45 cm (18 x 18 in), has yellow flowers and green foliage. Smaller still is 'Pink Kisses', which has bright pink flowers and grows to 30 x 45 cm (12 x 18 in). Cotswold Group hybrids include 'Cotswold Queen', to 1.5 m (5 ft) tall, which has apricot-flushed yellow flowers, and 'Pink Domino', to 1.2 m (4 ft) tall, which has rose-pink flowers.

Butterflies and other beneficial insects are attracted to the pale yellow flowers of *V. thapsus* (Aaron's rod, great mullein), 1.8 m x 45 cm (6 ft x 18 in).

KEY FEATURES
• Colourful flowers over a long period
• Easy to grow

PLANT
In full sun in well-drained soil

PROPAGATE
Seed in late spring to early summer; divide in spring

HARDINESS
Hardy to frost hardy; zones 5–9

PESTS AND DISEASES
Caterpillars, mildew

Verbena

▲ *Verbena 'Sissinghurst'*

Veronica

SPEEDWELL

▲ *Veronica gentianoides*

Of the annuals, perennials and subshrubs in the genus, the most widely grown are the colourful half-hardy perennials, mostly forms of *Verbena* x *hybrida*, which are often grown as annuals and used for summer bedding. They are usually compact plants, 25–45 x 30–45 cm (10–18 x 12–18 in), suitable for containers, windowboxes or the front of a sunny border. The group includes 'Imagination' (purple-blue), 'Lawrence Johnston' (bright red), 'Silver Anne' (pink) and 'Peaches and Cream' (pale orange-pink).

V. 'Sissinghurst' (syn. 'St Paul'), 20 cm x 1 m (8 x 36 in), is a mat-forming plant, ideal for the front of a sunny border. It bears corymbs, to 2.5 cm (1 in) across, of magenta-pink flowers from late spring to early autumn.

The borderline hardy *V. bonariensis*, 1.8 m x 60 cm (6 x 2 ft), bears clusters of tiny, purple flowers at the top of erect, branching stems all summer and well into autumn. The flowers are attractive to butterflies, and plants will self-seed, even in areas where they are not hardy, making them useful additions to a wildlife garden.

KEY FEATURES
• Perennial
• Flowers over a long period

PLANT
In sun in well-drained soil

PROPAGATE
Seed in spring; divide in spring

HARDINESS
Hardy to frost tender; zones 5–9

PESTS AND DISEASES
Aphids, slugs and snails, mildew

The annuals and perennials in this genus can be grown in mixed and herbaceous borders, and the smaller species are suitable for rock gardens.

The hardy perennial *Veronica gentianoides*, 45 cm (18 in) high and across, has dark green, slightly scalloped leaves. In early summer it produces pale blue or white flowers in erect racemes, to 25 cm (10 in) long. 'Variegata' has blue flowers and white-variegated foliage, and the compact 'Nana' has pale blue flowers.

V. longifolia, 1.2 m x 30 cm (4 x 1 ft), is also a hardy perennial with mid-green leaves. In late summer to early autumn it produces long erect racemes of lilac-blue flowers. 'Blauriesin' has deep blue flowers, and 'Rosea' has pink flowers. 'Blauer Sommer', 50 x 30 cm (25 x 12 in), has clear blue flowers.

The spreading and usually evergreen *V. beccabunga* (brooklime), 10 cm (4 in) high, is a marginal aquatic, best in water to 8 cm (3 in) deep. The small blue, white-centred flowers are borne on creeping, rooting stems.

KEY FEATURES
• Annual or perennial
• Easy to grow

PLANT
In sun in well-drained soil

PROPAGATE
Seed in autumn; divide in spring

HARDINESS
Hardy to frost hardy; zones 4–7

PESTS AND DISEASES
Mildew

Viburnum

Vinca
PERIWINKLE

▲ *Viburnum tinus*

▲ *Vinca major* 'Variegata'

This large genus includes both deciduous and evergreen shrubs. Evergreen plants make good specimens and rarely need pruning. Prune winter-flowering deciduous shrubs in spring and summer-flowering shrubs in midsummer, after the flowers have faded.

The evergreen *Viburnum tinus* (laurustinus), 3 m (10 ft) high and across, has dark green leaves. Small white flowers are borne in clusters in late winter to spring, and they are followed by black fruit. 'Eve Price' has pink buds, and 'Variegatum' has leaves with cream-yellow margins.

In winter the deciduous *V. x bodnantense*, 3 x 1.8 m (10 x 6 ft), produces strongly fragrant red-pink flowers. 'Dawn' has pink flowers, and 'Deben' has white flowers. *V. carlesii*, 1.8 m (6 ft) high and across, has fragrant white or pink flowers in spring; the leaves turn red in autumn.

The deciduous *V. opulus* (guelder rose), 5 x 4 m (15 x 12 ft), has flat heads of white flowers in late spring, followed by red berries and red autumn foliage.

KEY FEATURES
- Deciduous or evergreen shrub
- Winter or spring flowers
- Berries

PLANT
In sun or shade in moisture-retentive but well-drained soil

PROPAGATE
Seed in autumn; greenwood cuttings (deciduous) or semi-ripe cuttings (evergreen) in summer

HARDINESS
Hardy; zones 7–9

PESTS AND DISEASES
Aphids, honey fungus

These spreading evergreens are useful groundcover. Although they are often grown as groundcover in shade, they produce more flowers when they are in sun. Plants that outgrow their allotted space can be cut back in spring.

The species *Vinca major* (greater periwinkle), 45 cm (18 in) high, produces blue flowers over a long period from spring to autumn. It has glossy, dark green leaves. The leaves of the cultivar 'Variegata' (syn. 'Elegantissima') are edged with cream-yellow, and the blue flowers are produced in early summer. 'Alba' has white flowers.

V. minor (lesser periwinkle), 20 cm (8 in) high, has dark green leaves. It is the parent of several good garden plants. *V. minor* f. *alba* has white flowers, and the dainty *V. minor* f. *alba* 'Gertrude Jekyll' has mid-green leaves and cream-white flowers. 'Aureovariegata' (syn. 'Variegata Aurea') has blue flowers, and the leaves are edged in cream-yellow. *V. minor* 'Multiplex' (syn. 'Burgundy') has double, plum-red flowers. 'La Grave' (syn. 'Bowles's Blue', 'Bowles's Variety') has lavender-blue flowers.

KEY FEATURES
- Evergreen subshrub
- Easy to grow
- Vivid blue flowers

PLANT
In sun or partial shade in moisture-retentive but well-drained soil

PROPAGATE
Divide in autumn; semi-ripe cuttings in summer

HARDINESS
Hardy to frost tender; zones 5–9

PESTS AND DISEASES
Trouble free

Viola

Weigela

▲ *Viola* 'Jackanapes'

▲ *Weigela florida* 'Foliis Purpureis'

This huge genus contains 500 or so species, ranging from annuals (pansies), to biennials, perennials and alpines. Many are short lived, but some of the species, including the delightful *Viola labradorica* (Labrador violet), which has bronze-tinged spring leaves, will self-seed.

The appealing *V. sororia* 'Freckles' has pale, purple-flecked flowers from late winter to spring above heart-shaped, dark green leaves. Grow it in sun or partial shade and it will get to 15 x 30 cm (6 x 12 in).

V. biflora (twin-flowered violet), 8 x 20 cm (3 x 8 in), has pale green leaves with slightly scalloped edges. In late spring and into summer it bears lemon-yellow flowers, delicately marked with purple-brown.

The pretty little hybrid evergreen *V.* 'Jackanapes', 12 x 30 cm (5 x 12 in), has yellow and brown petals, the lower, yellow ones streaked with purple. 'Huntercombe Purple' has spurred purple flowers. 'Maggie Mott' has silver-mauve flowers with cream centres. 'Moonlight' has scented, cream-yellow flowers. 'Irish Molly' has yellow-bronze flowers.

KEY FEATURES
• Annual, biennial or perennial
• Flowers over a long period

PLANT
In sun or partial shade in fertile, moisture-retentive but well-drained soil

PROPAGATE
Seed in spring; divide in spring

HARDINESS
Hardy to half-hardy; zones 5–9

PESTS AND DISEASES
Slugs and snails, mildew

Weigelas can be grown in borders or woodland gardens. If necessary, prune after flowering. Cut some of the old shoots back to ground level, and shorten any strong stems by cutting them back to an outward-facing bud.

The species *Weigela florida*, 2.4 m (8 ft) high and across, has dark green leaves on arching shoots. Pale pink, funnel-shaped flowers, each to 3 cm (1¼ in) long, open from dark pink buds in late spring to early summer. It is the parent of the compact 'Foliis Purpureis', 1 x 1.2 m (3 x 4 ft), which has deep pink flowers and purple leaves. Think carefully about neighbouring plants and the overall colour scheme before you dig the hole.

W. 'Florida Variegata', 1.2 m (4 ft) high and across, is perhaps the best cultivar. Its leaves are edged with white in spring, deepening to cream-yellow as the leaves mature, and in spring pale pink flowers are borne in clusters.

In a white garden, grow *W.* 'Candida', 2.4 m (8 ft) high and across. It has dark green flowers and pure white, bell-shaped flowers in late spring to early summer.

KEY FEATURES
• Deciduous shrub
• Spring flowers

PLANT
In sun or partial shade in fertile, well-drained soil

PROPAGATE
Greenwood cuttings in early summer; hardwood cuttings from autumn

HARDINESS
Hardy; zones 5–9

PESTS AND DISEASES
Eelworm, honey fungus

Wisteria

Zantedeschia
ARUM LILY, CALLA LILY

▲ *Wisteria sinensis*

▲ *Zantedeschia aethiopica*

Wisterias are probably the most beautiful of all climbing plants, producing long racemes of scented, pea-like flowers in late spring to early summer. They look best when trained against a wall or over a pergola. For best results, wisterias need regular and careful pruning. This involves establishing a framework of main shoots and laterals and then, on established plants, shortening laterals and, in midwinter, shortening them yet again.

The vigorous twining *Wisteria sinensis* (Chinese wisteria) can get to 9 m (28 ft) or more, and the racemes of fragrant, lilac-blue flowers, to 30 cm (12 in) long, appear in spring and early summer and may be followed by seed pods. 'Alba' has white flowers; 'Caroline' has deep purple flowers; 'Prolific' has lilac-blue to pale blue flowers.

W. floribunda (Japanese wisteria) is not as vigorous as its Chinese cousin, but it, too, bears racemes to 30 cm (12 in) long, of fragrant flowers in summer. 'Alba' has especially beautiful white flowers in racemes that may get to 60 cm (24 in) long, and the purple racemes of 'Royal Purple' may be 50 cm (20 in) long.

These tuberous perennials need reliably moist soil, especially during the growing season. They have large, arrow-shaped leaves and striking spathes, which are usually white but can be strongly coloured.

Zantedeschia aethiopica, 90 x 60 cm (3 x 2 ft), has glossy, bright green leaves, to 40 cm (16 in) long. In late spring to midsummer the large white spathes surround the pale yellow spadices. Although it is not absolutely hardy, when it is grown in water to a depth of 30 cm (12 in), it will be hardier. Plants grown in the garden need a thick winter mulch. The cultivar 'Crowborough' has large white spathes. 'Green Goddess' has green and white spathes.

Several cultivars have been developed from *Z. elliottiana*, including 'Anneke', 50 x 10 cm (20 x 4 in), with claret red spathes; 'Aztec Gold', 55 x 20 cm (22 x 8 in), with yellow spathes; 'Cameo', 50 x 10 cm (20 x 4 in), has pink spathes with a contrasting black throat.

Z. rehmannii (pink arum), 40 x 28 cm (16 x 11 in), has a red-pink spathe around a yellow spadix in summer. This is tender and should be grown as a container plant.

KEY FEATURES
• Deciduous climber
• Fragrant flowers

PLANT
In sun or partial shade in well-drained soil

PROPAGATE
Layer in autumn

HARDINESS
Hardy; zones 4–10

PESTS AND DISEASES
Aphids, honey fungus

KEY FEATURES
• Perennial
• Large spathes

PLANT
In full sun in moisture-retentive soil

PROPAGATE
Ripe seed; divide in spring

HARDINESS
Hardy to frost tender; zones 8–10

PESTS AND DISEASES
Aphids, fungal problems

Plants for special purposes

▲ *Salix caprea 'Kilmarnock'*

▲ *Blechnum penna-marina*

▲ *Helleborus foetidus*

▲ *Clematis montana 'Elizabeth'*

TREES FOR SMALL GARDENS

Abies balsamea (balsam fir)

Acer japonicum 'Orange Dream'

Amelanchier lamarckii

Betula pendula 'Youngii'

Cercis siliquastrum

Chamaecyparis nootkatensis 'Pendula'

Crataegus laevigata

Cryptomeria japonica 'Elegans Compacta'

Halesia carolina (snowdrop tree)

Kalopanax septemlobus

Laburnum x *watereri*

Magnolia x *soulangeana*

Malus zumi 'Golden Hornet'

Nyssa sinensis (Chinese tupelo)

Picea glauca var. *albertiana* 'Conica'

Pinus mugo (dwarf mountain pine)

Prunus serrula (Tibetan cherry)

Salix caprea 'Kilmarnock' (Kilmarnock willow)

Sorbus hupehensis (Hubei rowan)

Syringa reticulata 'Ivory Young'

Tsuga mertensiana 'Glacua'

Ulmus x *hollandica* 'Dampieri Aurea'

GROUNDCOVER PLANTS

Ajuga reptans 'Catlin's Giant'

Artemisia stelleriana 'Boughton Silver'

Blechnum penna-marina

Cotoneaster dammeri

Cyclamen cilicium

Cytisus x *beanii*

Epimedium perralderianum

Hedera helix (common ivy)

Heuchera sanguinea cultivars

Hosta species and cultivars

Hypericum olympicum

Juniperus horizontalis (creeping juniper)

Lamium galeobdolon (yellow archangel)

Lysimachia nummularia 'Aurea' (golden creeping jenny)

Oxalis oregana

Ruscus hypoglossum

Saxifraga x *urbium* (London pride)

Symphytum x *uplandicum*

Taxus baccata 'Repandens'

Vinca major (greater periwinkle)

EVERGREEN PLANTS

Abies koreana 'Silberlocke'

Artemisia schmidtiana

Bergenia cordifolia cultivars

Calluna vulgaris cultivars

Chamaecyparis lawsoniana 'Aurea Densa'

Chusquea culeou

Cordyline australis

Daphne odora 'Aureomarginata'

Epimedium x *perralchicum*

Festuca glauca (blue fescue)

Gaultheria mucronata

Hebe 'Great Orme'

Hedera species and cultivars

Helleborus foetidus (stinking hellebore)

Heuchera species and cultivars

Ilex aquifolium (common holly)

Juniperus species and cultivars

Lavandula angustifolia

Mahonia aquifolium (Oregon grape)

Ophiopogon planiscapus 'Nigrescens'

Osmanthus delavayi

Phormium tenax (New Zealand flax)

Picea pungens 'Montgomery'

Santolina chamaecyparissus (cotton lavender)

Taxus baccata 'Fastigiata' (Irish yew)

Tsuga heterophylla (western hemlock)

BEST CLIMBERS

Actinidia kolomikta

Actinidia polygama (silver vine)

Clematis (large-flowered hybrids)

Clematis alpina

Clematis montana

Hedera colchica 'Dentata Variegata'

Hedera helix cultivars

Humulus lupulus 'Aureus'

Hydrangea anomala subsp. *petiolaris*

Ipomoea indica

Ipomoea tricolor

Jasminum officinale (common jasmine)

Lathyrus latifolius

Lonicera x *heckrottii*

Lonicera periclymenum (woodbine)

Parthenocissus henryana (Virginia creeper)

Parthenocissus quinquefolia (Chinese Virginia creeper)

Passiflora caerulea (blue passionflower)

Rosa (climbing roses)

Trachelospermum asiaticum

Wisteria floribunda (Japanese wisteria)

Wisteria sinensis (Chinese wisteria)

▲ *Genista hispanica*

▲ *Lobelia cardinalis*

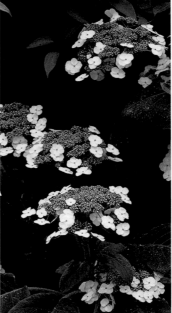
▲ *Hydrangea aspera*

▲ *Primula vialli*

PLANTS FOR DRY AREAS

Alchemilla mollis

Allium karataviense

Armeria maritima

Elaeagnus angustifolia (oleaster)

Eremurus x *isabellinus* cultivars

Euonymus fortunei

Garrya elliptica (silk tassel bush)

Genista hispanica (Spanish gorse)

x *Halimiocistus wintonensis*

Iris foetidissima (stinking iris)

Juniperus communis cultivars (common juniper)

Lavandula angustifolia

Nerine bowdenii

Papaver rhoeas (corn poppy)

Pelargonium cultivars

Ruscus aculeatus (butcher's broom)

Santolina chamaecyparissus (cotton lavender)

Stachys byzantina (lambs' ears)

Verbascum chaixii cultivars

PLANTS FOR BOGGY AREAS

Aruncus dioicus (goatsbeard)

Astilbe x *arendsii* cultivars

Caltha palustris var. *palustris* (king cup)

Cimicifuga simplex 'Atropurpurea'

Filipendula ulmaria (meadowsweet)

Gunnera manicata

Hosta species and cultivars

Iris pseudacorus (yellow flag)

Ligularia dentata (golden groundsel)

Lobelia cardinalis (cardinal flower)

Lysichiton camtschatcensis

Lysimachia nummularia 'Aurea' (golden creeping jenny)

Mimulus cardinalis

Myosotis scorpiodes (water forget-me-not)

Primula japonica (Japanese primrose)

Ranunculus lingua (greater spearwort)

Rodgersia podophylla

Trollius chinensis

Zantedeschia aethiopica

PLANTS FOR ACID SOIL

Athyrium niponicum (Japanese painted fern)

Blechnum spicant

Calluna vulgaris cultivars

Camellia cultivars

Crinodendron hookerianum (lantern tree)

Deschampsia cespitosa

Erica carnea cultivars

Eucalyptus gunnii (cider gum)

Gaultheria mucronata

Hamamelis mollis (Chinese witch hazel)

Hydrangea aspera

Kalmia latifolia (calico bush)

Lilium (Oriental hybrids)

Magnolia species and cultivars

Meconopsis betonicifolia

Nothofagus antarctica (Antarctic beech)

Nyssa tupelo (black gum)

Ophiopogon planiscapus 'Nigrescens'

Pieris species and cultivars

Tsuga canadensis 'Pendula'

Vaccinium corymbosum (highbush blueberry)

PLANTS FOR SHADE

Adiantum pedatum (maidenhair fern)

Cyclamen hederifolium

Dicentra spectabilis (bleeding heart)

Digitalis purpurea (common foxglove)

Doronicum pardalianches (great leopard's bane)

Dryopteris affinis (golden male fern)

Euphorbia amygdaloides var. *robbiae* (Mrs Robb's bonnet)

Hedera helix 'Oro di Bogliasco'

Helleborus foetidus (stinking hellebore)

Hosta species and cultivars

Lamium maculatum

Lilium (martagon hybrids)

Meconopsis cambrica (Welsh poppy)

Primula vialli

Pulmonaria officinalis (Jerusalem cowslip)

Ruscus aculeatus (butcher's broom)

Saxifraga x *urbium* (London pride)

Skimmia japonica

Thalictrum delavayi

Trillium sessile (toad-shade)

Plants for special purposes

▲ *Anthemis tinctoria*

▲ *Erigeron karvinskianus*

▲ *Primula vulgaris*

▲ *Fuchsia* 'Admiration'

PLANTS FOR FULL SUN

Agapanthus 'Bressingham White'

Anthemis tinctoria (golden marguerite)

Artemisia 'Powis Castle'

Aster alpinus

Canna cultivars

Cistus x *purpurea*

Cosmos bipinnatus

Crinum x *powellii*

Delphinium cultivars

Gazania cultivars

Iberis sempervirens

Ipomoea tricolor

Lilium auratum (golden-rayed lily)

Malva moschata (musk mallow)

Melianthus major (honey bush)

Nandina domestica

Nerine bowdenii

Onopordum nervosum

Passiflora caerulea (blue passionflower)

Pelargonium cultivars

Phlomis fruticosa (Jerusalem sage)

Solidago cultivars

Stachys byzantina (lambs' ears)

EASY-CARE PLANTS

Acanthus mollis

Armeria maritima

Bergenia cordifolia

Buddleja davidii cultivars

Campanula 'Birch Hybrid'

Carex elata 'Aurea'

Choisya ternata

Cotoneaster frigidus 'Cornubia'

Echinops ritro

Erigeron karvinskianus (wall daisy)

Garrya elliptica (silk tassel bush)

Geranium ibericum

Helianthus annuus

Iberis sempervirens

Ipomoea tricolor

Juniperus communis cultivars (common juniper)

Lavatera 'Barnsley'

Malva alcea (hollyhock mallow)

Pelargonium cultivars

Saxifraga x *urbium* (London pride)

Sedum spectabile (ice plant)

Stachys byzantina (lambs' ears)

Symphytum officinale (common comfrey)

Verbascum chaixii cultivars

Vinca major (greater periwinkle)

PLANTS FOR BUTTERFLIES AND BEES

Achillea 'Moonshine'

Aster novi-belgii (Michaelmas Daisy)

Buddleja davidii (butterfly bush)

Calendula officinalis

Centaurea cyanus

Centranthus ruber (red valerian)

Coreopsis verticillata

Crambe cordifolia

Digitalis purpurea (common foxglove)

Dipsacus fullonum (common teasel)

Echinops ritro

Eupatorium purpureum (Joe Pye weed)

Geranium sylvaticum (wood cranesbill)

Hebe x *franciscana*

Hypericum species and cultivars

Hyssopus officinalis

Kniphofia cultivars

Lavandula angustifolia

Lupinus hybrids

Monarda didyma (sweet bergamot)

Nepeta x *faasenii*

Oenothera biennis (evening primrose)

Papaver rhoeas (corn poppy)

Primula vulgaris (primrose)

Scabiosa atropurpurea

Sedum spectabile (ice plant)

Solidago cultivars

Verbena bonariensis

PLANTS FOR CONTAINERS

Acer palmatum var. *dissectum* (cut leaf maple)

Begonia 'Champagne'

Cistus 'Peggy Sammons'

Convolulus tricolor

Crinum americanum (Florida swamp lily)

Diascia rigescens

Erica carnea cultivars

Festuca glauca (blue fescue)

Fuchsia cultivars

Galtonia candicans (Cape hyacinth)

Gazania cultivars

Hebe cupressoides

Helichrysum petiolare

Hosta species and cultivars

Lathyrus odoratus (sweet pea)

Lavandula stoechas

Lobelia erinus

Muscari latifolium

Myosotis sylvatica

Ornithogalum nutans

Pelargonium cultivars

Phormium tenax (New Zealand flax)

Phyllostachys nigra (black bamboo)

Pieris formosa var. *forrestii* 'Jermyns'

Salvia splendens (scarlet sage)

Scabiosa columbaria

Senecio cineraria

Skimmia japonica 'Rubella'

Tulipa species and hybrids

Verbena x *hybrida*

▲ *Daphne cneorum* 'Eximia'

▲ *Berberis thunbergii*

▲ *Skimmia japonica* 'Rubella'

▲ *Dahlia* 'Worton Aileen'

PLANTS FOR SPRING COLOUR

Anemone blanda

Bellis perennis Pomponette Series

Chionodoxa luciliae

Corydalis flexuosa

Crocus tommasinianus

Daphne cneorum

Deutzia x *elegantissima*

Dicentra formosa (wild bleeding heart)

Doronicum orientale 'Magnificum'

Forsythia x *intermedia* 'Lynwood Variety'

Galanthus nivalis (common snowdrop)

Gentiana verna (spring gentian)

Kerria japonica

Leucojum vernum (spring snowflake)

Muscari armeniacum

Myosotis sylvatica

Narcissus species and cultivars

Pieris 'Forest Flame'

Prunus cerasifera (cherry plum)

Pulmonaria saccharata (Jerusalem sage)

Pulsatilla vulgaris

Scilla siberica (Siberian squill)

Tulipa species and hybrids

PLANTS FOR AUTUMN COLOUR

Acer japonicum (Japanese maple)

Amelanchier canadensis (shadbush)

Aster novae-angliae (New England aster)

Berberis thunbergii

Callicarpa bodinieri var. *giraldii*

Ceratostigma willmottianum

Colchicum autumnale

Cornus alternifolia

Cotinus coggygria 'Royal Purple' (smoke bush)

Cyclamen cilicium

Gentiana sino-ornata (autumn gentian)

Helenium autumnale

Malus 'John Downie'

Miscanthus sinensis

Nandina domestica

Nyssa 'Jermyns Flame'

Parthenocissus species

Photinia villosa

Pyracantha cultivars

Sorbus 'Joseph Rock'

PLANTS FOR WINTER INTEREST

Arundo donax

Aucuba japonica 'Golden King'

Betula utilis var. *jacquemontii*

Camellia x *williamsii*

Chimonanthus praecox (wintersweet)

Cornus alba 'Sibirica' (red-barked dogwood)

Cortaderia selloana 'Sunningdale Silver'

Cyclamen coum

Erica x *darleyensis*

Garrya elliptica (silk tassel bush)

Hamamelis x *intermedia*

Helleborus niger (Christmas rose)

Ilex aquifolium (common holly)

Jasminum nudiflorum (winter jasmine)

Juniperus chinensis 'Aurea' (Young's golden juniper)

Mahonia x *media* 'Charity'

Miscanthus sinensis

Phyllostachys nigra (black bamboo)

Prunus x *subhirtella* 'Autumnalis'

Rubus cockburnianus

Sarcococca confusa

Skimmia japonica 'Rubella'

Viburnum x *bodnantense*

PLANTS FOR CUT FLOWERS

Allium christophii

Alstroemeria aurea

Anthemis tinctoria 'Sauce Hollandaise'

Briza maxima (greater quaking grass)

Chelone oblique

Chrysanthemum cultivars

Coreopsis grandiflora

Crocosmia x *crocosmiiflora*

Dahlia cultivars

Delphinium cultivars

Echinops bannaticus 'Blue Gold'

Galegia x *hartlandii* cultivars

Gladiolus cultivars

Helenium autumnale

Hemerocallis cultivars

Iris (bearded)

Lychnis coronaria (dusty miller)

Miscanthus sinensis 'Malepartus'

Pennisetum alopecuroides (fountain grass)

Penstemon hybrids

Rudbeckia fulgida (black-eyed Susan)

Scabiosa caucasica cultivars

Stipa arundinacea (pheasant's tail grass)

Trollius x *cultorum* cultivars

Tulipa species and hybrids

Acknowledgements

Executive Editor Sarah Ford
Editor Alice Bowden
Executive Art Editor Karen Sawyer
Designer Claire Legemah
Picture Researcher Sophie Delpech
Production Manager Ian Paton

Picture Acknowledgements

Andrew Lawson 5 bottom right, 6 top right, 11 left, 16 left, 17 left, 17 right, 23 right, 31 left, 32 right, 34 left, 36 right, 38 right, 46 right, 48 right, 55 left, 66 left, 71 left, 77 left, 83 top right, 89 left, 94 right, 95 right, 97 left, 98 bottom left, 108 left, 109 right, 117 left, 118 left, 120, 120-121, 121 top right, 122 left, 124 left, 135 left, 137 right, 143 left, 145 right, 149 left.

Garden Picture Library/Howard Rice 80 left; /J. S. Sira 61 right; /Mel Watson 129 right; /Didier Willery 91 right.

GardenWorld Images 4 top right, 30 right, 35 left, 38 left, 50 left, 50 right, 65 left, 66 right, 67 left, 79 right, 81 left, 93 right, 107 right, 110, 116 left, 136 right, 144 left; /Anthony Baggett 49 left; /Rita Coates 111 top right; /Charles Hawes 11 right.

Harpur Garden Library 18 left, 119 left, 140 left; /Jerry Harpur 23 left, 47 right, 85 right, 114 left; /Marcus Harpur 2, 4 bottom right, 5 centre left, 7 bottom right, 25 right, 43 right, 52-53, 53 top right, 58 left, 63 left, 81 right, 88, 91 left, 99 top, 99 bottom left, 100 left, 113 right, 117 right, 121 bottom right, 126 right,144 right.

Octopus Publishing Group Limited 3, 4 centre right, 5 top left, 5 bottom left, 6 bottom left, 7 top, 8 left, 8 right, 9 left, 9 right, 10 left, 10 right, 12 left, 12 right, 13 left, 13 right, 14 left, 14 right, 15 left, 16 right, 18 right, 19 left, 19 right, 20 left, 20 right, 21 right, 22 left, 24 right, 25 left, 26 left, 26 right, 27 left, 28 bottom left, 29 top left, 29 top right, 30 left, 31 right, 32 left, 33 left, 33 right, 34 right, 35 right, 36 left, 37 left, 37 right, 39 left, 39 right, 40 top left, 41 top right, 41 bottom right, 41 bottom left, 42 left, 42 right, 43 left, 57 left, 69 top right, 78 left, 78 right, 79 left, 82 bottom left, 83 bottom right, 92 left, 93 left, 118 right, 119 right, 125 left, 133 top, 140 right, 141 left, 141 right, 157 right; /Michael Boys 24 left, 54 left, 62 right, 70 left, 71 right, 75 right, 84 left, 84 right, 106 right, 109 left, 110-111, 127 right, 131 right, 139 right, 151 right, 153 left, 154 centre right, 155 left, 157 left, 157 centre right; /Jerry Harpur 15 right, 44 left, 45 left, 45 right, 56 left, 56 right, 57 right, 59 left, 59 right, 60 right, 61 left, 62 left, 64 left, 65 right, 67 right, 68, 69 top left, 69 centre right, 69 bottom left, 72 right, 73 left, 73 right, 74 left, 74 right, 76 left, 77 right, 82-83, 86 left, 87 left, 89 centre right, 90 left, 94 left, 97 right, 98 top right, 101 left, 102 right, 103 left, 103 right, 104 left, 105 right, 106 left, 107 left, 108 right, 115 left, 116 right, 122 right, 123 left, 123 right, 124 right, 125 right, 128 right, 130 left, 130 right, 135 right, 136 left, 142 right, 143 right, 145 left, 146 left, 146 right, 147 right, 148 left, 148 right, 149 right, 150 right, 151 left, 152 left, 152 right, 153 right, 154 left, 154 centre left, 155 right, 155 centre left, 155 centre right, 156 left, 156 centre left, 156 centre right; /Neil Holmes 60 left/Andrew Lawson 40-41, 51 right, 72 left, 138 left, 154 right; /Howard Rice 104 right; /George Wright 46 left, 47 left, 51 left, 54 right, 63 right, 64 right, 70 right, 76 right, 80 right, 86 right, 96 left, 96 right, 101 right, 126 left, 127 left, 128 left, 129 left, 132 bottom left, 134 left, 137 left, 156 right, 157 centre left; /James Young 44 right, 48 left, 49 right, 53 bottom right, 55 right, 85 left, 100 right, 102 left, 105 left, 112 left, 112 right, 113 left, 131 left, 132 top right, 133 bottom right, 134 right, 138 right, 142 left, 150 left.

Science Photo Library/Claude Nuridsany & Marie Perennou 115 right; /Dan Sams 147 left; /Adrian Thomas 27 right, 75 left; /Nick Wiseman 114 right.